"Eva and Manfred Krutein have joined voices to create a vivid memoir of adventures in their new homeland, America. Their family life with five active children, Manfred's double life as a spy, Eva's love affair with music — the story of becoming true American nomads is filled with wonder and the joy of living, and will delight readers both native and new."

— Marjorie C. Luesebrink
Professor of Languages & Humanities
Irvine Valley College

"A wonderful story! A page-turning memoir which adds a necessary dimension to the 'immigrant' picture, one that we rugged individualists of America need to take a good look at. An educated, sophisticated family deals with an unfamiliar and often hostile culture, meets the challenges, copes with the complications. They become valued, trusted citizens of a nation that is not grateful enough."

— Florence Cohn, book reviewer
National Council of Jewish Women

"If all human beings were endowed with a writer's talent, the world would be filled with an incalculable number of profoundly fascinating autobiographies. Realistically, this will never come to pass. However, Manfred, a scientist, and Eva, a musician, prove themselves to be exceptions. In their collaborative autobiography, AMERIKA? AMERICA! they tell their life story with disarming openness, rich detail and passion, always connecting their personal narrative to the events unfolding around them: VietNam, the Kennedy assassinations, feminism, U.S./Soviet relations, the emergence of Buddhism in the U.S., the rise of the youth culture, etc. Their work is highly recommended. I read through the entire text in one sitting."

— Rev. Tetsuo Unno, adjunct professor
Institute of Buddhist Studies/Graduate Theological Union

"Another colorful, heart-warming tale of the Krutein family's life adventures — this one addresses immigration to Amerika and the process of becoming American. It's a wonderful book!"

— Dr. Gay Irons, psychotherapist

"A whale of an exciting, romantic, true story. A spy thriller, a beautiful love story, family challenges and a happy ending. I read this through at one sitting."

— Martin Hebeling, professor emeritus
Cal State Fullerton University
former U.S. Military Intelligence Officer

"...entertaining, humorous, informative. As a fellow one-time immigrant, I appreciate anew the early impressions I had of this Republic of ours: twin beds, no bidets, not shaking hands, older folks going back to university, and so on... The raising of a Soviet submarine by the Glomar Explorer from the depth of 16,500 feet, at the height of the Cold War... all this will be of particular interest to those who can remember the past... This shows how immigrants can become loyal Americans who are eager to do something for their country... Non-stop reading."

— Dr. Hans Askenasy, author of CANNIBALISM,
ARE WE ALL NAZIS? and HITLER'S SECRET

"Journeying from the ruins of Poland and Germany to Chile and California, then to the bottom of the North Pacific, AMERIKA? AMERICA! is a wonderful book and I hated to see it end."

— Theodore Taylor, author of THE CAY
and fifty-one more books

AMERIKA? AMERICA!

From Immigration to Espionage

Eva and Manfred Krutein

 Published with prior approval of the U.S. Government.

Printed in the United States of America
First Printing, 1997
ISBN: 0-938513-23-0
Library of Congress Catalog Number 97-75249

AMADOR PUBLISHERS
P. O. Box 12335
Albuquerque, NM 87195 USA
www.amadorbooks.com

To our children:

Lilo
Urs
Ronnie
Wernher
Irmie

Table of Contents

Introduction

"You and Eva," our mutual publisher told me, "my only two women authors so far, have been the most aggressive about your book projects." There was an edge of complaint in his voice. We were readying my novel to go to press and I was completing my various assignments so quickly that Harry hardly had time to breathe — and he hadn't quite recovered from a similar round with Eva a few months earlier when EVA'S WAR was published. I was too anxious about my book to have much sympathy for him, and I was happy to have a kindred spirit in the otherwise unknown Eva Krutein. I resolved that hers would be the next Amador book I would read.

Studying the introductory material to EVA'S WAR, I was struck by what an unlikely pair of bookends Eva and I made — a seventy-something German-born gentile and a thirty-something American-born Jew. If my childhood ethnic indoctrination had fully taken, I'd look upon Eva as the enemy. Instead, I found in her an ally. She, like me, had an affiliation broader than German or Jew. She, like me, was engaged in the process of trying to heal the scars of history through personal reflection and writing. Eva's post-WWII memoir provided vivid, heart- wrenching counterpoint to my own family's story. Clearly, no one group had cornered the suffering market.

Eva and I ganged up on Harry again three years later when publication of my ANCESTRAL NOTES overlapped that of Eva's second memoir, PARADISE FOUND, AND LOST, which chronicles the Krutein family's relocation to Chile. Again I found in Eva's unaffected, novel-like narrative a keen observer of the world around her. And again I was impressed with how Eva, buffeted by circumstance and serendipity, always managed to land on her feet.

Meanwhile, Eva's husband had set to writing a spy thriller based on his U-boat experiences with the German Navy. I found myself feeling uneasy about the project, entitled HITLER'S LAST GASP and slated as Amador's next publication. The kinship to Eva I so readily recognized faltered upon direct confrontation with Manfred's military past. But Manfred's well-plotted spy story proved as enlightening as it was entertaining. As fictional but believable characters acted out the great rift which existed between the fascists of the Nazi party and the patriots of the German armed forces, my heart synchronized to what my mind had always told me. The sense of kinship returned, stronger, enfolding Manfred as well. I realized that while my battle with anti-semitism had been fought, and very nearly won, even before I was born, Eva and Manfred and so many others must suffer a lifetime of suspicion and stereotyping...

Except that "suffer" is not a term one readily applies to the Kruteins. It would be hard to find two people more filled with *joi de vivre,* as I discovered in the fall of 1995, when Eva and I participated together in a lecture program. We met for the first time the afternoon of the performance, two diminutive women in purple — bookends indeed! That evening, we enjoyed an all-too-short but uproarious meal together. Our party filled the restaurant with the boisterous energy of a family reunion. I doubt anyone would have guessed that some of us had met only hours before.

Still, I must admit, I quailed somewhat at the idea of writing this introduction to AMERIKA? AMERICA! It was my own suggestion that the book have an introduction, but I intended that it be written by someone who had known Eva and Manfred for many years. I told Eva, "People who haven't read EVA'S WAR or PARADISE, or who don't know you personally, may not appreciate what complex and amazing events led up to your moving to the U.S., or what intrepid, energetic and determined people you and Manfred are. You need to have someone paint a bit of a picture of you. Without some background, I'm afraid your narrative could seem rather unbelievable."

And Eva said, "That's very good, Zelda. You will write it?"

So, I am writing. Because, if nothing else, I know this about Eva Krutein: She is a woman who always says, "Yes!" to life — and never takes, "No," for an answer.

— June, 1997
— Zelda Leah Gatuskin, author
The Time Dancer: A Novel of Gypsy Magic, and
Ancestral Notes: A Family Dream Journal

P.S. Believe it!

Prologue

Santiago de Chile, October 1957

One fabulous day in 1957 a man-made moon appeared in the blue sky and began to orbit our planet every 96 minutes. It was spring in South America, the month of October, and romantics interpreted the event as the beginning of a better era. The new satellite, a bit larger than our children's beach ball, emitted a low-pitched "beep-beep-beep," which could be heard by electronic engineers around the world. *What musical note?* I pondered. *Too bad, no information about that. Well, who besides me would care?*

The Chilean newspapers said the Russians called their little moon *Sputnik*, meaning travel companion, and were basking in triumph; the North Americans, jolted out of their beauty sleep, suddenly saw themselves as number two in space. Dr. Wernher von Braun, their head of missile development and our son Wernher's godfather, was called to Washington D.C. to explain why America was behind in the space race. (Money, money, money!)

Far away from the two competing superpowers, I took delight in this first step into space, recalling von Braun's prophetic words about "humanity's indispensable liberation from its cosmic cage." I hoped this was the beginning.

What I didn't know was that *Sputnik* would profoundly change our family life.

Arrival in America

1 August 1960

"We are encountering turbulence," the pilot announced through the intercom. A moment later the DC6 began to jerk up and down like a roller coaster. Horrified I clutched at my seat arms as if they were life preservers and stared ahead as if this was a way to steady the plane.

"Fasten your seat belts!" the pilot shouted as lightning flashed through the clouds enveloping the plane.

My heart was in my throat. We had hit a thunderstorm! Only minutes before landing in Miami. I quickly turned to my two small children to help them buckle up, put my own seat-belt on and saw my three older girls across from me doing the same.

It was terrifying: the plane bounced around while the attendants rushed along the aisle, checking, helping, calming. We all were at the mercy of the raging elements. One woman screamed, another curled up as though in a shell, a baby cried, a man shouted. *Oh God, will we make it to Miami?* I prayed. *You know I never wanted to go to Amerika, but now please let us land quickly!*

As an answer the plane was tossed more violently. A feeling of great helplessness engulfed me. *I'm going to throw up!* But my hands were clenched on the seat arms and I couldn't reach for the bag. As the plane jerked up again I saw one stewardess fall to the ground.

"Mommy!" my five-year-old cried.

Clenching my teeth, I reached over to her. This calmed her down. *Don't think of yourself. Your kids need you!*

As if my touch had magic power not only for my daughter but also for the elements, the airplane's shaking softened, the clouds swirled and finally gave way to reveal a sprawling city with skyscrapers spread out beneath us — Miami, Florida!

The events which led us here to the U.S. passed quickly through in my mind.

In the final agonizing months of WW II, fleeing the marauding Soviets who stormed into my hometown of Danzig, on the Baltic Sea, my baby daughter Lilo and I had smuggled ourselves on an oceanliner, which was many times overloaded with refugees. We survived the Russian torpedo attacks against the rescue ships. Terrorized by air raids and horrified by the sight of a sinking ship and the drowning people in the icy water, we finally reached the western part of Germany.

My husband Manfred found us in the chaos of Europe, and together we began a new life in Wilhelmshaven on the North Sea. A naval architect, he started a shipyard from scratch and built up a splendid existence, while I worked as an opera coach and had two more children.

When the Soviets seemed ready to overrun western Europe, we decided to leave the troubled continent and emigrate to the United States. Manfred sold his shipyard and we prepared for the U.S. Alas, we had no sponsors and therefore couldn't get visas. So we chose Chile, the South American Switzerland that had welcomed Germans for centuries, and in 1951 we sailed to South America.

We indulged in Chilean hospitality and the makeshift arrangements of everyday life. Manfred became a mining engineer while I worked as an opera coach. We had two more children, and all five of them and I became deeply rooted in wonderful Chile.

Not so Manfred. He felt he couldn't apply his talents in this non-industrial country and kept longing for the USA.

He was lucky. When the Soviet Union launched Sputnik, the startled U.S. called up its scientists and engineers and even issued visas to foreigners in order to meet and hopefully surpass the Soviet challenge in space. Manfred soon left our second homeland, Chile, to immigrate to California. His life-long desire to work in and for the highly advanced American technology sector had been granted.

Left behind in Santiago, and condemned to wait for notice from him about his first job and a copy of his working contract — requisites for getting visas for the rest of us — I converted our two-story house, hidden by pines and persimmon trees, into a warehouse. I squeezed everything from a piano to a can opener into the spacious living room and put a sign, "*Se Vende* — For Sale," in front of the long grape-covered pergola, and sold everything.

Two weeks after Manfred left I received his letter from San Francisco, California.

Palo Alto, May 12, 1960

Hurrah! Within one day I got a job as a design engineer with Utah Construction and Mining Company in Palo Alto, a suburb of San Francisco. I'm enclosing a copy of my contract. Take this to the American embassy and apply for visas and make reservations for your flight. Hurry up! It's great here and I'm waiting for you!

Love, Manfred

"Hurrah!" I echoed. "Goodbye, Chile," I mourned. I felt immensely torn apart by my joy about his new job and my despair in having to leave the country I loved. Here, among the friendly, carefree Chileans I felt grateful, acknowledged, protected. Would I experience the same thing in Amerika? That ragged letter "K," like in Ku Klux Klan, expressed all my fear and resentment about my imminent transplantation from South to North Amerika. Would Amerika ever become America for me?

With a heavy heart I entered the Amerikan embassy to apply for visas which would uproot and transport us to a strange land. Was there ever a human who asked for exile?

Our family still had German citizenship and, therefore, had to apply for those all-important rubber stamps. Manfred as an engineer had received one in a flash. I was neither an engineer nor a scientist, just a pianist and an opera coach and the mother of five children.

"The German quota is closed," the immigration officer said.

I felt as if he'd slapped my face. "When will it be open?" I stammered.

"Call in from time to time to see if there's been a change."

Every week, I checked with the immigration officer. The answer was always: "No change."

Desperate after two months of fruitless inquiring, I decided to make an extra effort to shake up the Amerikan bureaucracy and wrote to President Eisenhower for help.

Two weeks later I received a note from the Embassy to appear before the immigration officer. A copy of my letter to Eisenhower lay on his desk. The officer told me he had received orders to help me. He could give visas to four of us but not the rest.

Is the man crazy? I thought.

He explained Lilo and I were born in Danzig, the former Free State. Under Amerikan law the two of us still had this citizenship. The Danzig quota was open and my two Chilean-born youngest had free entry into the USA. But for my two German-born children the Embassy could not issue visas since the German quota was closed.

I felt the blood rush to my face. I was ready to strangle him until I grasped that the culprit was not this squat man, but the damned Amerikan bureaucracy — Amerika, not deserving a "c" in its name. Fuming with rage, I shouted at him until, apparently prompted by the noise, the consul himself, an elderly, gray-haired giant, entered the scene. I stopped screaming and broke into sobs. Through my tears I saw the two men talk. The consul briefly looked at me, then told the officer, "Let this woman take her five children and leave!"

The officer immediately issued the visas — I had won the battle! The three-month wait was over, and the taut rope I'd felt around my throat was loosened.

Now we had landed in Miami, Florida, America. Or Amerika? No matter. I sighed deeply and smiled at my five children.

"We made it," Lilo, 16, said as the airplane taxied on the tarmac.

A repulsive stench spread out over the entire plane. "Boo!

What a stink!" Ursula, my 13-year-old daughter shouted.

"Maybe a doctor has broken a bottle of medicine," I said.

"No!" Lilo pointed to the exit. "The stewardess is spraying us South Americans with a disinfectant."

Humiliated, I was ready to fly back to Chile. Yet people behind me were pushing, and I stumbled forward into the country that had the reputation of welcoming immigrants.

Coming suddenly out of the dry Chilean winter into Miami's humid summer heat, we trudged towards the airport terminal, while in my mind a funeral march was playing in time with the beat I marched. With my fur coat hung over my shoulders, feeling the sweat running down my back, I automatically counted over my five children — Lilo (LEE-loh), 16; Ursula, 13; Renate, 10; Irmgard, 5; and my son Wernher, 6.

Inside the airport building, I read the big letters above a door: IMMIGRATION. Armed with visas and chest x-rays, we entered a small, well-lit room. Behind the only furniture, a lectern, stood a tall, gum-chewing officer, ready to check our worthiness. I handed him our passports.

He counted the children. "All yours?"

"Yes."

He shook his head, then brusquely asked, "...Communist Party?"

So far I understood only one or two words of a spoken sentence in Amerikan English, so I thought he was trying to recruit me to his Communist Party.

I shook my head. "No."

"...pneumonia?" I was prepared for this, and showed him our six x-ray films.

"...husband?"

"Manfred Krutein in Palo Alto, California."

The officer grinned, returned our passports to me, made a joke, which I didn't understand, chuckled and finally let us pass.

Outside we became part of the milling crowd. How tall the Amerikans were! I, five-foot-three, had to look up at the pale-faced, straw-blond, blue-eyed giants. And now the first blacks and more and more of them, dark-eyed and somewhat aloof, looming even over the tall whites.

Routinely, I counted my kids: One—two—three—four—oh God, one was missing! "Where's Wernher?" Terror seized me. He was kidnapped — that's what they did in this country, after all! My blond, blue-eyed son, cute and smart, but these characteristics couldn't be as sensational here as they'd been in Chile...

Lilo pointed at the open door to the street. "There he is!"

"Lilo, watch the kids," I said to my motherly daughter and rushed to the door. There stood my little son in eager Spanish conversation with a pretty, black-haired stewardess from LAN, the Chilean Airline.

She motioned at me. "*¿Tu mamá?*"

"*Sí.*"

"*¡Adiós, churro!*" she said, using a Chilean term for "handsome," blew him a kiss, grabbed her traveling bag and left. Chilean spontaneity even here! Wernher beamed.

Lilo, my eternal substitute in caring for the four younger children, walked up with her three sisters in tow. I sighed with relief, and together we stepped out into the stifling heat toward a line of taxis.

We hired one, and the driver took us to a playground with moving cars and trains, bought ice cream cones for the children with his own money and introduced us to the immensity of a supermarket, over-stocked and air-conditioned.

Inside we gaped as a fat, pale-white man, clad only in swim trunks, pushed a shopping cart with a toddler half-buried in packaged food; his woman, in a bikini and gum-chewing, trudged behind the push-cart. In Chile such quasi-nudists would have been jailed!

On the tarmac a propjet was waiting for us. We had never seen such a huge plane before. Excited, we climbed the stairs to our space-vehicle, while heavy but warm rain poured down on us. Be it rain or sweat, we were always wet in Florida. Inside, we snapped our seat belts on while the plane whistled and grumbled. *A high F and a low B,* I heard.

"Did you see that, Mom?" Lilo marveled. "The stewardess just pushed a button and the outdoor staircase moved up! And it even folded and closed the door!"

I nodded and smiled. "Amerikan technology." Silently I added: *the United States' advanced technology must compensate for all the hardships we'll encounter here in Amerika!*

The jet zoomed into the clear sky toward Chicago—the only route to California the travel agent in Santiago had found. When the lights were dimmed I kissed the children good-night.

"I'll dream of my new doll Daddy has promised me," Irmgard said.

I nodded. "He said in his letter that the doll is waiting for you at the entrance window." Irmgard smiled and fell asleep.

Grateful to be sitting in a vehicle worthy of the 20th century, I pulled out Manfred's detailed letter, which I had received the day before our departure.

How many years had I waited for this day, to sit in a jet on my way to New York! To find work in the country I admired so much because of its technological achievements. Would I find an interesting job as an engineer? I yearned to be involved in important projects where I could use my experience in different engineering fields. My disillusion in Chile had been too great, not finding the recognition of my knowledge as an engineer and a naval architect.

I'd heard so much about California where the climate was supposed to be similar to Central Chile's. But would California really be the best state in which to live?

In New York I took a Greyhound bus to San Francisco. The almost uninterrupted ride across the continent lasted four solid days. One doesn't imagine such a large country! In San Francisco I rode in streetcars and buses to get an overview of the city—it's as scenic as I'd been told.

Next day I followed a newspaper ad to Palo Alto, a university town south of San Francisco. There, I found a job in the engineering division of Utah Construction and Mining Company. Right on the first day I befriended an Hungarian engineer, Jerry de Pottere, who invited me to stay with him and his family instead of having to live alone in a hotel. 'You'll need help to quickly adjust to this country,' Jerry said. 'Everything here is so different from life in Europe. First you need a driver's license. Then you must have credit cards. Without credit cards you are nothing in this country. In Europe you save money and then buy a car or whatever. Here we borrow on our credit cards and slowly pay off the debts. Next thing: buy a car. Next: look for a house. Rent one and then buy furniture. That all takes weeks of your free time after work. My wife and I will help you take step after step so that you have a home for your family ready when they arrive.' You can't imagine how much this generosity helped me! Without Jerry and his wife Madeleine I wouldn't have succeeded with my preparations for you and the kids.

Three things are very important here in America:

1) Since English is not phonetic you need to spell out names or countries, which we never had to do in Chile or Germany.

2) Say 'thank you' to everyone and everything.

3) Use a deodorant. Americans are very sensitive to smell. Even the slightest body odor is perceived as 'evil.' Because, the Puritans said, 'cleanliness is next to Godliness.'

Now about my job. I'm working with about 50 engineers on a project to design the processing plant for a mining facility in Perú. It's quite different from my work as a naval architect in Germany. Fortunately, in Chile I had adjusted to the mining industry and had become familiar with my new field. Here, every single employee is very friendly and cooperative. These two qualities seem to be typical for Americans at large.

But an unpleasant surprise: engineers get only two weeks of vacation per year! When I told my American colleagues that this, compared to most other countries, was a real outmoded treatment, they told me that until a few years ago engineers had no rights to a vacation at all. And there was no insurance for illness or unemployment.

Notwithstanding these drawbacks, my beloved, I'm ready to pick you all up in San Francisco! I can hardly wait!

Hugs and kisses, Manfred.

My hands let the letter sink into my lap. Manfred's image rushed in from the Pacific like a fresh breeze. I heard his stormy steps, his artistic whistling, his laughter. I saw his handsome face smiling at me, his blue eyes radiating confidence and determination. I heard his tender voice, "My little Bear." I sighed. Three months had passed since he had departed from Chile, and I finally had left the *country* I loved for the *man* I loved.

I hoped this eternal flying would soon come to an end. Thirty-six hours of flying and changing planes and hanging around airports had passed; twelve more were before us. I was tired to the point of offering my soul for a bed. Crouched into their seats, the children were asleep, and I passed out as well.

When I awoke, I spotted beneath us a flat, but dense cloud formation like a wad of cotton-wool covering a treasure. We penetrated the fluffy layer and emerged above the precious object: San Francisco. We landed at its International Airport.

Exhausted, we trudged towards the airport building, and inside met a huge crowd. Where was Manfred? At the same moment I heard the whistling of Richard Wagner's "The Flying Dutchman," our recognition signal. And there he was: Manfred, my handsome husband, who had lured us all to the unknown of the northern world. In his tanned face, darker than his blond hair, his white teeth flashed in a radiant smile that seemed to light up the air. Forgotten was the tiredness, my heart pounded wildly, and I took in his beloved face with its angular chin, his smiling mouth, his perfect nose, his radiant blue eyes, and rushed the last steps toward him right into his arms.

He tried to embrace the six of us at once while we all talked to him at the same time. "Now I recognize my family," he said, smiling.

In my happy muddle I confused dollars with cents and offered the black porter three shiny copper coins, thinking they were dollars. He refused to accept the pennies and left without so much as a glance at me.

"Mami!" Lilo called to me reproachfully. Too late to cure it. The man was gone. I hoped he didn't feel too insulted by my ignorance.

Manfred walked before me, flanked by Lilo and Ursula. He no longer towered above short Chileans, but with his five-foot-ten equaled most Americans. Was it true he was walking in front of me, but why couldn't I touch him? I heard his voice with the British R he had picked up somewhere in his childhood, but alas, he wasn't talking to me, just to our two oldest children. Even so I felt like walking on a cloud, focusing my eyes on his figure, his lordly bearing erect with nobility of mind and health, but at the same time he seemed far away; I couldn't touch him. He was the draw that brought us to the United States, and with our three youngest children I was now following him into the new world.

He led us to the outside and presented his dark-green Ford station wagon: Second-hand and larger than any car we'd ever seen. I was seated next to him, we were holding hands, and once in a while I looked at his profile, barely believing we were together.

Leaving the parking area, I told Manfred how the immigration officer in Miami had tried to enroll me in the Communist Party. "Is America going communist?"

He laughed. "Not at all. Do you know what the guy really said? All immigrants are asked this: 'Are you or have you ever been a member of the Communist Party?'"

"Why do they do that?"

"During the '50s they had a purge of communists here. So that question was left in the wake of it."

I shook my head in wonder. But onwards to Palo Alto! The suburbs between San Francisco and Palo Alto looked like one big park with bungalows sticking out from the greenery. Within 40 minutes we arrived in Palo Alto, a wealthy town of 50,000 with tree-lined streets and a private university. All the homes we passed looked like summer getaway homes. Where did people live the rest of the year?

"Is there a special 'tall tree' that gave Palo Alto its name?" I asked Manfred.

"Yes, an old redwood tree between town and university. It's a historical landmark already named in the 18th century. I'll show you the tree soon. But first I'll take you home."

On 235 Webster Street Manfred stopped in front of a small, dark-painted bungalow set back in the front yard — another summer-get-away house. Flanked with palm trees and adorned with paper garlands, its three steps led to a veranda, and in one of the large windows stood Irmgard's new doll with a raised arm, greeting her mother. Irmgard raced in, took the doll in her arms and kissed her. And I turned around to my husband, hugged and kissed him and didn't want to let him go. The family had landed.

Manfred took us around the two-bedroom house. He had accomplished an enormous task to furnish it and provide for seven people, although he'd had only time after work and on weekends. Everything he had purchased was selected with love and consideration. There was no piano though — my most important tool — but that would come later.

Strangely, our bedroom had only one wide bed. "Here in America married people sleep together in one bed," Manfred explained. I thought it was a joke. At least the children each had their own bed as the five bunks in their room indicated.

In the kitchen Manfred showed off just as a magician would. He lit the gas range without a match; he threw a potholder against the range, and miraculously it stuck; the toaster threw out the bread slices when ready and shut itself off. Holy American technology!

But when Manfred opened the refrigerator and I saw the prepackaged dishes, different ice creams and our preferred delicatessen, I broke down and cried and laughed by turns. The time had come when someone else was there to take responsibilities and lovingly provide us with whatever we could dream of. Gone were the three months of separation. Manfred held me tight. I was home. I could cry on his shoulder.

An hour later I examined the bathroom. "Where's the bidet?"

"There aren't any in this country," Manfred answered.

"God, how do people keep themselves clean?" No bidets, no maids, what else was missing here? *Definitely a bed for myself,* I thought. But soon, totally exhausted, I fell into Manfred's oversized berth without a wish or perplexity. I slept 14 hours.

When I woke up, I realized that Manfred had already gone to work. In the children's bedroom with the five bunks nothing moved, the kids were still asleep. As always, when I looked at them I experienced a feeling of achievement. Being an only child, I had missed siblings all my life. Now I had them — belatedly and moved-up one generation. All good and healthy; Lilo, 16, an artist and my assistant; Ursula, 13, down-to-earth and energetic; Renate, 9, gentle and considerate; Wernher, 6, smart and rebellious; and Irmgard, 5, soft-spoken and my little "red caboose." How grateful was I for having them! I only hoped that our move to Amerika would be good for their future.

Next day, Saturday, Manfred put the six of us in the station wagon and drove to The City, as San Francisco was called.

"Our first visit to California's capital," I said.

"San Francisco is not the capital; Sacramento is," Manfred said.

I shrugged. "In all those years in geography classes I never heard that."

"Get a refund of your school fees," Manfred said.

"School is *kaput*," I replied, thinking of the gigantic mound of rubble that Danzig, my native town, now was.

San Francisco turned out to be a jewel of a city with a thousand things to see and to do. As we were driving back to Palo Alto a kaleidoscope of impressions and musical themes swirled in my head and finally reflected in a letter to my friend Alicia in Chile.

> *Never have I seen a more beautiful city. I feel privileged to live here. But to appreciate all of it one needs years! Built on several hills, the streets go up and down so steeply that I swore I'd never try to drive on them. What do you do on a 30 or 40 degree incline and your engine doesn't make it and you roll down backwards, right into the oncoming traffic? God forbid!*
>
> *Uniquely, the celebrated cable car wobbles uphill and down on the steep streets. Late passengers hang from the cable car's doors, obviously having a good time, not the least because of the car bells' clang-clang-clang. Besides, with the Amerikans' cultivated sense of humor, this is thoroughly accepted.*
>
> *Even the many half-idiots or people in strange outfits on the streets are tolerated as they loudly talk vis-a-vis to unseen companions.*
>
> *The famous Golden Gate Bridge may be a technical*

wonder, yet it's not golden at all, it's red! It's also a popular suicide place; once you jump from its 250-foot height into the cold Bay you are guaranteed to be dead.

It would take a lifetime to savor and explore San Francisco in its versatility. At 39, more than half of my life is over, so I have to hurry to explore The City and what else is in store for me.

My dear, I hope you keep your promise and come to see us soon!

Cariños, Eva.

How easy it was to write in Spanish! "My English is terrible," I said to Manfred one night.

He suggested I should take evening classes in English for the Foreign Born. They were even free! So I enrolled. Buried by nine years of talking Spanish in Chile, my German-high-school English only slowly reappeared from the abyss of my memory. With all the other immigrants I stammered through the evenings. The Asians struggled to mouth an L, never attempted before. The Germans were ashamed to pronounce a Th, because in Germany people with a lisp were everyone's laughing stock. And all of us croaked and choked, hopelessly trying to pronounce an Amerikan R. With all those co-struggling foreigners around, I yearned for Amerikan natives.

Next Sunday I watched in amazement how, after mass, worshippers rushed to a coffee pot and mounds of donuts. There I inconspicuously mingled with the hungry. I could haltingly say in English what I wanted, but I hardly understood their guttural Amerikan enunciation. Most spoke in a subdued manner, fast and sometimes joking, of which, of course, I never grasped the meaning. The feeling of being dumb overcame me every time someone spoke to me.

Asking for a school for my children, they all recommended the parish school. So I went to the rectory to talk to Father Donahue. From his Sunday sermons I never understood much more than "Dollars....dollars....dollars..." What money had to do with a Sunday sermon was beyond me. In any case, I was prepared for a high fee. Maybe I could offer myself as an organist for the several Sunday masses.

At his office, Father Donahue, portly, gray-haired and red-faced, sat at a huge desk, looked up when I entered and gestured to a chair across from him. I sat down and told him my name and request.

"Do your children speak English?" he asked as brusquely as the immigration officer in Miami had inquired if I were a communist.

"Very little."

"Then they are like deaf-mutes. They'd slow down the learning process of the others. Send them to the public school." He reached for his pen, indicating the discussion was finished.

Humiliation and anger fought within me. I yearned to shout at him, but the words escaped me. Handicapped by dumbness, I stumbled out.

Once outside, I leaned against the church wall and felt the tears run. Abruptly I pulled my handkerchief and wiped my eyes. Dammit, this wasn't the end of the world. Maybe the public school was really the best for our children. But the priest's rough treatment had inflicted a deep wound in me.

After Labor Day our five children found a place in their respective schools. The counselors discovered that with the European school system in Chile our children were way ahead of their Amerikan counterparts and let them skip one entire year. Everyone was happy.

But during the day my nest was empty, housekeeping was boring and the hours stretched endlessly. With threatening clarity I realized what I had feared when I left Chile: I was in exile. The mighty Andes, ablaze at sunset, the Chileans with their genuine interest in people, their hugs and kisses, all this was gone forever. And all my friends were down there, in the paradise I had lost.

Worse, each child came home from school crying. "I don't understand one word the teachers say," Lilo, the 12th-grader, sobbed. Her eyes were swollen.

"Everybody laughs at me," Ursula, the eighth-grader complained.

"Nobody likes me," Renate, the fifth-grader, wailed. "Nobody hugs and kisses us."

"I'm not going back to school anymore," Wernher, the first-grader, declared, his brows knit in anger. "They call me 'Wiener, Wiener with Kraut'!"

Irmgard, the Kindergartner, said nothing, but every day came home with wet pants.

So my bilingual children were laughed at! They spoke Spanish with each other and German with Manfred and me — a matter of course in Chile's upper and middle-classes; only this way children became bilingual.

"Soon all of you will be trilingual," I said. "The other kids will marvel at that."

But my consoling words had little persuasive power. In the long run, we were all in the same boat. As for me, I had recurring dreams of icy landscapes. Amerika was a frozen continent and the people were as cold as ice.

"How do you like it here in Amerika?" I asked Manfred one evening in the living room, when he was absorbed in reading *Die Zeit*, a prominent German newspaper.

He looked up, visibly perplexed by my sudden question. "Very much." He looked back at the paper.

"How do you like the people here?" I insisted.

He looked up only for a moment. "They're nice. And very polite. They always say 'excuse me, please' and 'thank you' for every little thing."

"But they don't like physical contact," I said. "They don't even shake hands with me. Do they shake hands with you?"

His newspaper article must have been fascinating; he kept reading, eventually looked up, but kept the paper in reading position. "We never shake hands at the office."

"Do you guys talk on the personal level at all?"

"Barely." He even put the paper down! "We're too busy."

"Don't you miss personal talk?"

"Not at all. Our engineering projects are very interesting. Way more interesting than those in Chile. It was worth coming to this country."

How different we were! I knew how little need he had for intimate discussions — a fact that kept me from confiding my misery to him.

Meantime, at school all our children received tutoring in English and slowly shed their image of being deaf'n dumb. I saw their relief as though through a veil. Unable to pull myself up from gloomy thoughts, I anticipated the lonely hours with horror, when shadows slowly but irresistibly seemed to fall over me. When the telephone pierced through the silence, I panicked. Fearing I wouldn't understand the caller, I crammed pillows on top of the phone to bury its ringing. Strangely, not being able to answer the phone was like being imprisoned or tortured. Crying was a comfort, and nostalgia for Chile was the only relief.

Moreover, another unexpected problem arose: how to handle the household chores, which in Germany and in Chile the maids had done. Now I made our seven beds and washed bedsheets and clothes in the kitchen sink on a washboard. While Manfred and the kids ate dinner, I served and removed dirty dishes until the family had eaten, but didn't leave anything for myself — another cause for self-pitying and crying. At the deepest point of my depression the thought occurred to me that dying would be a way out of my misery. But I didn't know how to do it myself and so I was damned to wait and wish for my death — or for going back to Chile. I could feel how that country far across the equator pulled on me. I created a fantasy that Manfred would walk into the house, saying, "Come on, let's go back to Chile!" I would jump up and leave without looking back.

Manfred never came to take me back to Chile, but letters from our friends in Chile were arriving, "Tell us more about life in the States!" Determined to tell them about the lonely life in Amerika, I pulled out the typewriter, more than ready to write about the neighborhood, Father Donahue and my suicidal thoughts. But after I finished, I discovered to my surprise that I had written entertaining descriptions. How was this possible? The next day I repeated this kind of writing, with the same result, even humor had crept in. For instance at Halloween, when the children went trick-or-treating, ten-year old Renate came home with three bags full of sweets and marveled, "The

Americans have such handy holidays!"

A hurrah to my children! They introduced a laundromat to me, and so I advanced from washboard-in-the-sink to laundry machines. A hurrah for American technology! And a second hurrah to my children!

I wrote to Alicia:

> *What a difference between Chilean and Amerikan culture. Chileans tend to have twelve to fifteen children, Amerikans in general only two or three. Remember, when I told people in Chile I had five children, they asked, horrified, 'Only five? Don't you have a husband?' Remember that? Now listen to what Amerikans say. When I tell them I have five kids they say, horrified, 'Oh my God! That many? What kind of a husband do you have?' No matter where I am, the number always creates a shock.*

Controversies

We soon received our first invitation, from Manfred's Hungarian colleague Jerry de Pottere, who lived with his wife, Madeleine, in Portola Valley, a woodsy, high-class suburb near Palo Alto.

Passing the tall but unimpressive original *palo alto*, a tall redwood tree, we drove through green, rolling hills, dotted with oak trees, which looked like crooked dwarfs. Soon we drove into a dense forest of redwoods and pines, their perfume wafting through the open car windows.

An opening in the trees led to a clearing with great homes, artistically designed and all different from each other. Manfred stopped in front of a stately one-story house with wall-sized windows, which seemed set into the woods. "This was my first home in California," he said.

We climbed out, walked to the house and knocked.

The door was opened by a balding man in his mid-forties, who said in German, "*Guten Tag*, Manfred! Come on in. Your wife too."

Manfred introduced me to Jerry, who shook hands with both of us. Although he was muscular, his shoulders were stooped, as though he were carrying a great burden. His wife Madeleine, a slim, dark-haired good-looking woman of about 40, joined us, smiled, shook hands with us and kissed me on my cheeks. What a warm welcome! Hungarian music began to sound in my head.

We settled in the rustic living room at a round table. The large open windows allowed a view into the backyard, which inconspicuously blended with the fragrant pine forest. Over Hungarian wine we talked German — what a relief! They told us that their three children had gone to the movies.

The de Potteres had, like us, fled the Soviets in 1945 and had immigrated to Amerika ten years before us. They could explain many things, enigmatic to us. I decided to ask what was on my mind so often. "Most Amerikans we meet just say, 'Nice meeting you,' but neither hug nor shake hands with us. Why's that? I often feel like a leper. Nobody wants to touch my hand."

"I've gone through that too," Madeleine answered. "Even if people touch you accidentally they apologize. The idea is that any touch could lead to sex, and sex is the root of all evil, as the old Victorians said."

"And that nonsense is believed in the 20th century?"

Jerry chuckled. "Nonsense can linger for eternity."

"I'd always thought the Amerikans were modern and tolerant," I said.

"Some are, but others are not," Jerry said. "You have to be careful with what you say to somebody. You'll see how guarded Americans are when they talk to each other, careful not to say anything anybody might find offensive."

"How boring!" I said.

"On the other side it's very considerate," Madeleine said. "It *is* boring sometimes, but you'll get used to it."

"Was it hard for you at the beginning?" I asked.

"Immigration is always painful," Jerry said. "We were uprooted by the war. Now we're clinging to a different culture like stag ferns to a tree."

"Do you like it here now?" I asked.

"Oh yes. Climate, wide space, interesting people. Of the fifty states California is the most modern one, trend-setting. Here lies the future of the world."

Madeleine bent over to us for emphasis. "Rock 'n' roll was born here. We have holistic healing, acupuncture, yoga and a thousand other things."

"How interesting!" I said. "Do you participate in any?"

Madeleine laughed, and her dark eyes were sparkling. "No. I just mentioned to you a few unusual things here. California definitely is the best place to live." She got up and carried the empty wine bottle to the kitchen.

Seeing a chance to talk to her in private, I followed her. "I have a strange question: Why can't a married person have his or her own bed here?"

Madeleine smiled. "In the same bed it's easier to make love."

"I see, but it's no fun to sleep under the same cover when tossing and turning. One takes the cover away from the other."

"You've got to get used to it, my dear." She picked up a fresh bottle of Green Hungarian.

I sighed. I hardly did anything else besides getting used to the new life. How difficult was life in Amerika! At 39, was I too old to adjust?

Back in the living room, I heard Jerry say, "California definitely is the best place to live."

"If you make enough money," I said.

He put his glass down. "Want me to tell you how to make money on the side? Teach Spanish or German! There's a demand for foreign languages now."

I was startled.

"Not a bad idea," Manfred said.

"Put an ad in the local paper," Jerry continued, "and see what happens."

Soon we said goodbye to our friends. I felt enriched, bestowed with their friendship, undeserved and unexpected. Although of the same age, they seemed to be our parents.

On our way home Manfred and I discussed the idea of teaching German and Spanish.

"Why not?" Manfred asked. "Let's try it."

We followed Jerry's advice and put an ad in the *Palo Alto Times*. Within a few days Manfred got one lady for German and I one for Spanish.

One more lady called, Anne Fenton, a "real" American, because she was born in the U.S. She knew some German, wanted to improve it, and we agreed on a certain time. I was looking forward to working with her, when she called to cancel her first lesson. "I really can't afford it. I have to pay a dental bill..."

Frantically I searched my brain for a lure to keep her on the phone. Flash! "Would you teach me English in exchange?"

She took the bait. "Not a bad idea. But I've got two kids."

She paused, obviously thinking it over. "We could have a lesson during their naptime. I live just five blocks from you. Could you walk over to my apartment?"

Could I! Next day I hastened to her modern apartment building. At her first-floor flat I rang the bell. A woman, looming well over six feet, slim and athletic, opened the door and radiantly smiled at me, which reminded me of her dentist's bill. She was barefoot and soon I learned that she always went barefoot, sometimes even on the street.

Anne had planned her children's naptime so efficiently that for an entire hour we were undisturbed. Anne was great at correcting every wrong English word I spoke, and I did the same with her German.

I felt strangely fascinated by this intelligent, good-looking, athletic woman. How different she was from people I had met in this country! Independent, barefoot, always ready for a smile or a joke. How privileged I was to know her!

"Tell me where you are from," Anne said.

"I was born in a state which no longer exists."

"Where in the world is that?"

"The Free State of Danzig. At the Baltic Sea. Next to the corridor between Germany and Poland. It's now part of Poland and called Gdansk."

"How did that happen?"

"On September 1, 1939 Hitler annexed Danzig to Germany and marched into Poland. That's how WW II began."

"Did you have any bomb attacks?"

I smiled. "For six years we didn't have any at all. We thought we were spared because nobody would dare to destroy our 1000-year-old city with all its medieval towers and Renaissance cathedrals."

A light went on in Anne."Oh, I remember I've seen pictures of them in art books. So, no bomb attacks?"

I shifted uneasily in my comfortable chair. "Well, something happened on July 10, 1943. In the middle of the day the sirens began to howl, indicating an air attack. We thought somebody had pushed a wrong button. I went out, looked at the sky and saw one single plane. Suddenly it dropped one bomb and flew away."

"Didn't you run into a shelter?"

"No time for that. Everything was over before we could even think of running. One house was destroyed and that was it. Compared to the thousand bombers dropping 20,000 bombs over other German cities every night, you couldn't call this an air raid."

"Why didn't the Allies come with more bombs?"

"We know now that they couldn't fly that far with a lot of bombs. Technology wasn't developed enough yet. We never heard the sirens again and soon forgot the whole thing."

"So you were spared the nightly howling of the sirens..."

Like a howling siren a cry came from the children's room. "Mommy!!"

Anne jumped up and rushed to the children's room. A moment later she appeared with her two-year-old girl in her arms, her mother's look-alike, including her black hair and dark eyes. Anne's attempt to put her down was thwarted. The child begged until Anne took her up in her arms again.

"Look, Beanie, this is Eva. Say hello to her."

Beanie wouldn't even look at me. My mere presence threatened to take her mother's attention from her. Wide-eyed I observed how the child ordered her mother around for whatever wish came to her mind.

"I want a cookie!"

"Not now, Beanie," Anne said in a soft voice as if to not hurt the child's feelings.

"I want it now!!"

Anne sat down on the sofa. Beanie crawled on her lap, slung her arms round Anne's neck and sobbed, her tears running down her cheeks.

Anne smiled thinly to me. "What can I do?"

"Tell her: NO!"

Anne sighed. "I'm powerless before her tears." She got up and offered the cookie jar to the girl. "But only one!"

When Beanie reached out for a second one, the piteous cycle began again. I got up, unable to witness more of this. "Obvious the naptime is over," I said.

"Obviously," Anne corrected. "Are you going to come back next week?"

Only without another tyrannical-child-vs.-abused-mother scene, I thought. Instead I said: "Wednesday. Same time."

Later, in stores and even on streets I observed with shock similar spectacles between headstrong children and indulgent mothers. Even a child's shout to its mother: "I hate you!" was not punished, but simply accepted. I decided to bring this up next time we were together with the de Potteres.

That time came soon as the four of us were sitting in Jerry's station wagon on our way to Mount Hamilton, fifty miles southeast of San Francisco. The Mount held the famous Lick Observatory on its summit, our goal tonight. The car was inching up the narrow, bumpy, winding road that was lined with crooked oak trees which cast long shadows in the last rays of sun. Now the trees had lost their leaves, and gnarled trunks and bare branches formed bizarre shapes, worthy of a Picasso.

When we found a flat spot at a curve, we stopped for a picnic. Blood-red, the sun had set and taken the warmth with it, so we put our jackets on and enjoyed Madeleine's fruits and sandwiches.

Jerry raised his beer can. "To California and its great mountains." We followed his toast.

"I agree as far as the sceneries are concerned," I said. I told them about my observation of disobedient children.

"Americans are extremely indulgent of their children," Madeleine replied. "They even obey their children."

"How did it come to this?" I asked.

"The pendulum has swung from one extreme to the other," Madeleine said. "I've read about the time when babies weren't touched and older children were disciplined. Then Doctor Spock, a pediatrician, came along and preached against authoritative child rearing. He said, 'Be more flexible with your child,' and, 'Let the child decide what it wants.' That, in turn, led to the extreme you described."

"With this lack of discipline in childhood, how come Amerikan adults are so polite and self-controlled?" I asked.

Jerry took over. "The kids are allowed to express themselves as long as possible to rid them of their tensions. Later, when they are getting their first jobs as teenagers, they learn quickly what society accepts or not. Any undisciplined behavior can lead to being fired from the job at once."

"A harsh experience," Madeleine inserted.

"But it works," Jerry said.

Darkness took over, and we continued driving up to Mount Hamilton's summit. Here, at over 4,000 feet, stood the buildings of the Lick Observatory, which housed seven telescopes. We were lucky to be the only visitors tonight.

"This reflector is now directed at a galaxy 10,000,000 light-years away," the young crewcut astronomer said, as we took turns gazing through the eyepiece. "What you see now is not what that galaxy really is at this moment, but what it was 10,000,000 years ago. So what you are doing now is looking into the far past."

A light exploded within me. We were seeing time, not space! Along with this we were reduced to ridiculously tiny bugs cast against the universe's infinity. Thank you, Amerika, for letting me experience this!

We left the observatory, but not before I turned around for a long, last look. Fascinated with the solar system as a child, I dreamed of becoming an astronomer, but gave it up when my father told me that field was only reserved for good mathematicians. I barely made it through school with low grades in math but excelled in music instead and never left the world of harmonies.

Since our trip to the observatory I understood more about the ingrained indulgence of Amerikan mothers, and I saw to it that Anne's and my mutual lessons were finished before the first "Mommy!" cry sounded. Her second child, a baby boy, slept longer and was invisible most of the time when I visited Anne.

Anne not only had a clear diction that delighted the opera coach in me, but her vocabulary was so rich and her choice of words so striking that she absolutely was a perfect English teacher for me. We now met three times a week, and I had come so deeply under her spell that I couldn't imagine a week without her.

Being complimentary to one another with languages, we were able to discuss historical, political and psychological issues. She told me about the great communist purge in the fifties. "Senator Joseph McCarthy accused thousands of people of being communists. Many lost their jobs because of this."

"How could the nation let this happen?"

"People were afraid they'd be accused of being communists too, if they stood up against McCarthy."

"Hadn't they learned from the Nazi persecutions?"

"No one ever compared the two."

"Nations never learn from history," I said.

Anne sparked me in so many ways, and in time she became the personification of Amerika to me, yet the letter K was beginning to wobble.

Even so I reacted wildly after a conversation about German child rearing. "As a child I was spanked for disobedience with a leather whip at least two times a week," I said with a contemptuous grin.

Anne's dark eyes widened. "Those cruel Germans! That's why they could torture the Jews in the concentration camps."

A shock hit me. Never before had I been confronted with the atrocities in the SS camps. I was at a loss how to react.

"Eva, did you understand what I said?"

"Yes. But the camps weren't my fault."

"Whose else then?"

"That of the SS."

"But you all supported the camps."

I felt blood rush into my cheeks. "The average concentration camps were political prisons. Most cities had one and families often had a relative or a friend in there as we had." My cousin's image arose before me. Once drunk in a bar, he had sung the national anthem in parody, was immediately arrested and sent to a concentration camp. "Yet the extermination camps with the gas chambers were something else," I continued. "They were in Southern Poland. Poland was hermetically sealed off; you couldn't put a foot into it. We didn't know about their existence until after the war."

Anne crossed her long, tanned legs. "No one will ever believe that."

"You don't believe me neither?"

"Either. I don't believe you either."

My voice became louder. "You think I'm lying?"

She looked at her knees for a moment, then straight into my eyes. "I think the Germans are trying to evade the issue and slowly forget what happened."

That was no answer to my question. Yet the accusation remained and I felt deeply insulted.

I went home, looking forward to having the de Potteres over tonight, and rushed through my evening chores. When Jerry and Madeleine arrived and sat down in our small living room for a glass of California wine and pretzels, Madeleine asked, "What's new with you folks?"

We shared our small daily problems: Phone calls that made no sense to us or Bible pushers at the door. Then I told them about Anne's accusations.

A bitter smile appeared on Jerry's face. "They all know much better than we what happened 10,000 miles away from them, twenty years ago. The war propaganda was so intense, and Americans believe everything the media say."

"But that was twenty years ago. Why still talk about it?"

"Oh, this will go on for a long time. The Germans are a handy scapegoat. It proves the Amerikans were right to fight against the Germans. And so they curse them over and over again."

Oh, what country had we come to? I closed my eyes. The image of Chile's people, who lived for the moment alone, arose in my mind. I conjured up the alpenglow of the Andes, which cast an instant spell on me. As I opened my eyes the lure disappeared.

Madeleine must have seen my withdrawal. "You have to get used to this, Eva. Try to avoid conversations like that. You'll never persuade people who have been brainwashed for years and years."

"You know," I said, "as long as I can think back, in

Germany there was never any bad word spoken against Americans. But here I get the impression that the Americans think all Germans are bad and all were Nazis."

Jerry shrugged and took his time to light a cigarette. "Let's change the subject. Now everybody debates the two presidential candidates. Kennedy and Nixon."

"Be sure to watch the debate tomorrow night," Madeleine said. She looked around. "Where's your TV? In the bedroom?"

I felt slightly embarrassed. "We don't have one. We don't understand what's being said, our English isn't good enough."

"Well, you don't miss much," she consoled me.

"We've seen five minutes of a Western at a neighbor's," Manfred said. "A scene where one Indian was hanged on a tree branch. They showed his agony for five minutes. We got sick and left with an excuse."

Jerry laughed. "Tough luck. But tomorrow night's debate is really important."

Parental warmth radiated from the de Potteres, and I felt grateful for having them as friends.

Since no plans were made to buy a TV set, we watched the debate at Anne's home. Her husband was out of town.

Unfortunately we didn't understand one word. We only saw Kennedy look convincing and Nixon sweat.

Eventually Kennedy won. Anne was jubilant.

Instead of buying a TV set we finally went to purchase a piano. My musical memory could create music in an instant, and some melodies, harmonized or not, were always sounding in my head, but to let anyone else hear them I needed a piano. At the music store the owner led us from grand pianos to uprights, and I tried them out, one after the other. I played classical music, jazz and pop, and Manfred softly whistled to all of them. How fun to make music with him! His pure pitch perception and his musical memory were outstanding though he had no formal training.

It didn't take long to decide on a used upright with a sound that pleased me. The owner had stepped into his office. When we entered he was talking on the telephone. "She plays the piano unusually well," I heard him say. After listening he said, "All right," hung up and looked at me. "I just talked to Henry Holt, our local music director. He wants you to call him. Here's his phone number." The jubilant victory chorus from *Aida* sounded in my head.

Even before the "new" second-hand piano was delivered I arranged to meet Henry Holt, the director of Palo Alto's Opera Company. When I arrived, a jolly, well-rounded man received me with unusual warmth and cordiality. He turned out to be an Austrian who had changed his name to an American pseudonym. Witty, jovial and enthusiastic about music, he seemed to be delighted that I had contacted him.

"We have no orchestra in our productions," he explained. "We play the orchestra part of the operas on two pianos. Let's hear how you play." He opened an opera score randomly and put it on the piano rack. "Play," he commanded.

Just after a few bars I realized I was playing Verdi's *La Traviata.* No problem.

"Good!" Henry exclaimed. "You're hired. Let's start working tomorrow. Can you?" Of course, I could. "You also have to play the orchestra part with me during all rehearsals and performances." No problem either, I had done this hundreds of times in Germany and in Chile.

We discussed the pay, but it didn't matter to me how much he paid me. The main thing was I had returned to the world of music-making.

As an opera coach I didn't have to do too much coaching for *La Traviata*, since Henry had done most of it before I appeared on the scene. Yet the prima donna had some musical, not vocal, problems; she needed help with hitting the highest notes, Henry said. I asked him who was singing Violetta.

"Rosita Corano."

I was thrilled. "The famous coloratura?" He nodded.

So I called the prima donna and asked her to come to my home for coaching. I had seen pictures of her galore and expected to see the pretty young woman I knew from the magazines. Yet how shocked was I when I opened the door to an obese woman of about forty in a wide, flowered cotton dress. Her black hair and eyes showed her Italian background. But such a heavyset woman singing the title role?

After introductions and some small talk we opened our vocal scores.

"Let's do the end of Act 1," she said.

"Where you come in with *'Sempre libera degg'io*?' (Let me live for pleasure only?)" I asked. She nodded.

I opened the vocal score and played the introductory measures. She sang and I was mesmerized. Her voice was lovely, she knew her part well and I wondered why she wanted to work on this particular part. It didn't take long until she got to the coloratura part, which went up to a high C, and she hit neither the C nor the neighboring high notes.

I stopped playing. "Let's try it again. This time from *'dee volar.'* (Let my star lead)."

She tried it again and failed the second time. I thought she would be embarrassed by now, but to my surprise she smiled and said, "This time it will go well with a little help." She opened her handbag and took out a small bottle with the label COGNAC. She took three sips, replaced the bottle and sang the coloratura, hitting the high notes without a problem.

"No wonder it went well," I said. "But what are you going to do on stage?"

"Each time I walk offstage I take a few sips. You see, my dear, when you get older you need a little help. I need it only for notes above high B-flat."

I felt sorry for the prima donna and her decline. For a moment I was at a loss how to deal with this. Then I decided to test her ensemble capabilities and asked her to sing her part while I sang the tenor's lines and played the orchestra accompaniment. It worked well.

When she was gone, I shook my head. A drinking soprano! There was always something new. Yet I decided to discuss this with Henry.

"That slop!" he shouted. After a moment of thinking he said, "I don't see any cure for it. After all I couldn't easily find another soprano who could sing that role. So I guess you have to make sure the *schnapps* bottle is filled until she dies," referring to Violetta's death from consumption at the end of the opera.

Soon we had the first stage rehearsal with a young, thin, long-legged director, named Isabella. The singers, expected to memorize their musical lines by now, listened to Isabella's instruction on how to act out their roles on the stage. This was the most tedious part of the rehearsals for Henry and me, playing the orchestral music on two pianos. The director interrupted the singing every minute to redirect the singers about their steps, gestures and facial expressions. Each time Henry and I had to stop, return a few pages and give the singers the entrance words, back and forth, back and forth. I easily memorized the often repeated music. Yet to prevent chaos Henry and I had to be glued to the stage direction every moment. This was the most stressful but inevitable part for the rehearsal accompanist.

By and large all rehearsals went well. Between the acts I made sure Rosita had always enough *schnapps* in her bottle, and we looked forward to opening night.

On opening night the theater hall of Palo Alto's community center was filled to capacity with opera fans, who were dressed up in evening gowns and tuxedos for the occasion, making our suburban playhouse look like New York's Met. Seat neighbors and friends chatted excitedly, and the air was enhanced by the ladies' perfumes. As an extra bonus for my participation in the opera I received free tickets for Manfred and our three oldest children just as I had at the Chilean opera house. At 18 (Lilo), 14 (Ursula) and 11 (Renate), and after my thorough introduction to plot and music, all four of them would be able to enjoy the production.

Down next to the stage stood our two grand pianos face-to-face, their wing-like lids wide open so Henry and I could have eye contact with each other. As we started to play the overture the audience was hushed. The curtain rose and the stage began to fill with guests of the great courtesan, while the famous prima donna got her first applause without even opening her mouth. Throughout the opera she sang beautifully, and I helped her reach the high notes by making sure she could reach the *schnapps* bottle backstage during intermissions.

Henry not only played the orchestral part with me but also gave soloists and the chorus entry signals with his right hand, while the left one kept playing. In spite of his corpulence his gestures were fast and precise, and he had no worries about one hand leaving the keyboard, because I was playing all the notes.

A feeling of satisfaction filled me. I was playing music, Verdi's beautiful music, my coaching had worked and the performance was going along smoothly.

But then in Act Two when the chorus, clad in gypsy costumes, danced and everyone had to sing different lines and words, Henry gave his signals too vigorously. He accidentally hit his score and caused it to fall down. Henry stopped playing and quickly picked it up. Immediately I played twice as loud to make up for his silence and gave the "gypsies" entry signals. Henry hastily put the score back on the rack, thumbed through the pages to look for the right place to come in again and continued playing.

At the *finale* Henry again gestured too forcefully and knocked his sheet music down. Again I took over for him, and after seventeen measures the opera ended, the curtain closed, the wildly clapping audience rose to their feet, and the popular conductor got extra applause.

Rays of Hope

Besides Manfred's and my mutual love for music, I had a burning desire for space flight. While in Chile in the 1950s we had read several of Wernher von Braun's books on space flight with great enthusiasm, and when our son was born in 1954, we named him Wernher after NASA's director, Dr. von Braun. I wrote to him, asking him to be little Wernher's godfather, and graciously he accepted the honor.

And tonight was the night to see the famous rocket scientist in person and to find a way to approach him. Jerry de Pottere had managed to get tickets for us for this event in Palo Alto, and now we were sitting with 300 people, engineers and their spouses, at long white-covered dinner tables in the multi-purpose room of a high school, poking at tasteless food and drinking beer or iced water.

On the stage sat a row of NASA engineers. Unceremoniously, NASA's director von Braun appeared from the wing and sat down in their midst. We observed that someone brought a letter to him, which he opened and read. He beamed and looked searchingly down at us, gesticulated with the letter and avidly talked to his neighbor. The letter had been written by our son Wernher and said in German:

Dear Uncle Wernher! Fine that you are here! May I see you tomorrow? *Your godson Wernher.*

But now it was time for von Braun's speech. He was introduced and then climbed to the speaker's desk. He spoke good American English with a German accent, interspersed with the jokes Americans love. He talked about the state of rocket production and showed slides.

After his talk we pushed our way to von Braun, who was quickly surrounded by people who apparently had invited him for tommorow, and I heard him say three or four times, "I'm very sorry, but tomorrow I'm flying back to Huntsville."

As soon as his giant escort grabbed his arm to pull him away, von Braun cast a glance at me. I seized the moment. "I'm your godson's mother," I quickly said in German.

He stopped immediately and turned to me. "I have received his letter, and I want to meet him."

"We won't bother you for too long," I said. "Two minutes will be enough."

He turned to his escort. "How can we do it timewise?"

"Your flight leaves at 10 a.m.," the giant said.

The rocket man turned back to me. "Could you come very early to my hotel, at 7:45 in the morning?"

"With pleasure," I said.

At the same moment he disappeared backstage. We drove home through the warm, aromatic winter night.

Next morning the seven of us stepped into the quiet breakfast room of the luxury hotel, where the manager talked about us as "relatives of Dr. von Braun." As soon as our Wernher discovered a huge lit aquarium he dashed to it.

Suddenly the door opened and Wernher von Braun strode in. Tall, wide-shouldered and with a wide grin. He greeted Manfred and me with great warmth and cordiality as if we had known each other for a lifetime. We introduced our daughters to him, but when we called for our son, he couldn't tear himself from the aquarium. So the great rocket man stepped over to his uninterested godson and drew him into a vivid discussion about rockets, spaceships and the future moon flight. The tall Wernher held little Wernher's hands and talked insistently to our son, who, in contrast to his usual way, was rather self-conscious.

All of a sudden Irmgard, usually shy, put her hand on von Braun's arm and asked with big, begging eyes, "May I come along too?"

"But where?" von Braun asked with surprise.

"To the moon," Irmgard answered.

Von Braun looked at me with mock-desperation. "Well, what

should we do with her in the rocket?"

"I can cook," she suggested.

"That's a good idea!" von Braun replied. And from then on the trip to the moon was settled.

The rocket man also took time to ask Manfred about his work and plans, making suggestions, giving him names of important people.

While the two men were talking I studied the world-renowned scientist with intensity. His famous charming ways had always contributed substantially to all his victories in front of Congress as well as with his team members. His simple naturalness and his vivaciousness were disarming. And now I observed what I had read about him when he spoke to someone: He listened to his partner as if no one else existed and as if the other's words were of utmost importance. This ability to respect others added to his popularity.

I had brought along von Braun's book "The Exploration of Mars." I opened it to page 75 and said, "We admire you because of this remark (I pointed to the last sentence): "...in a few decades humans will step on Mars."

Immediately, he took out a pen and wrote: "...and then we'll take my dear godson Wernher Krutein along. Wernher von Braun." He smiled. "You and I are the only Wernhers in the world who write their name with an 'h'!"

In the following months Wernher and Irmgard started every other sentence with, "When I'm flying to the moon with Uncle Wernher...."

Three months after our encounter with the rocket scientist President Kennedy showed America and the rest of the world the way to the future: "I believe that this nation should commit itself to achieve the goal, before this decade is out, of landing a man on the moon and returning him safely to Earth."

We understood: Wernher von Braun's appearance in Palo Alto had been one of many successful publicity events for a flight to the moon, and President Kennedy could now put final approval on the project.

Meanwhile, Manfred's short but concentrated conversation

with Wernher von Braun soon bore fruit. Manfred received letters from shipyards in Seattle, Washington, phone calls from the Polaris Center near Palo Alto, and references to San Diego, where experiments with new submersibles were being conducted. He collected and weighed the offers without committing himself to any one of them.

At a church meeting we met Dr. Ken Copenhagen, the director of Stanford University's famous linear accelerator. Learning that Manfred was a "German engineer," — magic words in North and South America — he invited us to see the accelerator. Delighted, we accepted his invitation.

Inside the long tube red signs warned: "Dangerous radiation! Radioactivity! Emergency switch here." The air smelled of ozone and the needle in the Geiger counter in the director's hand reached 200, the highest reading. Fear flooded through my body.

Ken must have seen the horror in my face. "We could endure this radiation for about an hour without getting sick." Nevertheless he ushered us out into the fresh air and with relief we inhaled the cool, clean oxygen.

That's when he asked Manfred if he would like to work here. To my surprise, Manfred turned down the offer as he had done with all the other invitations.

Back home I prepared tea, and we sat down in our two simple armchairs. I asked him why he declined all those fantastic job offers.

He emptied his tea cup and put it down with a clang. "I have something else in mind. There's a new field emerging. Ocean mining. It's still in an embryonic stage, but it could be the future."

"What's ocean mining?"

"Mining the ocean floor for minerals. With special ships and special equipment. All that technology has to be developed yet."

"How did you get into this? You never told me."

"Some literature exists about this. As I said, the matter has still not progressed beyond the early stages."

"And why do you think this would be something for you?"

"Because I am a naval architect and a mining engineer as well. And I'm interested in new things and work on the future.

That's why I always wanted to be in this country. No other country has the means of developing technology."

"How about the Russians?" I asked. "Aren't they ahead of the Americans?"

"At the moment perhaps. But I want to be here and nowhere else."

My arguments were exhausted. Besides, I had to drive to the theater for a rehearsal of *Rigoletto,* so I let the discussion go.

In spite of coaching and accompanying singers I more than ever felt like a wanderer between different worlds, with my body in Amerika and my heart in Chile. The message I received from the Amerikan culture was: *Shut off your feelings and use your brain only. Don't bother anyone with your own problems.* Desperately in search of help, I thumbed through Lilo's college textbook, *Introduction to Psychology.* Lucky Lilo who could take a course in psychology! I envied her.

In the index I found the page with the subject "Nostalgia." It was listed under "Maladjustments" and stated, that "persons suffering from this self-centered feeling are victims of the charitable deceptions of nostalgia."

I was shocked to the bottom of my heart. *So, that's how people like me are judged by this cold society! How can one live here and not freeze to death?* My dreams of an icy landscape and frozen people intensified — if I slept at all.

I decided I needed tranquilizers and finally went to the nearest pharmacy, asking for such pills. The pharmacist said I needed a prescription from a doctor.

"In South America I got tranquilizers without a prescription," I argued.

With utmost contempt in his voice, he replied, "We're not in South America."

His arrogance made me feel like a shooed-off beggar. So I thought I should ask Anne about a doctor.

On a morning when I tried to shake off the memory of another icy dream, a visitor knocked at the always unlocked front door and entered. Anne Fenton walked in, barefoot, hand-in-hand with toddling Beanie and, strapped to her back, six-month-old Chris — all three with black hair and eyes and deeply tanned. For a second I thought I was in South America.

"Hi, buddy. Did I wake you up?" Anne asked.

Immediately I felt uplifted. Anyone calling me "buddy" and visiting without being invited certainly was a good friend. The ice of my dream began to melt.

"No," I answered, "I've already fed my gang and sent them off. Sit down. What's up?"

She carefully laid her kids aside as if they were expensive clothes. The baby's mouth was plugged up with a pacifier. Beanie groped about, inspecting my humble living room.

"You don't listen to the radio, do you?" Anne asked.

"We don't even have one."

"The East Germans have erected a long, guarded wall through Berlin."

"Whaaat?" I was startled. "What for?"

"To keep the East Germans from fleeing to West Berlin. See? You were lucky to leave Europe."

A memory of WW II floated in. "In Germany we believed war was an act of God. So we took the slaughter for granted like sheep at the shearing."

Anne shook her head. "Unbelievable." She leaned back in her arm chair. "Let's change the subject. Tell me about your kids."

"Do you want me to rattle off the list?"

"Anything goes."

"Lilo is in college. She also works for the telephone company. Ursula joined a bowling club and does a lot of babysitting. She even stays overnight on weekends. Renate has a chum next door, a Japanese girl who is in her class. They do everything together. Renate and Wernher play the recorder in a recorder orchestra."

"Wow!"

"Irmgard also has a friend across the street, a Chilean girl who is in her first-grade class."

"I see, you folks stay international. Anyway, they all seem to have found their niches."

With baby asleep and Beanie absorbed in books, Anne now switched to German to give me a chance to feel knowledgeable. I then asked her about a doctor, and she gave me the name and address of her physician, Dr. James Baldwin.

"I prefer women doctors," I said. "They are more sensitive."

A bit standoffish, she replied, "In this country doctors are men."

I shook my head. Backwardness showed more often than I could digest. But I knew I couldn't do anything about it. I made an appointment for the next day.

At Baldwin's office, the nurse made me undress and put a white smock on. Just for getting pills!

Soon after, a short, young man in a white coat entered and said, "I'm Dr. Baldwin. Please lie down and put your legs up here."

What a country! I thought. Just to get some pills I needed a gynecological exam. And the gynecologist was a man! Oh, why hadn't I stayed in Chile?

The doctor shook me out of my daydreams. "You have several tumors at the cervix," the doctor announced. "How old are you?"

"Thirty-nine."

"Do you want more children?"

"No, thank you," I replied.

"You need a hysterectomy." Whatever that was! He thumbed through his calendar and scheduled a date for the surgery. It took a lot of phone calls between him, Anne and me until I understood what a hysterectomy was. Surrendering to my fate, I prepared for my stay at the hospital.

My worries about my family's well-being during my absence were blown away by a never-before-seen offer.

A church member called me. "Eva, make sure that somebody is home in the afternoons. When you are in the hospital, church members will bring pre-cooked meals for your family. For two weeks you won't have to worry about food."

I was stunned. What a co-operative attitude, what generosity! Whom could I thank? Thank you, America! Immensely relieved, I checked in at Stanford hospital.

When I awoke Manfred was there with our five children. He had brought red flowers, but before I could identify them I slipped back to sleep. Eventually I stayed awake and enjoyed talking to my family. Because of my high pain tolerance I felt only a little discomfort.

"Should I bring you something to read?" Manfred asked.

I pondered it and said, "The vocal score of *Tristan and Isolde*."

A few hours later he brought the score along. From then on I read it, enchanted, translating the notes in my mind into orchestra and vocal sounds. Unfortunately the music kept playing in my head, keeping me from falling asleep, yet luckily the night nurse was generous with sleeping pills.

A week later I was released. Finally I received my prescription for a tranquilizer. What a detour! My daily exercises helped me to recover from the partial hysterectomy. Meanwhile, the church members kept bringing casserole dishes and desserts, and for the first time our refrigerator came close to bursting.

While I was doing my exercises in the tiny backyard under the plum tree, whose fruits had long been eaten or canned, Manfred told me I missed two events — one good, one bad.

"The good one, Astronaut Alan Shepard has become the first American in space."

"Wow!" I felt like I had received a personal gift.

"The bad news, Freedom Riders in Mississippi were attacked, beaten and arrested." Inside, the telephone rang and Manfred rushed to pick it up.

What riders? I wondered. Horseback riders? I surely took freedom for granted, but why would horseback riders be arrested? Manfred stayed on the phone for a while so I couldn't ask him about those riders and soon forgot about them.

Meanwhile, Anne Fenton remained instrumental in providing fascinating experiences. After my recovery she came over one day, barefoot, hand-in-hand with Beanie, baby strapped onto her back. As usual, she put her precious brood on the floor, Beanie with a picture book and Chris with a pacifier.

She sat. "How would you like to go to Yosemite with us?"

My jaw dropped. The famous park in the Sierra Nevada! The idea left me speechless.

"Wouldn't it be fun together? Each family in their own car. You in your station wagon, we in our Porsche."

"What a great idea!"

It would be a camping trip, Anne said. We discussed the details. They had tents for our two families, and we'd have to buy sleeping bags and non-perishable food for ourselves. Patiently we waited for the weekend.

Saturday morning we drove to the Fentons, who became our guides to world-famous Yosemite. Trailing the red Porsche, we passed endless cotton fields and wound through wooded areas. We inhaled deeply the wonderful aroma from the redwoods that fanned into our station wagon.

Suddenly, the engine sputtered, slowed and finally stopped. No cranking, no fist-hitting and no praying helped.

The Fentons had seen us stop and came back. After checking under the hood Manfred and Doug decided the car should be towed to the next village.

"You need a tow truck," Doug said.

"How do we get one?" Manfred asked.

"I'll stop a car," I said, stepping nearer to the middle of the road and holding my hand up as a signal for help.

It wasn't long before a Ford stopped. "Need a ride?" the middle-aged driver asked.

I pointed to our stranded group. "Our station wagon broke down. Could you take me to the next village so I can get a tow truck?"

"Come in," the man said and opened the door.

I climbed into the passenger seat, smiling and stammering my thanks.

"What's your accent?" the man asked. I told him.

"Where are you from?"

Uncomfortably I shifted on my seat. "Danzig. Nobody knows where that is."

"Oh, I know where it is," he said firmly. "During the war,

did you have any air raids?"

"No," I answered, automatically suppressing the cloudy memory of that single bomb in July of 1943.

For a fleeting moment the driver turned his face to me. "Madam, you're wrong. You had an air raid on July 10, 1943."

Horrified I stared at the man. "How do you know?"

"I dropped that single bomb on Danzig," he said.

Almost unbelieving I sat there, letting California's pine trees rush by, with a man next to me who tied himself and me to the past, far removed in place and time. Finally I found words. "How come that strange bombing happened?"

"I was a pilot in WW II. Stationed in Scotland. One morning my superior called me to his office. He showed me a map of Central Europe, pointed to Danzig and said, 'Danzig has never had an air raid. But the people there shouldn't think we've forgotten them. Figure out how many bombs you can carry to Danzig and come back.' I made the calculations and came to the conclusion that I could take only one bomb along." He gave me a quick look. "And I dropped it, as you know."

Struck dumb, I remained silent. The horrible war, the escape, the chaos and the years of famine imposed on the Germans as punishment — the memories returned with force, preventing me from feeling safe in this beautiful place.

In the next village the WW II pilot helped me find a gas station that owned a tow truck. I thanked him, and he drove off. Only later I wondered why I hadn't asked for his name.

Unfortunately, this meant the end of our Yosemite trip. We said good-bye to the Fentons and the station wagon was towed to the next village to a gas station. Manfred rented a motel room and stayed with Wernher in the village to supervise the car repair. The rest of us took a bus to Fresno, flew to San Francisco and took a Greyhound bus to Palo Alto.

Yosemite remained unreachable.

Ideals and Reality

Two days later our two men came back in the repaired station wagon. At the dinner table Manfred made an announcement. "Soon we're going to have a radio. Built from a kit."

Six open mouths gaped at him.

"Whenever Mom is out to her opera rehearsals the six of us are going to build the radio," he continued. "Tomorrow, right after dinner, I'll take you all to buy a Heath kit."

Next afternoon, Irmgard asked for permission to walk over to her Chilean friend's house.

"You must be home by six," I told her. With a second thought I asked, "Do you know when it's six o'clock, Irmgard?"

She shook her head.

Ursula came to her rescue. "When the Three Stooges are on you'd better get your tail home right away."

Irmgard nodded and left.

With surprise I realized how well-informed the children were in regard to TV programs without us having a set. They obviously watched in their friends' homes.

Lilo made herself heard. "I won't be here tonight. I have a date. Joe and I are going to see a movie."

"Who's Joe?" I asked, astounded.

"He's in my English class."

"I thought you were dating Jay."

"I do. But tonight I'll go to see *Psycho* with Joe."

So Manfred would have only four assistants tonight.

Some hours later I came home from the rehearsal, earlier than usual, and found the kitchen transformed into an electronic workshop. Cores, tubes, switches and resistors with multi-color markings lay on table, cooking range and kitchen counter.

"I've got great co-workers," Manfred told me. "Ursula reads

off the directions for the assemblage. And Renate, Wernher and Irmgard put all the mysterious things together."

"And you?" I asked, joking.

He chuckled. "I'm the supervisor."

Surely, a complete picture of domestic harmony. But now it was bedtime.

"Leave all your electronic parts where they are now," Manfred said. "We'll keep working over the weekend."

After the usual jostling in the bathroom the children, except Lilo who hadn't come home yet, were finally tucked away in their beds. I kissed them and turned off the ceiling light.

When I entered the children's bedroom the next morning I saw one bunk empty. Lilo was missing! Oh my God, she hadn't come home from her date! I felt choked. Yet a second later I found her in Ursula's bed, both girls in spoon fashion and sound asleep.

I slightly touched Lilo's shoulder to wake her up.

When her eyes were open and she recognized me, she cried, "Oh, Mom, *Psycho* was horrible! I was so scared when I came home I couldn't be alone in my bed. So I crawled to Ursula for protection." Tears came to her eyes.

"It's daylight now, Lilo. You don't have to be afraid. Just get up."

All five children jumped out of their beds at once and raced to the only bathroom — with the exception of Renate, who first took care of the two canaries, feeding them and refilling their tiny bowl with water for the day. I smiled. She had an exceptional sense for the well-being of others. Just to help her friends who had a hard time pronouncing "Renate," she'd changed her name to Ronnie. The name change was contagious in so far as her two sisters demanded the same privilege. Ursula became Urs, and Irmgard became Irmie. In turn they changed "Papi" to "Dad" and "Mami" to "Mom." Only Wernher held on to his name, because its unusual spelling immediately referred to his famous "uncle."

One morning Ronnie hesitated for a second before asking, "I

have a question, Mom. Are we poor?"

"Not quite. Why are you asking?"

"Because we five kids sleep together in one room. Only poor people do that."

"We just immigrated, Ronnie, and the others didn't. Wait a while and each of you will have a separate room."

"Please don't tell anybody that we sleep in the same room."

I promised not to. Visibly relieved she went to the shower.

How can we create another bedroom? I pondered, scanning the bungalow's floor plan in my mind. *Give up the dining room, put in Lilo's and Urs's bunks and eat in the kitchen. It will be crowded, but hopefully we can give the kids some kind of a step forward. I'll discuss it with Manfred tonight,* I thought.

After breakfast the general exit took place.

Lilo's friend, Joe, rang the doorbell — medium-sized, blond, blue-eyed and radiant. "Hi, folks!" he greeted us with a cheerful voice as if we had been good friends for years. He escorted Lilo to his sky-blue Chevy. Another boyfriend! First Jay, now Joe.

Wernher and Irmie ran off to school. Ronnie was the last one to be ready. She was picked up by her next-door chum, Linda Toshitsune, a shy Japanese girl. Linda brought a message from her mother, asking if she could come and visit me this morning. I sent Linda back to tell her mom I'd be happy to see her.

Mary Toshitsune was about my age, 40, as small as her four daughters and as thin as a ten-year old. With her black hair and almond-shaped eyes she resembled the many Japanese who lived in this area. But she became the first one to whom I could talk.

She didn't come with empty hands, but with a homemade pound cake. "As an expression of thanks for the day your husband drove your daughter and Linda to school." She put the cake on the coffee table.

I was slightly embarrassed. "For a small favor, such a big cake?" I gestured to the armchairs. "Please take a seat."

She sat down. "It's not only for that, but for letting Ronnie go together with Linda."

"What's so special about that? They like each other, why shouldn't they be chums?"

"Not every Caucasian mother would let her child play with

a Japanese."

I was dumbfounded. "Caucasian? What's that?"

"Another word for 'white'."

"Why for heaven's sake wouldn't a white American mother let her child play with a Japanese child?"

"Because Americans don't like us." A simple statement.

"I thought you were American?" I asked, with a premonition of something serious and ugly.

"I am. I was born here. But during WW II this country interned us." She told me about the ordeal of herself and 120,000 other Americans' of Japanese ancestry in the relocation camps. "We were treated as war criminals." Tears were running down her cheeks. She pulled a handkerchief out of her pocket and blew her nose. "Our government said we were 'a subversive threat to the war effort,'" she continued. "The camp had watchtowers and five strands of barbed wire. Searchlights were going all night so we couldn't escape. They made head counts every night. Most non-Japanese people didn't know about our camps; information about them was restricted by the government."

My first reaction was: Why did the Japanese-Americans let this happen to them? But then I thought of the Jews in Germany who hadn't rebelled either, when they were transported to the camps. Misery here as there.

I told her about my mother's admiration for Japan. "She taught me that the Japanese had the highest culture in the world."

A bitter smile appeared on her face. "Here they don't think that way."

"I can't tell you how much I hate wars and all the evils coming with them," I said.

Briskly Mary put her handkerchief back. "I know you folks in Germany had terrible times as well. All the bombings."

"Not only that. My oldest daughter Lilo and I left everything behind and ran away from the Russians. After the war 14 million people were chased out of their homes in Eastern Europe for 'ethnic cleansing.' To hell with wars!"

Mary got up. "Let's hope we'll never have one again," she said as she left.

Deeply moved by Mary's tale, I realized how little nations knew about each other. No wonder prejudice, hatred and fear grew unbridled.

As if in a continuation of Mary's and my talk the *Palo Alto Times*' front page showed Japanese in colorful kimonos dancing in preparation for the Obon Festival at a Buddhist temple in town. Everyone was invited to see the dance and to tour the temple. "I've never seen a Buddhist temple," I said to Manfred. "America has everything!"

On that afternoon, our entire family went to attend the Obon Festival, including Lilo's new handsome escort Jay — who had replaced Joe. A low, stretched-out white Japanese building, sparingly adorned with dark-brown roof and beams and a stone-lantern in front, presented the background for booths and a huge crowd of people, white and Japanese. From a loudspeaker came Japanese music, its five-tone-scale immediately conjuring up Asia for most people. Oriental food, sushi, teriyaki steak and other, never-before-seen edibles, along with hot green tea, were for sale and we indulged ourselves.

As soon as chairs were put in rows we rushed to sit down. Five-tone-scale music sounded again, and men and women dancers in kimonos slowly moved to the gentle music. Exotic and fascinating. I was surprised how many "Caucasians" participated in the Japanese folk dancing. No prejudice, no fear nor hatred were present. The dancers, each with a fan in hand, formed a circle, dancing around in a single file, imitating the gracious movements of the leader.

When a tour through the temple was announced we joined the curious Caucasian crowd. A young Japanese, who introduced himself as Glenn Kameda, led us into the sanctuary. Looking over rows of benches, my eyes were enthralled by the abundance of gold around the altar and the beautiful flower arrangements. A gold-covered statue of the Buddha sat tailor-fashion in a shrine, squeezing thumb and index finger of one hand and holding up the other three fingers.

"Which god do you worship here?" I asked Glenn.

I saw how he tried to suppress a smile. "No god," he

answered. "We worship the teaching of the Buddha." His English was accent-free; he must have been born here.

"Oh, I thought Buddhists believed in many gods."

"No, we don't. But if you are interested in learning more about Buddhism you may want to attend our Sunday classes."

"I might. What time?"

"Service starts at ten. After that we teach classes."

My curiosity began to burn. For next Sunday I decided to go to mass early and afterwards to the Buddhist service and class. What an interesting experience that would be!

After Sunday mass at our parish church and coffee and donuts in the lobby I drove to the Buddhist temple. When I arrived at the parking lot a priest, round like a ball, in a black clerical gown with a brocade stole around his neck, hit a metal gong several times, calling for the service. When he disappeared into the building complex I entered the temple. All seats were taken and so I stood with other latecomers in the back and listened to the slow-changing harmonies, which a young woman played on the harmonium — a miniature organ I hadn't seen for decades.

Golden scenery at the front seemed to fill the entire temple. Everywhere I looked was gold, gold — the filigreed candle lanterns hanging from the ceiling, the candleholders in the form of a crane standing on a turtle, and the altar table, supported by boldly curved legs — all this appeared to be an overwhelming realm of gold. My eyes, scanning the myriads of gilded ornaments, finally came to rest on the dignified sitting-Buddha statue. Itself golden, it sat in a gleaming lotus flower, its bare torso reflecting the candlelight. Memories of my mother's admiration of Japan returned. In the 1920s, when many people didn't even know that a Japanese nation existed, she had ordered an exquisite tea set from Japan and cherished it until war bombs destroyed it with the entire house. At that pre-jet time there was no hope I'd ever meet a living Japanese.

Now, thirty years later, I was watching one. At the side of the altar, showing his profile, sat the black-clad priest whom I had seen in the parking lot. After striking a carved metal bowl he chanted Japanese syllables in a monotone, which at intervals were repeated by the congregation. I felt wonderfully tranquilized by it and wished this drone-like singing would go on forever.

During the chanting a strong scent of incense began to fill the temple. The worshippers, one by one, most of them black-haired, some blond, approached the altar, took a pinch of ashes from a bowl and strew it over a larger ash heap in which incense burned. Everyone except me participated; I didn't feel qualified.

"We have a special ceremony today," somebody whispered to me. I turned my head and recognized Glenn Kameda, the young Japanese guide from the Obon festival. "Four new teachers are being initiated."

The priest stepped in front of the altar, bowed with clasped hands, lit one candle from another and turned to us. The four aspirants, three short Japanese and one tall Caucasian, all male, each an unlit candle in hand, put themselves in front of the priest, who in turn asked each of them, "Are you ready to live according to the Noble Eightfold Path?"

"I am," each of them answered.

"Are you prepared to teach the Buddha's Four Noble Truths?"

"I am," the four replied.

The priest inclined his candle a bit so the four teachers could light theirs from it. "Then go and teach the *Dharma* to all those who want to listen." He shook the teachers' hands, smiled and said a few words. They walked up the aisle toward us and stood nearby to await the continuation of the service.

Once on the lectern, the priest began a simple but humorous sermon. There was no mention of dollars, as in our parish church. I didn't always understand his words because of his strong Japanese accent, but the congregation seemed to have a good time. A hymn, sung in English, brought the service to a close. Everyone bowed with clasped hands in the direction of the altar and left.

I espied Glenn Kameda. "May I attend your class?"

"I teach only a children's class," he replied. "You may want to go to the adult class. The teacher is Bob Burch. I'll take you there."

He ushered me into a small room where several seated adults, one black, the others white, turned to Glenn and me.

"Mr. Burch, this lady wants to attend your class," Glenn said to the teacher and left.

To my surprise the tall, thin Caucasian, who had just been initiated, stood before us. His longish face was pockmarked, but his dark eyes flashed and I thought a flame must be burning inside him. I said my name and sat down.

"We're just discussing the differences and misunderstandings between Christianity and Buddhism," Burch said to me, his large Adam's apple moving up and down. Then he turned to the rest of the class. "The Buddha is no god. He was Prince Siddhartha of the Sakya clan in Nepal, who through meditation achieved enlightenment and became a teacher who taught us the Four Noble Truths and the Eightfold Noble Path." He paused to let this sink in. After a while he added as a matter-of-fact, "At the temple we worship his teachings and nothing else."

Now my curiosity was aroused to hear about this strange religion that didn't seem to have a God or gods. How could it be called religion? Or was it only a philosophy?

Burch asked the class, "Anyone want to recite the Four Noble Truths so our new student can learn?"

The black man, age about twenty, answered, "The First Truth: All living beings are suffering."

Burch nodded at him and turned to the others. "Anyone for the Second Truth?"

"The cause of suffering is ignorance," said a pretty red-haired woman of about thirty.

A middle-aged man who looked like a warrior with his bushy eyebrows straightened up on his seat. "The Third Noble Truth: Ignorance can be overcome."

While reflecting on these ideas I missed the Fourth Noble Truth, quoted by a matron. Burch had apparently observed my inattention and said to the lady, "Please say the Fourth Truth again."

"The way to overcome ignorance is the Eightfold Noble Path."

Burch handed a sheet of paper to me. "Here are the Four

Noble Truths and the Eightfold Noble Path. Take it home so you can study it."

I thanked him and put the slip into my handbag.

The class went on, discussing the different directions Buddhism had spread geographically and philosophically, depending which of the sutras — the Buddha's sermons — a sect was based on.

"Despite the different emphases in sects," Burch asked, "what are the fundamentals they all have in common?"

The young black man raised his hand. "All things are impermanent. No beginning, no end. No first cause, no creation."

Just like that! I sat startled.

The teacher smiled, turning to the others. "What else?"

The warrior-looking man cited, "No immortal soul. No self. Life is a temporary combination of items." He looked at me. "By the way, that's exactly what science confirms."

I had read this so often in popular explanations of physical and chemical news; after death, we, our molecules, decompose and combine with other compounds. Nothing in the universe is lost; it remains in changing form forever.

Burch interrupted my contemplation. "The Buddha's greatest noble demand?"

"Compassion for all suffering beings," the pretty red-head cited.

A goal I've been striving for all my life, I thought.

"You folks really have learned your lessons," Burch declared with a proud smile. "I hope our new student will catch up fast."

An hour later and the sheet with the wisdom of Buddhism in my handbag, I left and drove home, deeply touched by the Buddhist teachings. I felt I had stepped into a fascinating new world, but was well aware of my heavy Christian background. Raised as a Lutheran, I had converted to Catholicism twenty years ago, being attracted by the multi-colored world of the Catholic Church. For love of me Manfred had followed, and we had raised our children as Catholics, never turning back to the Lutheran faith. Now confronting Buddhism, would I be able to work out these discrepancies?

My studies of the most peaceful religion on Earth were brutally interrupted by Manfred, coming home from work.

"We are invading Cuba!" he shouted to me as he went to the kitchen to wash his hands.

"What for? Are they insane?"

"Cuba has gone communist. Kennedy wants to overthrow that government. It shouldn't take too long to capture it."

"A war! That's exactly what I hate. Have we come for this to Amerika?"

Manfred dried his hands on the kitchen towel. "We won't be touched by this. The Cubans can't shoot missiles at us. Watch out, in a few days we'll hear it's over." He was so sure and at the same time so uninterested, as if it were a matter of emptying a garbage can.

Hours later I dashed to Anne for clarification and found her busy with her clothes dryer. "Hi, Eva! What's up?"

"What do you think about the invasion of Cuba?" I blurted out.

"We're cleaning up that island," she said in a superior tone. "We don't want any communists eighteen miles off our coast." She began to wipe off washer and dryer with slow and detached movements and I thought if the Americans were to treat the Cuban communists this way, they might not succeed.

Anne's cleaning action was finished. She picked up the dried clothes. "By the way, Eva, I need a babysitter tomorrow night. Can you send Ronnie over? She's Beanie's favorite. And Ronnie has the patience of an angel." She laughed. "Not even I can handle Beanie. But Ronnie can."

How fast Cuba's invasion was forgotten! Thousands of deaths were involved, but its importance was wiped off like a washing machine. I deeply sympathized with the people of that small island, who now were exposed to horror and death because the politicians were unable to handle the situation in peace.

As it soon turned out, the attempted clean-up of Cuba failed at the Bay of Pigs.

I again met Anne at her service porch.

"We lost the battle," Anne declared, taking out clothes from the dryer, "or at least didn't pursue it any further."

"An unusual generosity."

She began to fold the clothes. "President Kennedy is supposed to have asked himself: 'How could I be so stupid?'"

"How do you know, Anne?"

"Gossip in Washington, D.C. My brother called from there and told me."

While preparing for the night I asked Manfred, "How could a sophisticated world power be humiliated this way?"

"By sending in poorly trained refugees instead of well-trained troops."

"I'm sure Kennedy's ashamed of the defeat."

He shrugged. "He's imposing an embargo against Cuba. No trade or travel." He hopped into bed.

I shook my head and laid down next to him, finally used to sharing his — our — bed.

"Good looks alone don't make an effective leader," I said. "By the way, what kind of education do these politicians actually have? After all, they have the power to send human beings in for slaughter by the thousands but never have to risk their own heads."

"You won't change that, Eve." He covered himself up to his chin.

"Too bad," I replied with anger. "If I had something to say, I would let the leaders of the nations solve their problems in duels. You would see how fast wars and duels would be eliminated."

He pulled me towards him and held me tight. "If you were on the ballot, I'd vote for you and no one else." He kissed me and I melted in his arms. How wonderful to have him and to be desired by him! I felt on fire, and war and politicians were forgotten.

Next afternoon I sat on the edge of our bed, happily remembering last night's delights, as the jubilant love duet of *Tristan and Isolde* sounded in my head. Suddenly I saw through the curtain Lilo coming home from college. That early? Then I heard her sob. Ice-cold fear touched my heart.

Crying, she came through the open bedroom door and fell in my arms.

"What is it, Lilo?" I asked softly into her disheveled blond hair.

"I'm pregnant."

A bomb exploded, shattering our family life to pieces. We fell into a black void, stifled to lifeless figures.

Lilo must have realized that I was in shock and unable to respond. She grabbed a tissue from my night table to wipe off her swollen eyes.

"Mom, I'm sorry," I heard her say as from afar.

Her words made me slowly come out of my shock, and I listened to her stammered revelations. It had been Jay, the tall, handsome young man whom I'd met when I was teaching German to his mother. Lilo had gone out with him several times. Both were eighteen.

The blackness within me had given way to grayness, but I still felt a heavy burden on my shoulders. What would Manfred say? Would he blame me for whatever reason? For not having protected her better?

Lilo kept silent. She got up and went to her room.

I stayed back, still sitting on the bed. The weight on my shoulders got heavier, and since I saw no solution to unload the burden, the thought crept in that it would be good to be dead. Not hearing anything, let life and its turmoil pass and dissolve into an eternal night. I finally fell asleep and woke up when Manfred came home from work.

"Lilo is pregnant," I said.

"Whaaat?" he almost shouted it. "Who's the guy?"

I told him.

"Now what?" he said, hopelessness in his voice.

I slowly shook my head. "I don't know."

Helpless, we kept silent. I strongly wished I were dead.

Finally I pulled myself up and went to the kitchen. Life was going on, and dinner had to be fixed.

While we were eating in the kitchen the telephone rang. Urs

went to answer it. It was Esther, Jay's mother. Was she trying to set up another German lesson? I went to the telephone.

"Eva," Esther's slow and clear voice said, "we learned that Lilo has talked to you about her and Jay's situation. I just want to tell you, whatever you and Manfred decide will be all right with us."

Startled by her friendliness and generosity I mumbled, "Thank you, Esther." With effort I added, "I'll let you know."

The only source we consulted was our parish's young vicar, Father Boyle.

"I'm glad the idea of abortion never came up," he said, and indeed, none of us had ever thought of that. So marriage was the solution and it was set up for November.

The first Yankee to join the family! Whatever I had seen around me had convinced me of the superior treatment of women in this country — one of the reasons why Manfred had dragged us to Amerika. As for Jay, he came from a fine family and so there was little to worry about this marriage, except the bridal pair's age.

"Together we are thirty-six," Jay consoled us.

The younger the mother the healthier the child, the statistics tell us, I thought. *Poor comfort.*

Esther, who so much resembled England's Queen in appearance and conservatism, not only cooperated with us but, knowing our tiny two-bedroom bungalow, offered their own spacious two-story house for the wedding party. As for the American custom to shower the bride with rice for fertility, she bought an Instant-Rice box. "To hurry it up," she said.

With such pleasant experiences we all looked forward to the wedding, when an atomic war threat rose on the country's border: Russian missiles in Cuba! Their range covered half of the United States and the American population lost its usual complacency.

"Oh my God, we'll all die!" I heard a customer cry at the supermarket's check-out counter.

"These damned communists!" another shouted. "We should drop a nuclear bomb on them!"

Our next-door neighbor, Mary Toshitsune, rushed over to ask me, "Do you think there will be a war?"

"No," I answered. "I don't think so. Kennedy will do something about it."

Her almond-shaped eyes became almost round. "How can you be so cool?"

"I've survived one war, I'd survive another. You too, Mary."

And Kennedy did "do something about it." American newspapers reported only that "President Kennedy demanded the removal of the missiles," while European papers wrote that "Kennedy had exchanged a removal of Russian missiles in Cuba for the removal of American missiles in Turkey."

"All Krushchev wanted was to get American missiles out of Turkey, right?" I asked Manfred at dinner.

"Looks like it. Anyway, for several days we were really on the brink of a nuclear war."

"I think we'll never have a nuclear war," I said. "The leaders fear for their own lives and switch to diplomacy for a change. It's close to what I mean with my dream for duels between those warmongers."

"My dear pacifist, would you pass me the salt?" he asked, sarcasm in his voice.

I was ready to throw the salt shaker at him, but saw the opportunity to give an example of pacifism. "Here's the salt, Lieutenant Commander," I said, tinting my voice with sweetness. "I'm glad you survived the war. Let's not have another one."

Lilo's wedding preparations brought a surprise for us. The American custom of bridal showers brought Ronnie's earlier statement to mind: "The Americans have such handy holidays!" They also had handy celebrations, I learned. One helpful church member invited her friends who "showered" Lilo with very much appreciated household goods. In America, it seemed, one had only to signal to friends who would then come and lavish goodies on the central figure.

More surprises: First, there would be a rehearsal of the wedding ceremony. Even without being spruced up Lilo looked fabulous, her blond hair stylishly done, her pretty face beaming, her blackened lashes framing her blue eyes. She neither resembled Manfred nor me — she carried her pleasing appearance as her own unique bearing.

The next surprise: The wedding ceremony dragged us back to the middle ages. While in old Europe bride and bridegroom together strode down the aisle to the altar, in modern America the bride's father walked his daughter down the aisle to "give her away" to her next superior. What degradation for the bride, what a shame! I felt like protesting, standing up for women's rights, but instead, I swallowed the visible insult and gave in to the general joyous mood of the participants. None of my children would probably mind this outmoded ceremony, especially not Urs and Ronnie who served as bridesmaids. One nice surprise was the music "Here comes the bride," from Wagner's *Lohengrin,* although in the opera it's sung after the wedding ceremony. No big deal.

The wedding party at Lilo's in-laws' spacious home was a great success. A big crowd had gathered, and champagne flowed in torrents. We couldn't have given such a glamorous party, I thought. All the more I was grateful to Esther for stepping in where we might have failed.

Meanwhile, Esther's Instant Rice was doing its job and in three months produced a healthy, blond, blue-eyed girl. She was named Yvonne, and Lilo took care of her as she had done so often with her younger siblings. I bonded with the baby as I always had with my five "other" children, and so Yvonne became "my sixth child." The thought that I was her grandmother didn't occur to me.

The young family soon moved across the street into a house Jay's parents bought for them.

Yet to become a mother-in-law was a painful experience. Whenever I stepped into their home Jay ignored me almost to the point of open hostility. Ignorant and well-meaning, I tried to compensate with doubled friendliness — without positive results and not comprehending that a mother-in-law's place ought to be *in absentia.*

Esther, now Lilo's mother-in-law, unknowingly came to my

rescue. She told me about her music appreciation class at nearby Foothill College. She was fifty, ten years my senior and still taking classes as people in this country could freely do, and therefore I thought it might be a good idea to learn English in a class whose subject I was familiar with. So I joined Music Appreciation 1-A.

At the college I had my first feeling of completely being at home. I was sitting on the grass by the buildings, waiting for class time as the Westminster chimes on the campus tower began to ring through the air and directly into my heart. Wonderful, these were the sounds of my parent's grandfather clock; I had grown up with them. Feelings of being home, and of pride, gratefulness and excitement filled me. I knew I belonged in this environment and joyfully I walked to the classroom, where I knew in advance what the instructor would teach. I grinned; could anyone during my teenage years have predicted that I, who considered high school a prison, would ever exult at being in college?

Besides learning English in a music class I was busy enough with my own family, driving Ronnie and Wernher to their recorder orchestra; teaching piano; coaching singers; playing the piano at the opera performances and harpsichord in Baroque groups. My life was filled with music. But I felt alone.

Regarding the West

I had lost Manfred to his marine world long ago; or had he never emerged from it, just sometimes showing his face? Our mutual interest in music occasionally brought us together, but with the sea and Buddhism we were alone in our respective worlds. I decided to satisfy my interest in Buddhism by playing the harmonium for the service and afterwards attending Sunday school.

What I missed at the Buddhist temple was the lack of rituals. I told Sunday-school teacher Bob Burch about it.

"I assume you'd like Zen Buddhism," he said. "Every Wednesday I drive with some of our class to San Francisco to participate in Zen meditation. Come along if you like."

So, on Wednesday night I joined the group I knew so well from Sunday school. In his VW-minibus Bob Burch drove us along crowded Bayshore Freeway. I sat next to him, wondering what had caused the pockmarks on his face.

Unaware of my musings, Bob was giving me instructions for the impending sitting session at the Zen Center. "While you meditate keep your eyes open all the time, otherwise you might fall asleep. Think of nothing. Empty yourself of all the crap we deal with every day. We'll drive home after about two hours."

In the late afternoon we entered San Francisco without seeing it, since dense fog was hugging hills and buildings. Driving along Van Nuys Street, we turned onto Bush Street and stopped in front of a gray, old, two-story building.

We entered it, and Burch said to me in a low voice, "From now on we keep silent. No talking. Follow us."

We walked through a corridor and entered a sparely lit room without furniture. Five people sat on the floor, in "lotus position," facing the wall, their legs crossed, knees wide apart, hands on their thighs, palms up. In one corner stood a short, dark-robed monk, motionless and fading into the background, apparently the Zen master.

Burch handed me a rolled-up bamboo mat. Following the others, I opened it, put it on the floor and settled into the crossed-leg position, facing the wall before me. I found sitting in this position easy and comfortable, but emptying my mind was a different story. I kept fighting the memories of the day — how to coach *Rigoletto*'s tenor so he'd safely reach the high C; what to cook for dinner tomorrow; had I paid the water bill on time? Also my mind sounded the theme of a Bach fugue and kept transposing it into another key. Where was the stillness I so strongly desired?

Suddenly I heard a noise as if someone had been slapped. What in the world was that? Wide-awake, I strained my ears. From the corner of my eye I saw the monk shuffling around the hall, his steps inaudible. Every ten minutes or so there was another slap. My curiosity went into a blaze. Not too much later I saw the person next to me bow towards the wall, his palms joined together. A moment later he received a slap with a thin wooden lath from the monk. Apparently the meditator had asked for it! But why?

I sat very still, thinking if I should give it a try. Not knowing where the monk was at the moment, I put the palms of my hands together and bowed. When I noticed the monk approaching me, I was prepared for the slap. He lightly hit me with his lath on my shoulder and then continued his walk. It hadn't hurt at all. It was more like a friendly pat, without sensation, more a reminder to meditate properly.

After about an hour the Zen master hit a gong, apparently indicating the end of meditation, because everyone got up, folded his or her mat and put them in a corner. A folding wall was removed, revealing a dark-green Buddha statue on a simple low stand. The group spread out around the altar and the monk began to chant monotonous syllables,

"Shiki soku ze ku. Ku soku ze shiki."

"Form is Emptiness. Emptiness is Form."

What a concept! The power of the contradiction continued to

keep me spellbound.

On our way home, I asked Bob about the Emptiness idea and the monk's hitting our shoulders with his lath.

"The words come from the sutra on which Zen is based," he said. "The meditator's bowing means to express humility and the slap to reinforce it." He gave me a quick look. "I hope you learned some of it." Bang! That was *his* slap regarding my lack of humility.

As for the regular sessions I regretted not having received the benefits one could get from proper meditation. I was too restless to sit still for hours. But I quite often thought of Bob Burch's "hope" that I learn some humility. Did I really lack it? I'd have to say yes, I was often judgmental and intolerant. One of the Buddhist teachings emphasized ridding ourselves of criticism. I resolved to work on it from now on.

Despite all my commitments and distractions I couldn't fail to notice that our Urs was suffering from teenage turmoil. With her blond hair and blue eyes inherited from Manfred, but taller and stronger-built than her siblings, she'd always seemed to be the most level-headed and energetic of our off-spring. All the more disturbing was her recent touchiness. Discontented, impatient and grumpy, she now saw her deliverance only in a life in Hawaii. For Californians the Hawaiian Islands were, by popular books and commercialism, The Paradise. Movies and advertisements extolled an exotic life under palm trees and an eternal sun with a Polynesian population doing little else but singing, dancing, surfing and love-making. A fantastic world for dreamers, a turf with endless amusements for rich vacationers and a no-no for us ordinary people.

Having dinner on the terrace in the backyard, I asked Urs what she wanted for her high school graduation.

"A trip to Hawaii!"

Everyone laughed except Manfred and me.

"Sorry, Urs," Manfred said. "This is out of the question. Can you think of something else?"

Brusquely she got up from the table and went to her room

and probably cried.

Poor Little Bear, I thought — no longer allowed to use her nickname. After dinner I went to her untidy room and saw her head with the blond ponytail bowed over books; she was doing mathematics.

"Homework?" I asked.

She shook her head, but didn't look up. 'When I have it up to here," she touched her nose, "I do math. Then everything becomes cool and clear."

I sat down on her bed and looked up at her. Her eyes were still a little red, probably from crying. "What a girl — math as a remedy! I wish I had your brain." I kissed her and left her to her higher domain.

Hours later, when I went to bed I found a small, green-covered notebook under my bedcover. I opened it and read Urs's outpouring of complaints and frustrations, of her vain efforts in dealing with family and friends. She recorded no dramatic events, only her feelings, and instead of a signature she wrote, "Please answer in writing." So the little green-covered notebook became a conversation vehicle between her and me, just as deaf Beethoven's conversation book had been with his visitors.

Unrelated to Hawaiian dreams or frolics I received an invitation I could hardly refuse.

On a Sunday, the Buddhist priest said to me, "Mrs. Krutein, we appreciate your playing the harmonium for our service. Our teachers are going to attend a meeting in Sacramento next weekend, and I invite you to go with them."

Flattered and excited, I accepted. What a chance, what an honor! Playing the miniature organ was such a trifle for me, I was there for Sunday school anyway. Besides, I was only a beginning student of Buddhism, and now I was invited together with the teachers! I felt immensely honored.

On the trip to California's capital I rode with the five Sunday school teachers in a van. Arriving in Sacramento, we walked to a high school, entered the multi-purpose room and joined several other Japanese groups from different areas until we were a crowd of about 100, all wearing western clothes. How comfortable, I didn't have to raise my chin to have eye contact, the Japanese were all as short as myself, except a white-haired giant in the back, who probably didn't even belong here. I enjoyed the pleasant noise of their soft speaking and their repeated bowing to each other. No one smoked — presumably not to bother non-smokers.

The program was interesting: Sightseeing the Capitol and the famous azaleas in bloom. Later, short lectures in Japanese and English, all in the multi-purpose room.

Particularly enlightening was a talk by Reverend Fujitani from Hawaii, first in perfect English, then in Japanese. Standing erect and commanding on the lectern, he appeared to be a resurrected samurai, radiating intelligence and power. In his speech he incorporated the pitfalls of daily life into modern Buddhism as I hadn't heard before.

"...To compare and compete is to create problems. When the sun shines, enjoy it; when it rains, enjoy it. All things in life, let them come and let them go. This is a secret of life that keeps one from getting upset or being neurotic. Sakyamuni Buddha said that all things in life and in the world are in constant change, so do not become attached to them. True happiness is not given to us — we create it."

What a philosophy, how different from the Amerikan stress on competition and winning!

As a gong sounded, the crowd moved without haste to a large table covered with what I thought was an art exhibit. Spellbound I stood before a display of Japanese culinary creations. Lacquer boxes with sushi, filled with colorful inserts, plates with flying cranes made of white, thin slices of fish, flowers with yellow petals of cooked bass with red tuna as seed-vessels. Small, vase-like bottles, themselves pieces of art, contained hot sake. Maple leaves and closed fans were the sparing decorations. After admiring the exhibit we all filled our plates with the delicacies.

Socializing was a delightful addition. Reverend Fujitani stood next to me and I could see his handsome, inscrutable face at close range. While selecting food, I said to him, "I enjoyed your talk, *sensei*," using the Japanese form of address for Reverend and teacher.

"Thank you," he replied softly. He kept sampling gourmet pieces. "Have you been studying Buddhism?"

"For many months."

He stepped away from the table to make room for others, signaling me to do likewise. "Have you ever been in Hawaii?"

"Not yet." I told him about Urs's Hawaiian dreams. "She's trying her utmost to go there."

"You've got to meet Mr. Harding, also from Hawaii," Fujitani said, leading me to the tall, white-haired Caucasian I had noticed before. He introduced us and added, "May I be excused?" He bowed slightly and left.

Unlike inscrutable samurai Fujitani, Ralph Harding's wrinkled face radiated warmth and friendliness. We shook hands. Among the short, black-eyed Japanese, this blue-eyed giant stood out from the crowd.

"Let's have some tea and sit down," Harding said.

We filled our tea cups, picked up a few salted Japanese cookies and sat down at a small table with a simple but artistic flower arrangement. Against a background of subdued talking we told each other how we had come to Buddhism. I learned that Harding's wife was Japanese, with whom he had four children.

His voice, unlike that of usual giants, was soft as those around us. "My oldest, Verne, is graduating from high school in June. He wants to go to college on the mainland. But he never asks how to finance it."

A flash as bright as a burning meteor hit me. "I have a daughter who wants to go to school in Hawaii. We certainly can't afford that. What would you think of a children's exchange?"

Harding, about to have a sip of tea, let the tea cup sink to the table. "Are you kidding?"

"I really mean it." He and I were companions in searching for the light, I thought, and we could trust each other. I invited him for dinner tomorrow night. I gave him the directions to Palo Alto and our house and could hardly wait to discuss my proposal with the family.

Next evening when Ralph Harding dined with us he described life in Hawaii. "In the summer the weather is hot and very humid. Whoever's not used to that should avoid the summer. We have no real racial problems in Hawaii. There are lots of Caucasians, Japanese, Chinese and Filipinos. All get along very well."

Manfred agreed with the swap. "And I think adding an American to our household will help us understand America better," he said. "And we'd have to speak English in the house."

Before young Verne arrived we moved to a two-story house about a mile away, where the boys would have one bedroom and Ronnie and Irmie another. All the children helped move. Manfred transported the piano himself. He put it on a dolly and pushed it by hand through the streets. When neighbors appeared with their cameras, I even played on it, while walking sideways like a crab.

By leaving the old neighborhood we also moved away from Lilo and "my sixth child" Yvonne. Then she and her family of three increased the distance between us by selling their house in Palo Alto and buying a walnut ranch in Northern California. Lilo was pregnant again and wanted to raise her children in the middle of the great redwoods. I felt as though I were giving up part of my tribe.

When Verne arrived, tall as his father and with black hair and slanted eyes from his mother, Urs left for Hawaii. I saw her go with sadness. I'd miss my Little Bear! Would she miss us? Or would she adjust?

Getting organized in the newly-rented house, we even bought a TV set after three years of resisting the "idiot box." With great anticipation we turned it on — and watched how President Kennedy was shot to death.

"My God, how can one kill a president?" I asked Manfred, incredulous. "Who in the world did it?"

"His enemies, of course. It's the common way to get rid of an unwanted politician. We'll see whom they decide to blame."

Although it was already late, we decided to see the de Potteres. Why did one have good friends if not for discussions?

In their woodsy home Jerry and Madeleine de Pottere sat in front of the TV, watching what probably the whole world was seeing now.

Jerry lowered the volume. "We have expected this to happen sooner or later."

"Why?" I asked with utmost surprise. "What in the world has Kennedy done that he had to be disposed of?"

Jerry contemptuously blew his nose. "He attacked Cuba. Lost the battle. Now he has secretly sent more than 15,000 troops to Vietnam, where we have no business at all. Congress is mad. Instead of only rapping him on his knuckles they killed him instead."

"Who's they?"

"His political enemies. He had many."

Madeleine took a wine bottle and glasses from a closet. "Everything is better to bear with wine," she said and began to pour Hungarian Green.

"How do you know about the 15,000 troops?" I asked Jerry.

"From European newspapers. Ours don't tell much."

Madeleine, turning to the over-and-over rerun of the murder scene, told us, "They say one man did the shooting. They already caught him."

"And soon they'll declare him insane and that's it," Jerry said.

Manfred put his emptied glass down with a bang. "Maybe they can even blame the Soviets for it."

Dirty politics, I thought. Don't soil your own hands. I wonder what Anne would say to the killing?

Next day, curious to hear her opinion, I rushed over to her place. It was Saturday and Doug was also home. The kids were playing in the backyard.

Anne was sad and Doug was mad.

"What a shame before the world!" Anne cried.

"Those lazybones police and FBI!" Doug shouted. "Not to clear the area of insane gunslingers!"

"You believe that one man alone did it?" I asked.

"Of course, only a moron would do this!" Doug shouted.

An old saying came to mind: When national pride or religion comes in, you'd better quit arguing.

I saw a book on the table. Maybe this could be a good digression. I picked it up. *The Feminine Mystique*, by Betty Friedan. I looked at Anne inquiringly.

"I bought this last week and read it," she said. "But nothing is important anymore after this awful mess in Dallas."

She sounded so miserable I almost felt like consoling her. "May I take the book home?" I asked instead. "I'll return it as soon as possible."

Anne gave a deep sigh. "You don't have to return it. We are moving within weeks. Doug got a transfer."

A bombshell! No, that couldn't be true! I just had found her and now she'd go away! My buddy, my teacher, my consoler, my comforter, my — I ran out of expressions. "Where are you going?" I managed to ask.

She sighed again. "Geneva, Switzerland."

A deep sadness filled me. Unable to say more, I stepped over to her, hugged and held her tight.

As if to make an end to our sentimentality Doug asked in his usual commanding way if she had picked up his trousers from the cleaners.

I felt superfluous. I said goodbye and left, taking Betty Friedan's book along. As so often in my life I decided to bury my sadness in reading a good book.

I devoured Friedan's book greedily. Society, she wrote, had put down women who left the kitchen for creative work. That was I. Making music outside my house, I had endured men's sneering remarks and women's envy in Germany and in South America as well. 'The heck with them!' Betty Friedan seemed to tell me. 'You were right — send the critics to hell!' A wonderful certainty overcame me: I had always known that the kitchen was not my destiny. But now an author told this to the whole world and liberated me. I took a deep breath, feeling the remaining doubt disappear. I'd never been that happy with myself before.

My happiness was soon overshadowed by the Fentons'

departure. After a long search I had made a good friend, and now she was leaving. "'Ships that pass in the night,'" I said to Anne.

"My whole life has been that way," she said. Even she who was so skilled in meeting life's challenges with a sense of humor, had lost it now. "I can't tell you how much I hate to move again. Never before have I had such a close friend."

"We'll write each other," I said. "I've never lost a friend because of distance. I'm sure we won't forget each other." Even so, writing was a small compensation for talking face-to-face.

Meantime Urs wrote glowing letters from Hawaii. She liked her adopted family and particularly Mrs. Harding who initiated her into oriental culinary art. On the pictures Urs sent us, her new half-Japanese family posed with her in front of their bungalow, surrounded by white orchids, red anthuriums and yellow hibiscus.

Ralph himself frequently wrote to us. One of his letters shook me to my bones: "Why did you send Urs away without any instructions about birth control pills or condoms? She wants to go out on dates and isn't protected..."

I sat thunderstruck, never having heard of those pills. Was this my responsibility? Yes, it was. Particularly with Lilo's experience, who hadn't been instructed either, I should have taken a stand long ago. Too late now. No, it was never too late! I should discuss the problem with someone. Anne and her family were already in Switzerland, and for some reason I didn't feel like discussing birth control with the de Potteres. Oh, I missed Anne!

Before I could make up my mind a big event took up all my energies: We bought our first home, a typical California Ranch-style home on the south end of Palo Alto. The house stretched out to both sides. Three bedrooms and a converted garage as a fourth one provided ample space for all of us. A small grassy frontyard and a large backyard were bonuses.

As the agreed-upon time for the children's exchange had come to its end, Verne took up residence with a friend near his college.

When Urs returned from Hawaii she happily took charge of her own room. She was full of energy and pride. She cooked a delicious Japanese dinner for us, "Beef Tomato," using chopsticks for cooking and eating. Then she prepared a surprise for us. She pushed the living room furniture to the walls, had us take a seat and disappeared. Soon Hawaiian music from the record player filled the room and Urs appeared in her floor-length mu'umu'u and danced for us, using her hands and arms for imitative gestures that meant paddling, swimming or diving. Wernher had quickly gotten his camera and shot his sister's every movement. How much she had learned in Hawaii!

Regardless of Urs's Hawaiianization my bad conscience reminded me of the new birth-control pills. Not knowing whom to ask about them, I had put this problem on the back burner. Because of our move Urs, like her siblings, had to change schools and make new friends — no small task for a sixteen-year-old girl. But dates were no danger at this point.

The greatest threat now was the escalating war in Vietnam. At one Saturday luncheon we were seated beneath a white canvas umbrella on our sunlit wood deck.

"How a giant like the U.S. can relentlessly bomb a small agricultural country is beyond me," I said. "Johnson should be ashamed of himself. What's the excuse for the shooting this time?" I asked, biting into a cheese sandwich.

"To curb communism."

"Those were Hitler's words too. America could have fought at his side."

Manfred ignored my sarcasm. "With this new Tonkin Gulf resolution the question is: How many more troops will Johnson send to Vietnam? The draft calls have already increased by a hundred percent."

Wernher interrupted his chewing and said, "I'll never be drafted. I'll be a conscientious objector."

I smiled. "That's my son! You hate the war as I do."

"I hate to kill people. And animals," he said.

Ronnie fixed her big brown eyes on me. "I'm against the war

too, Mom."

Urs began to collect the empty plates. "I'm also very much against war. But that's not enough. We have to let Johnson know that he's doing a dirty job."

"How are you going to do that?" Manfred asked.

"Go on protest marches." She stood and carried the dishes out.

The war escalated more and more, the population began to protest on a wide scale, and candlelight marches increased. The hippies conquered San Francisco; rock concerts with lightshows and smoking pot became the standard entertainment of the young people. The generation gap widened, the students of UC Berkeley started the Free Speech Movement and the blacks awakened and fought for their rights. In a word, the nation was in a cultural turmoil, which, I thought, was necessary and gave hope of more tolerance for all the people who — like myself — by nature deviated from the standard population.

Struggle and Determination

The first day of 1966 sneaked in. Still half asleep, we all went to mass to begin the new year with a spiritual effort. Our parish church was crowded and we had to stand. Dissonant organ noises whined through the house of God which made me shudder.

"What a jangle!" Manfred whispered in my ear.

At one point of the service the congregation was called on to recite the Creed. Since I couldn't say it by heart in English I made it a point to listen to the recitation and, wondering how much of the Buddhist teaching had influenced me, to check up on my own beliefs. The jubilant music of Beethoven's *Gloria in excelsis deo,* Glory to God, impressed itself on my mind, the melody in D-major storming up.

"I believe in God." *Oh God, do I really?* I asked myself, appalled.

"The Father almighty, creator of heaven and earth." *No creation, no beginning, no end...*

"In Jesus Christ..." I sighed with relief. *Like the Buddha, preaching the same fundamental commandments, full of compassion...*

"...conceived of the Holy Spirit, born of the Virgin Mary..." *Sorry, that's a legend.* The music stopped.

"...suffered under Pontius Pilatus, was crucified, died and was buried..." *Yes, all beings suffer, even He...*

"...descended to the dead, rose again, ascended into heaven, seated next to the Father..." *No, I didn't believe that.*

Horrified, I realized I was as unbelieving as I had been before I converted from the Lutheran Church to Catholicism. Ironically, Beethoven's *Gloria* began to sing in me again, nagging, incessant. As the mass continued I recalled my first shock when

I saw how different American Catholicism was from that in South America: The Virgin Mary enthroned, no street processions, no mysticism, no union with the state. I had felt pushed back into the paleness of Protestantism. Therefore my curiosity and eagerness to study another religion. The Buddhist philosophy had blended with my view of the universe, was unintrusive, non-missionary and consoling. And now, confronted with the Christian Creed, I realized that Catholicism to me was a borrowed religion and that my metamorphosis had begun and was still continuing. I felt dizzy, pushed into chaos, loaded with responsibilities and consequences which I wasn't able to foresee. Silently I went home with my unsuspecting family.

My pangs of conscience left me sleepless the following night; not even the tranquilizers helped. When I got up on Monday morning I was tired, had a headache and felt listless. I remembered I had to attend a Parent Teacher Association meeting at Irmie's elementary school in the evening, and drowsy with tiredness I dragged myself to the school and into the multi-purpose room, which was already crowded with people. I had difficulty finding an empty seat.

A psychologist, Dr. Judah Landes, was the guest speaker. Middle-aged, bald-headed and quite overweight, he talked about how marital problems affect the children. Suddenly I was wide awake. Here was someone who understood those problems and, as he recommended, seeing a counselor — like him — could help. After the speech I approached him and asked him for his business card.

On my walk home I asked myself what marital problems I had. Manfred was a fine, honest, intelligent and hard-working husband; so what in the world did I miss? *Communication*, it sounded within me from all sides, *communication, communication!* Yes, that's what it was. Manfred gave commands and briefly answered questions most of the time, but he rarely asked questions and when he did, listened only with half an ear.

When we went to bed, I told Manfred about Judah Landes. "This man could be a tremendous help for people with marital problems."

"Probably," he replied. His interest in psychology was as skimpy as in the changing temperatures on the planet Mars.

My total exhaustion from balancing marital and religious problems proved powerful enough to make me sleepless at night. I kept reading books or musical scores while Manfred next to me was snoring the hell out of the bedroom.

At five in the morning my resentments were so strong that I brusquely got out of bed. All the books I had been reading during his beauty sleep lay scattered around on my side of the bed. Furiously I grabbed one and threw it at him. It hit his shoulder. His snoring stopped, but he still wasn't awake. My anger grew into rage. The musical score of *Tristan and Isolde* lay there, just waiting to be grasped. I picked it up with both hands and threw it at his head.

He jerked up and stared at me. "Are you crazy?"

"I just want to wake you up," I said, shaking with fury.

Bewildered, he looked at the clock, obviously trying to remember why I had wakened him. He stared at the scattered books and then at me. "What's the matter?" He got up from the bed, knocking off the *Tristan* score. My beloved score! I picked up another book, but before I could throw it at him he'd come around and pulled it from my hand. "Stop that! And tell me why you're doing this?"

With utmost anger I shouted, "I can't sleep! It's five and I haven't slept at all!"

"That's enough!" he yelled. "Let's see that counselor. Do you still have his name?"

His sudden decision made me speechless. So he had already considered counseling, otherwise he couldn't have come to this conclusion so quickly.

"Do you really want to see that psychologist?" I asked.

He got up from the bed. "Yes. I want to see why you have so many problems and I don't." He disappeared into the shower. During breakfast we didn't talk much. As Manfred went out the door he said, "Don't forget to make an appointment with that psychologist."

"I won't," I said, suppressing a smile.

I called Judah Landes, and set the time for our first encounter at 7 P.M. on Thursday.

On that evening, we arrived at Landes's office on time. Subdued light fell from several table lamps in the corners onto the comfortable scenery — a sofa, three arm chairs surrounding a small table on whose middle stood a box with tissues.

The bald-headed counselor heaved his enormous weight from the chair to greet us with a handshake. We sat down.

After preliminary questions, Landes asked Manfred to tell him about his life. Manfred gave a detailed description of his youth, Navy time, marriage and his work on three different continents and his future plans.

When my turn came I began with "We have five children —"

"Whaat?" Landes interrupted me, turning to Manfred. "You have five children and didn't mention them at all?"

That question made a deep impact on me and also on Manfred as I later learned.

The second jolt came from Landes's question, "What are your responsibilities at home?" He gave each of us paper and pens to make lists. My list contained 22 items, Manfred's only one: Take out the garbage cans.

Judd, as he wanted to be called, became a central figure in our lives, and in the course of months we learned from him how to talk to each other and so handle our problems. He encouraged us to buy a TV set, "That way you see the good and the bad things of our society," he said. We had to make up a written budget, and he urged us to have as much sex as possible. "Because that's one activity that brings people together," he said. In each session he asked us, "Have you had sex?" We had.

After counseling we always drove to deserted places, the palm-studded boulevard to Stanford University or the winding road along Palo Alto Creek, and talked and talked and talked. It was as if we were trying to catch up with all those years without real communication. He even called me Little Bear again — which I had missed hearing for ages!

However, although we made progress through the counseling,

it was painful for each of us. Notwithstanding my open-mindedness there were still areas in which I wanted to hold back, but, encouraged by Judd, had to speak up. How much harder must it be on Manfred, who was taught as a child never to talk about inner feelings, not even about his beloved mother's death!

Although Manfred had opened up quite a bit, he suddenly seemed to be absent-minded again. He frequently flew to Los Angeles or San Diego for a day, and, at home in the evening, buried himself in extra work.

"What are you up to, Manfred?" I asked him as we had dinner on the backyard terrace under the ornamental-banana tree.

He hesitated for a moment, then said, "I'm very involved in ocean mining. Looking for minerals, manganese mainly. It comes in nodules, which contain important elements such as nickel, copper and cobalt. But the mining process is still experimental."

"And what's your part in all this?"

Decisively he put his fork down, and I knew he would now forget to finish his meal. "The whole field of ocean mining is complex and requires a diversity of knowledge — experience in mining on shore and knowing how to construct a ship and how to operate on and in the water. So I think that's a field where I could put to use all my experiences. And the field is new and all the more exciting."

What a revelation! "So how do you go about studying where everything is new?"

"In conferences for ocean-related projects there are often papers read on ocean mining. I've persuaded my company to let me get information on ocean mining. Now they are sending me to all those conferences." He took a deep breath.

"Will you ever go down to the bottom of the ocean?" I asked, hearing Handel's *Water Music* ring out in my head.

He smiled. "The Pacific drops down to 38,000 feet at one point. About seven miles. East of the Philippines."

"Oh my God! But you won't get down that far, will you?"

He laughed. "No, my treasure, I promise, I won't." He got up, came around, kissed me and said, "Let's go for a walk."

We left dinner and dirty dishes behind, walked to the well-known creek and talked and talked. *Thank you, Judd!* I thought. Handel's music was still with me.

Independent of our marriage counseling, I discovered a linguistic problem within the family. We'd been in the States for almost five years, and I noticed that our children avoided speaking Spanish with each other. Particularly Ronnie resisted Spanish. For a while they spoke a gibberish of Spanish and English, but lately they spoke only English.

"What can we do about it?" I asked Manfred, as he was watering a spot in the backyard that wasn't reached by the automatic sprinklers.

Manfred turned off the hose. "Sorry, Bear, I have no answer to this problem."

A few days later the church office called to ask if we could house a Mexican student for two weeks. I perceived this as a gift from heaven and said yes.

We hurried to prepare a room for the new house guest, and soon Luís Martínez moved in, the fourth child of a doctor's family in Mexico City. His features were Latin, his manners gentleman-like, and for me he was surrounded by mariachi music sounding through my head. Every day he joined fellow students working at various projects together with people of the community.

At the end of the two weeks I asked Luís what his impression of America was.

After a moment he summed it up, "When talking to Americans I often found them sloppy or uninterested. But I learned it's only their informality. Besides, they show a great friendliness and cooperation to strangers, which we in Mexico are used to only from long-term friends. All in all I think they are great people."

He invited us to visit him and his family in Mexico. Through the church office I checked out the reputation of the Martínez family and got excellent reports of their piety, sophistication and good financial status. It didn't take too many letters to arrange for Ronnie to spend the summer vacation with the Martínezes.

Ronnie turned sixteen, and as summer began she flew to Mexico City. She called once and described her new family and their reception with glowing words. I sighed in relief.

Urs graduated from high school and went to work for the telephone company. Bilinguists were hired on the spot, trilinguists even sooner. The endless summer vacations were a good opportunity to make and save quite a bit of money.

Two months later Ronnie came home from Mexico. She appeared at San Francisco International Airport, with her dark brown hair and eyes resembling the Mexicans, and said goodbye to her co-passengers in Spanish. She turned to us and greeted us in German. She looked radiant, more self-assured than before.

Urs switched to English and Ronnie answered in English.

I sighed in relief. She was trilingual again. And she was home! "What was the highlight of your trip?"

She smiled. "The days in Acapulco. The Martínezes have a house on the beach. And the ocean is so warm down there."

When I asked her about the Martínez family she said everyone was fine. "Luís has a younger brother. His name is Manolo. He's 18." And with a softer tone in her voice she added, "Manolo and I are in love."

A jolt hit me. Again I had sent away one of my girls without thinking of possible love affairs and their dangers. How naive could I be? No letter had arrived from Mexico like Ralph Harding's from Hawaii, scolding me about my head-in-the-sand policy in regard to my daughter's prospective sex life. I tried to picture Ronnie and her "boyfriend" together on Acapulco's beach. Feeling immensely guilty of negligence, I closed my eyes. What could I do now?

Only later Urs told me, a bit contemptuous, "Ronnie told me about herself and Manolo. In Mexico young people are never left alone for a minute. She and Manolo couldn't even kiss, could only hold hands."

Urs, my down-to-earth daughter and the very image of her father, gave me relief and absolution for my negligence! As for now, there were no boyfriends around my daughters. But the day when young men appeared on the horizon, would I be ready to handle the situation? Yet before I could find the answer an urgent matter pushed itself into the foreground.

We applied for citizenship. After the required five years of adjustment to the American culture, the ugly "k" had finally transformed into a "c." Manfred thought he knew what he was supposed to know for the oral exam of citizens-to-be, but I took a citizenship class to learn what our children already knew about U.S. history and politics.

On a trip to the ocean with the de Potteres I shared with them my surprise about the emphasis the teacher gave on colleges. "The teacher talks about an electrical college all the time."

Jerry broke out in laughter. "I'm sure he said, 'electoral college'! But that has nothing to do with school. He explained to me that this was an outmoded body of electors chosen by the voters in each state to elect the President. How much did the other people in my citizenship class understand, if they didn't have friends to explain the political gibberish to them?

Besides, endless questionnaires had to be filled out. The ever-present question: "Are you or have you ever been a member of the Communist Party?" was already a nuisance. Yet the question: "If married, have you ever committed adultery?" was something new. From time to time I told this to our American friends, who, of course, had never been exposed to such a question. It provoked different reactions; embarrassed grins, cynical remarks or loud laughter.

Manfred, who had arrived in America months before us, became the first American citizen in the family. When the big day came for me to drive to San Francisco to take the oral exam before a judge, I felt somewhat uncomfortable. Knowing that these government officials probably had little sense of humor, I wished I were already back home. I entered the judge's reception room. I didn't have to wait very long and was called into the judge's office.

As I walked into the crammed office a very tall, thin, bespectacled gentleman got up from his chair, mumbled his name, shook my hand and said, "Please raise your hand and repeat my words." He raised his own hand and spoke words that resembled an oath. Shocked, I forgot to raise my arm. But he laughed, grabbed it and pushed it up. I babbled his words, hardly understanding what was really said. So much for truth under oath. He grinned and gestured to a chair across from his desk. I sat down.

He could be my grandfather, I thought. Before him lay my long questionnaire. "You are under oath," he said. "I'm going to read the questions and you answer them to confirm what you have written." He began to read off the questions with lightning speed. I was sure he had it up to his ears with rattling off the same sentences day after day. I answered like a parrot.

When he asked, "Did you ever commit adultery?" I replied with mock sadness, "No. And now it's too late."

With equally mocking concern he looked at me and put his hand on mine. "It's never too late as long as you enjoy it, kid."

What a game! I thought and decided to parry. "How can I enjoy it when it's a crime?" I asked.

He withdrew his hand. "Listen, kid. It's a crime only when you're caught." He winked and then continued his routine inquiry. At the end I had to sign the questionnaire, and he released me with a grin. *It sure was child's play to him!*

A week later our four children (Lilo exempt from us) were summoned to the County Seat and thoroughly fobbed off with fine words. As the judge read something out loud about "equal races and pure blood," he shocked 10-year-old Irmie by asking her brusquely, "Do you have pure blood?"

As she stared at him uncomprehending, he took a red pen, poked a bit at her earlobe, reddening it, and then examined the tip of his pen. "Good blood," he announced.

A few days later a ceremony converted our family and about a hundred co-foreigners into American citizens. Coming home I found a pot with yellow chrysanthemums in front of the door — a heart-warming gift from my friend Anne in Switzerland. I was genuinely touched. How thoughtful of her to remember this day! Our friendship was alive and well.

Shortly after we became Americans, Urs, in college now, started dating a fine young man, Jeff Sylvan, with whom she had classes together. One evening he came to pick her up. Urs introduced him to us.

I had to look up at his 6'1" height. With his blond hair and blue eyes he fit right into our family. Even his eyeglasses concurred with my own nearsightedness; only he wore glasses and I wore contacts.

"When do you want me to return Urs?" Jeff asked.

I was unprepared for that. "Eleven."

They left and I sat down to contemplate. Now the time had really come to handle the "love situation."

Next afternoon I summoned Urs and Ronnie to the living room and announced, "I have to tell you something important."

Both girls sat down opposite me and were all ears.

"For a long time I was at a loss how to help you to avoid Lilo's experience with her unwanted pregnancy."

Four eyes widened.

"There seem to be birth-control pills around, but you get them only with a doctor's prescription. I don't know how they work, because after my hysterectomy I didn't have to worry about getting pregnant again."

The girls kept waiting.

"So tomorrow I'll call Dr. Kielty, whom you both know. He's not only a family doctor but also a gynecologist. You can see him for learning about the Pill. And when you need them he can prescribe them to you. He can send me the bill."

The girls seemed shocked. Had I been too blunt? How else could I have said it? Honesty had always been my best friend.

Urs was the first to speak. "Well, that's all okay. Only I don't need the Pill now."

"That's your own business, Urs," I replied. "And so is it yours, Ronnie. You don't ever have to tell me about your experiences, if you don't want to."

Ronnie said, "Mami, you worry too much about us. I really appreciate your concern, but I don't need it."

I got up, smiled and said, "Make of it what you want to," kissed them, and we all went back to our daily routine — until it was drastically interrupted by Manfred.

San Diego Beckons

"Sit down, Little Bear," Manfred said when he came home from work. "I've some news for you."

Burning with curiosity I followed him into the living room and took a seat.

"We might have to move to San Diego."

I swallowed. "Moving again? What for?"

"As you know, I want to do ocean mining. After all the research I've done, Utah Construction and Mining Company has decided to keep their operations on land and not to try mining the ocean."

With heart a-flutter I asked, "And now?"

"I've contacted General Dynamics in San Diego. That is a big company with shipyards. They build submersibles, underwater vehicles for research. I wrote to G.D. about the research I'd done. They are interested in my ideas and asked me to fly down on Friday to talk to their vice president."

My thoughts raced like stirred-up ants in their hill, but subsided at the picturesque image of the sea-port San Diego.

"San Diego has the best climate in the States," Manfred said, and I heard the lure in his voice. "The beaches are white and clean. There's even an opera house. And the Mexican border is near."

I closed my eyes and imagined moving again, as we gypsies had done so often, and admittedly always with a glorious outcome. The image sparkled until I thought of the other side of the coin. "I'd have to give up my piano students, my college classes, my opera coaching." I could already feel the pain of the loss. "And what about the children?" I continued. "They just changed continents and cultures."

Manfred kept silent, letting me rattle off the list of difficulties of the prospective move. But I knew that when Manfred once made up his mind, he tenaciously pursued his goal. Defeated, I knew in my heart that one day we'd all end up in San Diego.

Friday came and Manfred flew to San Diego. In the evening I picked him up at the San Francisco Airport.

He was beaming and hugged and kissed me. "All worked out well. The vice president likes my ideas, and I got a contract right away."

Walking to the parking lot and unable to say anything, I had the feeling we were drifting aimlessly in the crowd.

"Little Bear, I know what you are feeling. This is the month of March. How about this: I move alone to San Diego and you and the kids follow in June when school is out?"

My heart was too heavy to answer. We discussed the many possibilities until we arrived home. Our gourmet chef, Ursula, had dinner ready, and we sat down to eat.

"Dad is going to work in San Diego from now on," I said. "He's moving soon. We have to stay here till June."

"I want to go with him!" Wernher exclaimed, shoving his long, blond hair behind his ears.

"You can't," Ronnie said. "We are practicing with the recorder orchestra for the concert in May."

"I'll stay here," Urs said with certainty. Everyone knew she didn't want to give up Jeff.

Irmie's tiny voice managed to be heard: "Can I go with Dad?"

Laughter and unrestrained chatter followed.

Yet I had heard the little voice. I knew how hard it was for her to stand up to all those siblings and her brother's constant gibes. When there was a breather, I said, "Irmie has asked if she could move with Dad to San Diego. What's wrong with that?"

Sudden silence. They all began to think about their little sister who for eleven years had stood in their shadows.

Protests: "...she can't be alone all day long..." "...she doesn't know anybody down there..." She couldn't do this and she couldn't do that.

I took the situation in hand. "If Dad could rent an apartment near an elementary school, she would spend much of her day at school."

"I can cook until he comes home," the little voice said.

Ursula, the kids' leader, suddenly sided with her sister. "I can make you an easy-to-read cookbook." Irmie's green eyes shone.

"You would keep Dad company every evening," I said. "And on weekends you fly home with him."

Dismay crossed her round face. "Then I have to stay in Palo Alto again?"

"No," Manfred said. "On Sunday evening we both will fly back to San Diego." So, Manfred had accepted her company.

Irmie got up. "I'll pack my clothes now."

I just caught her and held her hand. "First Dad has to find an apartment and a school for you. Then you can go with him."

Her eyes sparkled again.

Mine didn't, because Manfred and I would be separated again for a while. My "baby" was leaving too and I had even sponsored her departure!

A week later Manfred called from San Diego and when Irmie came home from school I told her the news. "Dad has found an apartment in San Diego. He's moved in today. It's just two blocks away from your new school. Dad already talked to the fifth-grade teacher. She's waiting for you."

Her small, freckled face, alert and tense, turned up to me, and I thought I could see how she was already mentally preparing her move.

While she was running to her room to pack, I realized that I had ignored my own feelings about sending my "baby" away. For sure I'd miss my little golden-haired, green-eyed girl, but the thought of having eliminated the war between her and twelve-year-old Wernher pushed my own grief to the back burner. She'd be Manfred's "only child," and she'd be allowed to establish more self-esteem than at the tail end of the family chain. She'd always been overpowered by her older siblings. Her move was worth my grief.

There wasn't only one winner from the unusual move but

two. "You can't imagine how lucky I am to have Irmie around," Manfred acknowledged one weekend as he and Irmie were visiting us.

"Before I leave for work in the morning," Manfred told me, "Irmie packs a brown bag for me with a huge sandwich and a fruit, and she always writes 'Manfred' on the bag. " He looked at her. "We haven't told Mom yet what else we do before bedtime."

"We paint pictures," Irmie burst out. "Dad paints flowers and I paint stars."

When the children were in bed and Manfred and I had settled in the living room with a glass of wine, I finally could ask him about his work. "How's your research coming along?"

"Very well. I wrote a proposal last week." He got up, rummaged in his briefcase and handed a binder to me.

I read: "Plan For Accurate Statistical Exploration Of The Ocean Floor Using Research Submarines."

I lifted my glass for a toast. "Submarines again! Your fate is definitely under water."

He told me about General Dynamics' deep-submersible vehicles, with which they could start the research for ocean-mining at the depth of 200-600 feet.

"Are you going down there too?" I asked.

He laughed. "Of course! In the war I've been under the Atlantic. Now I want to see the bottom of the Pacific." He swiftly turned around to face me. "Too bad I can't take you along. But I can take you to bed." He smiled.

Together we went to the bedroom, undressed and rushed onto the solitary bed I had long accepted as a comfortable love place. Feeling his warm body against mine I wished he'd stay with me and I could keep him from descending into the abyss of the Pacific Ocean.

Love was everywhere. Urs, coming home from college, asked me if we'd be home next Saturday. "Jeff and I want to be married sometime in the future," she announced in a matter-of-fact voice. "He wants to formally ask Dad for my hand."

I sat there, dumbfounded. Our written communication in the

little green-covered book had ended since she started dating Jeff. I could have seen this development, but hadn't thought this would come so soon. My second child was leaving home for good!

On Saturday, Jeff, looking very correct in a beige suit and dark-blue tie, appeared exactly on time, sat down with Manfred and me and, well-mannered and soft-spoken, point-blank asked Manfred for Urs's hand.

"We are planning to get married in two years. I've been drafted and probably have to go to Vietnam."

To Vietnam, oh my God! What are the chances of surviving that messy war?

"I'm leaving for the service next week," Jeff continued. "So I decided to talk to you before I go."

"I appreciate your coming, Jeff," Manfred said, as formally as his prospective son-in-law. "I'll give you what you asked for, our daughter, Ursula."

"Thank you very much," Jeff said and got up.

Both exchanged a few more polite phrases and Jeff left. Through the window we saw Urs leaving with him.

Manfred lit a cigarette. "Let's talk about our future plans, Little Bear. It's May now. When are you moving to San Diego?"

For a moment I closed my eyes. More drastic decisions. I'd just had it up to my neck with changes!

"Schools are out in June," I said without enthusiasm. Suddenly a ray of hope entered my head, putting off the dreaded move a bit. "We can't all live in your apartment. We have to put this house on the market and find one in San Diego."

"No problem, there are plenty of homes for sale. I'll have a realtor show me around and then buy one."

Just that, as if it were a pair of shoes! But I realized that buying a house was no problem for a man who once had built up a shipyard from scratch and now was preparing to invade the Pacific to explore for precious nodules from the sea floor, which no one had done before.

Not only had he ready plans for work and home in San Diego, but his next remark showed his new level of responsibilities. "Our marriage is in pretty good shape now. And in San

Diego we have to see how it goes. In case we need more counseling, there will be lots of psychologists around."

I smiled at my "new" husband. "I agree. Okay, I'll get ready to move down in June."

So easily said, but so hard to break away! Although I had moved umpteen times in my married life, I still felt awful when I thought of losing my friends and having to walk into another level of my life. Shouldn't I have gotten used to this gypsy lifestyle? Couldn't I keep in touch with my old friends and look forward to new chapters? I sighed. *I'll miss the Buddhist temple and its Sunday school. But I'll try, try hard again. After all, I've seen America only from one point — Palo Alto. Let's see what San Diego has to offer, the southern-most city in the U.S.*

I felt my despair turning into curiosity.

San Diego Delivers

In June — finally, nevertheless with a heavy heart — I said goodbye to my friends and my students in Palo Alto, packed our belongings and put my dream house on the market.

Urs decided to stay in the house as long as it wasn't sold. Her college work and Jeff kept her in Palo Alto, and sooner or later she and Jeff would get married. With Lilo gone, Urs staying behind, and Irmie already residing in San Diego, I had only two children with me: Ronnie, full of expectations, and rebellious Wernher, who announced he'd do anything to stay in Palo Alto. I instructed Urs, who was taking us to the airport, to help me keep an eye on Wernher until we entered the airplane. To our surprise he showed no resistance but silently followed us, his head hanging low.

After an hour and a quarter of flying we looked from the air at the harbor of San Diego. It was interspersed with rivers, canals and bays, crowded with ships and sailboats. No wonder Manfred was in his element here.

The plane landed. As we walked into the airport building I spotted Manfred, a bunch of red roses in hand, and Irmie, in a new green outfit. An abundance of hugs and kisses united us again.

In his new Mercury Manfred took us within minutes to the prestigious peninsula, Point Loma, and drove up one of the many steep streets, to almost the top, where our new two-story corner house beckoned. We climbed up a stony, shrub-lined outdoor staircase and entered our new home.

The spectacular view from the living room to the bay and its warships and aircraft carriers kept me spellbound.

"All schools are only a few blocks away from our house," Manfred said. "And I drive to work in ten minutes."

There was no reference to my workplace, I noticed with a shiver. *Am I supposed to sit in front of the living-room window and stare at the bay for hours? Oh no, I'm going to find work as quickly as possible!*

Suddenly we heard a roar in the distance. While it was swelling up fast Manfred pushed us onto the balcony.

"What in the world is that?" I asked.

From the balcony we looked straight down at the airport's runway, which pointed directly to us. Right after its take-off a jet came roaring at us, quickly increasing in size and sound. The airplane seemed to aim at us, ready to destroy our house. In fear the children pressed themselves against me, and I in turn grabbed Manfred's arm. A second later the jet, spanning the entire sky, thundered over us and was gone, and the roar diminished gradually.

My heart was still beating fast. "My God, how often does this happen?" I asked.

"Every few hours or so," Manfred replied calmly. 'The last plane flies out at 10 p.m. You'll get used to it."

I noticed a red light on top of the neighbor's house. "Why that red light?"

"For the pilots, so they know they have always to be above that light."

"Have there been any crashes lately?"

"Not during the two days I've been here." Lovely San Diego!

Summer school occupied the children in the morning, and in the afternoon we escaped to the beach, five minutes away. The sand was whiter than I'd ever seen — miles and miles of gleaming shore. Yet the ocean was as cold as in Northern California, chilling us to the marrow, but clearly refreshing one's mind, even forcing decisions on me — particularly about my professional life.

Soon I began to make phone calls for piano jobs. The Music Teachers Association gave me names and addresses of colleges of the San Diego area. I called their music departments, talked to the chairmen, who to my greatest surprise and joy offered me work as an accompanist. I also lined up for a solo recital at the

Library Concerts. Delirious with joy, I thanked Manfred in my mind for having dragged us to San Diego. Life here seemed to have a favorite disposition for our family.

Fortunately, the music world was as large as the planet, and all it's inhabitants liked it, needed it and hired musicians to create the art of sound. And I was one of the music makers who was blessed to generate joy.

While I played the piano in town, Manfred worked under the ocean in small research submarines.

"What do you do down there?" Wernher asked Manfred as he joined us on the beach after work.

"We have a small sub with manipulators," Manfred said. "It's an arm with a grappling device." He stretched out on the sand and put his hands under his head. "The next time we go down I'll arrange for you guys to watch the submersions." He got up. "Let's go swimming."

We all walked into the surf, the kids braved the smaller waves but stayed behind while Manfred and I swam out into the empty ocean. Easily thrilled in great water, I again felt the ocean was Manfred's world and I was privileged to swim in it. I also looked forward to watching him plunge into the ocean with the submersible.

So, next morning the children and I drove along Harbor Drive, the waterfront to the downtown facility of General Dynamics, passed the check points and were led to the company's harbor section. Across the bay an aircraft carrier peacefully lay at the North Island.

We looked at a dozen workers who were busy with a strange red apparatus, obviously ready for submersion. Manfred, now clad in a black overall like the others, was among the workers. When he saw us he stepped over to us. "You came just in time. We're boarding in a few minutes." He gestured to the red vehicle.

"It looks like a huge guppy," I said. "Complete with eyes and tail."

"The 'eyes' are portholes," Manfred explained. "So we can

see the things on the ocean floor."

At this moment the workers turned to us. A man, also in overalls, called, "Manfred, we're ready!"

"That's the pilot," Manfred explained, giving him the high sign. "We'll be under water for two hours. See you at home." He turned away and approached the red submarine.

First the pilot, then Manfred climbed up a small ladder to the vehicle, then down into the white turret and closed the lid above them. A crane lowered its swinging arm onto the submarine, grabbed, lifted, swung and lowered it into the water. Manfred now was where he longed to be, in the ocean.

Besides his underwater activities Manfred also led a busy life on the surface. "On Wednesday I'm flying to Santa Barbara for an ocean mining conference," he told me on a Monday as I was serving dinner. "On Saturday I'm flying to Houston, Texas."

"Anywhere else?" I asked, putting the plates down with a clang.

"Later this month there'll be a conference in Washington, D.C., next month one in New York —"

I covered my ears in mock terror. "Enough! Enough! I hope you marked your calendar and don't forget to look!"

He didn't answer.

Stop! I told myself and sat down. *What did you learn about communication? Be honest! You just used cynical language. Get on fair ground!* "I feel irritated by the thought of being left alone so often," I said.

That was the new, honest language we'd learned from Landes, and Manfred showed that he now was fluent in it. "My Little Bear, I understand your feelings. First let me tell you how I feel in those cities after the conferences are out and I go to my hotel room. My head is full of all the new ideas I've heard. I want to talk to you about it, but you aren't there. I'm alone in that room. I'm alone in bed, and at that point I detest those conferences. Then I pull my bedcover over my ears and fall asleep."

His revelations were a treasure for me. "I didn't know you ever thought of me in those places at all! Thank you for telling me." We looked at each other and smiled.

"Look, Bear, you're married to a man who has to be out on the water a lot. Right now I have to travel much, all in the name of the ocean. There will be a time when we always live together. I promise!"

We chuckled and began to enjoy our dinner. Between salad and main dish he told me that he had applied for three patents on a system, a method and a vessel for ocean mining. I praised the mealtime for presenting an opportunity to learn about Manfred's life. Would I ever understand where his unending energy came from?

The same day, a neighbor invited us to a cocktail party at the summit of our Point Loma peninsula. I squeezed myself into nylons and gloves, and we drove the few blocks to the elegant mansion. Its living room already accommodated about fifty people, who clinked glasses and filled the room with cigarette smoke. Consequently, my eyes began to burn.

We were introduced to several people who smiled and said friendly words. Then we met bald-headed Dr. Robert Teutsch, who held on to a pipe, sucking on it on and off. We learned that he was the chairman of the music department of Cal Western University.

Teutsch spoke German fluently, fast and pointblank. "So you're a musician? New here? What have you done so far?"

"Opera coaching, piano accompanying —"

"Do you play the organ?" he interrupted.

I grinned. "Well, how pianists play the organ..."

"...holding your foot above the C and when C comes you push it down?"

I laughed. "Just about."

"You're honest."

"That's my trademark," I replied, smiling.

After a puff on his pipe he asked me, "Would you be interested in teaching a beginning piano class at Cal Western?"

"Yes, I would," I stammered.

"Come see me tomorrow at two in my office." Abruptly he turned and disappeared into the blue smoke.

"See?" Manfred asked. "That's why one has to go to parties. Now get your papers together and meet him at Cal Western tomorrow. It's around the corner from here."

"Everything in San Diego is around the corner," I said. "A real handy city."

The campus of the private Cal Western University with its many flat buildings lay directly on the beach. Crowds of students milled around. At two o'clock sharp I entered the music department. Most windows had a view of the ocean. What a handsome campus! I knocked at the door with Teutsch's name on it, and his voice called, "*Ja*!"

As I entered he got up from his desk and said without formal greeting, "Let's go to a piano." Steadily sucking on his pipe, he led me into a tiny room with an upright. I opened the keyboard lid and sat down on the bench. He put sheet music before me, Beethoven, Sonata opus 111 in C-minor. "Play it," he said.

I played half the page when he interrupted me. "Now play this." He put another sheet of music on the rack, which looked like a witch's dance of printing ink. Used to playing from first sight I knew one couldn't play every single note, but rapidly had to filter an extract which should make sense of the music. With utmost concentration I managed the devilish task.

"Not bad," Teutsch said. "Now play a G-flat minor scale, harmonic." I played it.

"A diminished seventh chord on B." I played it.

"Enough for teaching a beginning piano class," he said. "I'll talk to the dean. If she agrees, I'll call you."

Despite the whirl in my head I managed to ask, "Wouldn't the dean demand a degree in music? I don't have one."

"We are a private university and don't necessarily ask for degrees in the Fine Arts. What counts is the know-how. Goodbye."

I stumbled out and went home. Next day Dr. Teutsch called and confirmed the assignment. Only then I jumped up and down with joy. *I'm going to teach at a university! What an honor! Will I be good enough? Dr. Teutsch said I am.*

Peeling potatoes in the kitchen, I told Manfred of my luck.

"Congrats, Little Bear," Manfred said, downing a beer. "Now you deserve something special."

"What is it?"

"You know that I always wanted you to have a harpsichord. As you know they are prohibitively expensive. Remember when you played on one with the Baroque group in Palo Alto? Even then I asked the owner where he'd bought it. He told me he'd assembled it himself from a kit he ordered from Boston. He gave me the address. Now I'll send for a kit and build you a harpsichord."

I didn't believe my ears. Knowing that he could do anything he wanted was one thing. Building a complicated musical instrument was another. "How could you ever —"

"Leave that to me," he interrupted. "I promise, in six months you'll own a harpsichord."

"When would you have time to work on it?" I finally asked, putting the potatoes into a bowl.

"On weekends," he answered matter-of-factly. He threw the beer can into the trash, indicating he had talked enough about his harpsichord plans.

True to his word, he ordered the kit. A few weeks later a huge package arrived, complete with pre-cut wood for the case, rolls of strings and assorted keys for the keyboard. Manfred submerged into the basement, transforming a small, damp storage room into a harpsichord factory.

Five and a half months later Manfred and Wernher carried the brand new keyboard instrument into the living room with the manufacturer's label, "Manfred Krutein 1966." They screwed in the three legs, and there it stood: A gleaming, light-brown, tiny baby grand in the shape of a laid-down *harp* that gave half the name to the instrument. On the keyboard, *chord*s could be played that gave the instrument the second half of its name — *harpsichord*.

Manfred opened the lid, and I could look onto the 56 strings, set lengthwise in order as on a harp. They would be plucked when I depressed the keys on the keyboard.

With the help of an electronic tuner Manfred tuned his new

instrument in octaves and then commanded, "Play it."

Enchanted, I sat down and played a few broken chords. Silvery sounds, pure and short, filled the room, invoking the 18th century with its candlelight and powdered wigs.

"Play a Bach prelude," Manfred said.

I played the E-flat-minor from memory, and when I finished I knew I'd never again play Baroque music on the piano, but only on the instrument for which it was written and whose period Manfred had conjured up by using his magical hands. Wordless and with tears in my eyes I threw my arms around his neck and kissed him.

Once the word spread that I owned a harpsichord, offers for concerts flooded in and also an invitation to join a new group. Together with the flutist and the violinist we called ourselves the "Colonial Trio" and played for the "Young Audiences" organization. We toured the county schools and played short recitals to educate the students in classical music.

Since my harpsichord's legs could be unscrewed, its body, ninety pounds, could easily be carried by the flutist and myself and laid down onto a two-wheeled, open trailer, which I hooked up to my Ford. And off we went!

During our first demonstration on stage I played the "Twinkle, twinkle" theme from Mozart's C-major sonata and then got up to explain the harpsichord with a few sentences. I then asked, "How many play the piano?" About a quarter of the audience raised their arms.

Then I told them, "I'm going to play for you Mozart's *Turkish March.* Listen to the sound of the harpsichord again. And if you want to try out the harpsichord come up here and play a short piece."

While I played the children could fight their stage-fright and get ready to volunteer. Then I let one student play a short memorized piece on my harpsichord.

"You should've seen the delight in her eyes," I told Manfred at home, when he helped me carry the instrument into the living room. "I hope she'll never forget the experience." We put the harpsichord torso on two chairs, screwed on the three legs and set it down at its place near the living room wall.

Carrying my instrument and with it my music, to young students meant more to me than a good opportunity. My ability to give students one of the most important treasures in life — good music — filled me with gratitude. I hoped I could do it for the rest of my life.

"I've got news for you," I said one day to Manfred. This time it was *me* telling *him* news. "Cal Western University has a branch downtown, called the School of Performing Arts. I'm scheduled to teach harpsichord there."

"Wow! Congrats!" he said and kissed me. We went to the kitchen to grab something from the refrigerator. "By the way, how are your piano classes at Cal Western?"

I took out two plates, filled them with ready-to-eat sandwiches and apples and sat down with him at the table.

"Fine," I replied. Then I told him about a strange experience I'd had. "The students had to learn all the different scales. So I tested them. Each of them had to play on a piano whose keyboard I couldn't see from my desk. They did well, until a student with shoulder-length hair sat down at the piano. I asked him to play the E-flat major scale, which is a bit more difficult than the others because of the black keys involved. When he played a scale I heard that it was the F-major scale which is much easier than the E-flat. Since I couldn't see the keyboard he'd never thought someone could have absolute pitch and hear the difference."

"Yours came in handy."

I nodded. "I told the student straight what he'd done. He turned red and apologized. Then Lori, the best student of the class, raised her hand and asked me to explain absolute pitch. I said it was an innate ability to recognize the exact pitch of a tone by ear. Of course, it's not the external ear but the auditory nerve that seems to be more refined."

Manfred put his napkin down. "Is it related to music only?"

"No, it isn't. I can distinguish between the noise of different porcelain plates or clinking wine glasses or bunches of keys —" A memory came back. "At grammar school each teacher carried around her own bunch of keys for all the different rooms and we heard them clatter from afar. Since we often were doing forbidden things, it was very important to know which teacher was approaching. My classmates always turned to me, 'Eva, who's coming?' They knew I was able to tell the difference." I bit in my apple slice.

"Don't you feel good to hear more things than most people?" Manfred asked.

"It's like seeing colored pictures instead of black-and-white ones."

"The students must be very impressed by your absolute pitch."

I shrugged. "Maybe. Yet I'm always afraid that one of them will ask me about my college degree and I would have to say that I have none."

He knit his brows, collecting his memory. "One of the engineers at work told me that his wife was back in college, working on a degree. Could you think of something like that?"

A glimpse of hope appeared at the end of the tunnel. *What an idea! To go back to college at a mature age! Only in America can this be possible.* In Germany people would laugh at me for thinking an "old" person of forty-five could still learn. "You can't teach an old dog new tricks," they would say. And men would add, "Only women can be that crazy."

Thank God I live in America!

However, I wasn't a hundred percent sure if it was really true or not. I lost no time in inquiring at the university's administration office and learned that for faculty members all courses were free. Not only was higher education accessible but even free! I was grateful beyond words.

So I enrolled in English, Speech and American History. And not only did I study seriously, but I experienced a tremendous thirst for learning with excellent instructors who had high expectations. I soon planned my future classes and began to look forward to getting my Bachelor's Degree one day.

Long before that day Lilo's husband Jay called from the

walnut ranch to tell us about the birth of their son, Jess, on Mother's Day. When we finally managed to travel to the ranch in Northern California to meet our first grandson, he was sitting in his parents' station wagon, dark-haired like his father, beaming from ear to ear and so fat he was already put on a diet. Little Jess got more kisses from us than he could weather.

We returned from the walnut ranch and adjusted to our daily routine, while Manfred immediately disappeared into his underwater world.

On one of his appearances on the surface — our home — his face showed the sagging lines of disappointment.

"Did anything go wrong?" I asked.

Without a look at me he slowly nodded his head. "Very."

I took his hand and pulled him to the loveseat, from which we could see the lit ships on the Bay.

"The Nixon Administration has stopped any funding for oceanography. That means the end of research in ocean mining."

I put my hand on his. "Isn't there another place for ocean mining?"

"Not in this country. Maybe in Japan. But the Japanese don't like foreigners in their research."

Downtown's lights sparkled as if there were nothing but joy in the world. "What will General Dynamics do?" I asked.

"Probably close the Marine Technology Center."

That meant he'd lose his job entirely. My eyes were clinging to the city lights' reflections on the Bay as if the problem's solution came from there. "I'm sure you'll find something exciting again," I said.

He didn't reply, and I thought he had fallen back into non-communication.

When he came home a few days later, taking two steps at once on the outdoor staircase, I knew that something positive had happened. He stormed into the kitchen and kissed me.

"Ocean mining on the agenda again?" I asked.

"Not exactly." He opened the refrigerator and took out a can of beer. "Something totally unexpected. Remember the famous French ocean explorer, Jacques Cousteau? He's dreamed up a new project." He swallowed the beer fast. 'He wants to make a documentary of all research submersibles."

Cousteau would later sell the documentary to TV stations, Manfred said. Cousteau had invited the eight existing companies from both coasts that own research subs to gather at Catalina Island because of the interesting underwater landscape there. He concocted a show with the eight subs and would start filming next week.

I put the meatloaf into the oven. "And you'll be in the movie?"

He straddled the kitchen chair. Not only that, he said. He'd be in the leading sub and would transmit between Cousteau and the other subs. "It will be real underwater choreography. Imagine: The steel arms with an elbow joint and tweezers will pick up stuff from the floor. That's what I've been doing the last months."

I stepped over and kissed his cheek. "That all sounds great. I'm so glad you are involved."

A shadow crossed his face. "It's only a temporary job. What comes then only the gods know."

In the meantime, Manfred and his pilot were invited by Cousteau to dine with him on his famous research vessel Calypso, where they discussed the details of the show, with good French food and wine.

During the next months the show was filmed underwater, edited by Cousteau himself and then sold to a TV station. When it finally aired I was on tenterhooks. With a bottle of French wine (in honor of Cousteau) and coke and popcorn for the children (in honor of America) we all sat comfortably before the TV set.

Cousteau's vessel, *Calypso*, white on a black base, appeared in full sunshine before the blue hills of Catalina Island. Captain Cousteau himself, in leather jacket, blue jeans and his indispensable red knit cap, showed his deeply-tanned face with the famous eagle nose to the audience. He gave a short introduction to the documentary in good English. The on-board camera showed the eight deep-sea submersibles—baby whales in luminous colors, some red, some yellow or even white.

"I'm in the last, the red one," Manfred said.

One after another, they submerged in the ocean. Then the scene changed to the green darkness of the ocean floor. Kelp forests swung in slow movements to and fro, passed through by single fish or schools. The first sub appeared, maneuvering to the far left side and settling on its keel.

"A green sub?" I asked in surprise.

"Colors underwater lose their intensity, and the eye sees mainly green," Manfred explained. "You can't tell one sub from the other. I'll tell you when mine is coming down."

The vehicles proceeded to their positions in the half-circle and at last turned their front sides toward the cameras so that they appeared as globes.

"That's us!" Manfred announced when the last sub sank to the far right side.

Amazed, we saw how one manipulator stretched out its arm and picked up a tube from the sea floor. Another operated a box and took off the lid and replaced it again.

A strange feeling of unworldliness overcame me. Manfred deep underwater, in that murky world, invisible in this inner-space vehicle — but, thank goodness, also next to me in his own flesh and blood.

After a few more of the tasks were accomplished, manipulators approached each other, two-by-two, grabbed their tweezer hands and shook them.

We burst out laughing. "Dad!" the children shouted. "What fun!"

"Whose idea was that?" I asked, still laughing.

"Mine," Manfred said. "Cousteau liked it and put it in his screenplay."

"That sounds like you!" I said, squeezing his hand. "A tense build-up and a happy ending like in a novel." I raised my glass, while the children toasted with their coke cans.

Onwards!

A rather conservative albeit joyful event was approaching — Urs' and Jeff's wedding.

Jeff had been drafted and thoroughly trained to fight in Vietnam. Urs, who had stayed in Palo Alto and continued college, had seen him transferred to Arizona's Fort Huachuca, where he became "the best soldier of the month and an honorary citizen of Tucson, Arizona." After that it was a matter of waiting day by day for his dispatch to the hellish war theater.

No one had anticipated how a silly mix-up could interfere in one's fate. There were two different lists, one called "L" for eligible and another called "7" for those who were not sent to Vietnam. Jeff was born as Jeff Tanner. When his father died, his mother remarried a man named Jack Sylvan who took Jeff on as his own child without adopting him legally. So Jeff grew up as Jeff Sylvan. Yet the "L" list showed only Jeff Tanner. Eventually, Jeff Sylvan, who didn't fit into any category, was dismissed and sent home, and he and a jubilant Urs prepared their wedding.

What a wonderful error! Such luck! And both deserved it.

They were married in the Unitarian Church in San Diego. No, I didn't play the organ. I leaned back in the pew and enjoyed the merry ceremony, listening to my colleague's playing Bach and Handel on the organ and watching my entire family. Lilo had come with her two offspring, five-year-old blond daughter, Yvonne, and twelve-month-old dark-haired son, Jess. We were united again!

As for the bridal couple, I anticipated that Urs would be very happy with Jeff. Nostalgia overcame me as this was the last time Urs allowed me to call her by her childhood nickname. And so I said, "Goodbye, Little Bear," as they climbed into their white

Chevy and happily drove to Disneyland and later to Arizona for their honeymoon.

The day after the wedding became an unexpected milestone in Manfred's life. As he lit a cigarette after dinner, Wernher, his long hair falling on his shoulders, put on a sad face and lamented, "Yesterday we rejoiced. But soon we'll have to say goodbye to a dead man."

All eyes went to our teenage son. "Whaaat?"

Wernher, his head low, continued. "By smoking cigarettes every day Dad will develop lung cancer and die."

"Wernher!" I shouted. "How can you say such things?"

"You're rude! Apologize to Dad!" Ronnie demanded.

Wernher, who had obviously anticipated this storm of protest, sat quietly and let everyone else go crazy.

Meantime, Manfred had built up his fortress, knocked the ash from his cigarette with dignity and said, "You're crazy, son. You don't know what you're talking about." He took another puff from his cigarette, got up and, erect and inaccessible, went to the living room and turned on the TV set.

No more words were spoken, and we all went our ways. I was furious at Wernher, but wasn't sure how to handle the situation.

When we went to bed, Manfred said to me, "I think Wernher was right. I smoke too much."

"That's not a reason to talk about your funeral. Besides, you're only a social smoker."

"He probably has heard about the research which links lung cancer to smoking. He's concerned; he doesn't want me to die prematurely. I think I'll reduce my smoking. It's just a bad habit."

In fact, next evening at the dinner table, Manfred said in front of the children, "Wernher, I thought about what you said about me smoking too much. I think you're right. I'm going to reduce the number of cigarettes."

"That's not enough, Dad," Wernher pleaded. "You have to give up smoking completely!"

"Well, that's too difficult. How about only one cigarette a

week?"

"Not enough!"

"How about one cigarette a month?"

"No. Not enough!"

Finally, Manfred, visibly tired of the debate, promised to quit smoking once and for all.

He kept his promise and never touched another cigarette again.

"Where would we be without our smart kids?" he asked.

"In the tomb," I replied.

In the now smoke-free house our shrunk family sat enraptured in front of the TV set, watching the American astronauts' long-awaited landing on the moon. When Neil Armstrong and Buzz Aldrin stepped on the moon and did their antics on the ghostly lunar surface, I felt that I myself had arrived at a goal which I had pursued since childhood — to explore the solar system. My strong desire for the stars had made me a voracious reader of science fiction as a youngster and later led us to Wernher von Braun, whose Saturn 5 rocket had made this flight to the moon possible. I was proud of my new country. This was what I'd expected from the USA: a bold and ingenious level of technology.

"Your dreams have come true," Manfred said to me.

I smiled. "Only one of them. I'm waiting for a flight to Mars."

Still down on Earth, I looked forward to finishing my classes for my B.A., which was to me the crown of all my studies. Never in my life would I have dreamed of getting a college degree at the age of forty-nine.

Before getting my certificate I had to see the dean for a signature. Dr. Kobe, slim, elegant and bespectacled and of about my age, didn't waste time with small talk. She signed the certificate, returned it to me and said curtly, "Congratulations. Are you going on for your Master's?"

Shocked, I asked, "Me?"

She looked at my grade sheet. "You got all A's. Why not go

for your Master's?" Speechless, I swallowed, trying to keep my bearings. "I've also done it late in life," Dr. Kobe said. "You can do it, too."

I staggered out of her office. Overwhelmed by her suggestion, elevated to boundless heights, I saw a life of lofty levels before me, which I'd never known existed. Somehow I got home without crashing into anything, but I made it, and that night I told Manfred.

"Sure," he said as if it were a matter of going to the movies. "I agree with the dean. You can do it." He got up and took a bottle of white Zinfandel from the refrigerator. "We have to celebrate that. I assume you've already decided, right?"

I sank into an armchair for support. "You really think I can do it?"

"Sure," he said again with a matter-of-fact voice. "Why not? I did it too."

"But you were twenty when you got started. I'm forty-nine."

"Universities in this country don't discriminate against age." He poured wine and we clinked glasses.

I felt undeservedly blessed. "It's as if a door has opened to a future I had never dared to imagine," I said. "I'm so glad you dragged us to America. Had we stayed in Chile I'd be an old lady now, sitting in an armchair and cultivating my illnesses." I raised my glass. "Thank you for ushering us to America!"

Then Manfred revived the dream I had repressed for a long time.

Europe

Go to Europe! Re-encounter your old friends! Find out how the old continent has changed and what impressions European daily life makes on me. Eighteen years ago we had left the old continent for Chile to escape a threatened Soviet invasion of western Europe. Now I gave myself four weeks to test out my new Americanism against the old world. Free from teaching during the summer, I looked forward to visiting my European friends.

One point in Europe, the best, the dearest in the world, my home town of Danzig, now Gdansk, was taboo. Having seen dozens of pictures of the heap of rubble to which the Russians had bombed it, I shuddered just thinking of it. So I preserved the image of Danzig's glorious Renaissance architecture and tried to forget the wasteland my beloved Danzig had become.

Manfred had no intention of visiting Europe at this point. Not wanting to interrupt his oceanic activities, he encouraged me to travel alone.

So in August I arrived in Frankfurt, West Germany. The airport and the railway station were teeming with brown-skinned people — Turks, who'd come to Germany to get jobs the Germans didn't want to do.

All my thoughts were with the friends I was now going to visit in West and East Germany, Austria and Switzerland—most of them people with whom I had grown up.

First of all: Heinz. We had met in the courtyard between our apartment buildings when we were both three years old. In contrast to my mother who managed our lamp shade factory, Heinz's mother was a homemaker. I ate my meals there and called her "Mama" and her husband, a customs officer, "Papa." Heinz was forever my brother.

War and wind had scattered us like leaves in a fall gale. Heinz, now a driving instructor, had landed in Mozart's Salzburg. Without fail *The Magic Flute*'s overture floated over me, and several arias rang out, one overlapping the other, and, unable to turn off the sound, I let the musical chaos be.

And there stood Heinz! Short like me, a bit stooped now and his gray hair receding, he greeted me with a bouquet of violets. We hugged for a long time, each of us feeling we had Danzig in our arms. And we cried.

We caught up with the events since my flight from the Soviet Army eighteen years ago, and we drank *Danziger Goldwasser,* Danzig goldwater, a choice Danzig liqueur with flakes of real gold. The Poles still produced it under the old German name, although with many fewer gold platelets swimming in the liquor. We laughed ourselves silly and went to sleep late.

On the next morning nothing could keep me from searching for Mozart and his world-famous town. I knew that Mozart never liked Salzburg because of the way he was treated by the ruling nobility there. Nevertheless, posterity now had made up for those "noble" lowbrows' misdeeds and established a stunning center for Mozart's immortal music in this castle town.

Accompanied by my "brother" Heinz, I walked through Salzburg's narrow streets. My eyes caressed all the buildings in which Mozart had lived, and my hands touched the harpsichords and clavichords in the apartments where he had composed — writing down every musical work that came from his genius brain in perfect form, never needing any corrections.

Heinz had silently accompanied me on my pilgrimage to Mozart's spirit, careful not to disturb my reverie. Suddenly he grabbed my arm and pointed to a huge advertisement on a window:

HERBERT VON KARAJAN
Conducts Mozart
Symphony Hall
Friday, 8 p.m.

"That's tonight," Heinz said.

With a hopeless gesture I replied, "Sold out for months."

"Sometimes people return tickets." Heinz had never given up when we played in Danzig and he hadn't changed a bit. He urged me to the box office, where we heard the sales clerk saying on the phone, "One? Yes, I'll take you off."

"You can sell it to me," Heinz said to the clerk.

Astonished that Heinz had quickly understood that one ticket had become available, the clerk sold it to him.

Heinz got his deserved hug.

That night I sat in the relatively small Symphony Hall and saw Karajan limping onto stage and platform. He bowed sparingly to the huge applause and without further ado lifted his baton for the first piece on the program, the Cassation K.99, a rather unimportant work by Mozart.

Used to listening to performances with a critical ear, I suddenly felt I was lifted out of my seat by the weightless sound the orchestra produced. The music floated in the air like veils wafting in the wind. I'd never thought Mozart could be played that way, that light, that charming, that elegant, that wondrous — the right way, the only way. I felt as if Mozart himself were here, raising the music to the heights he expected. Of course, he was here in spirit as always when his works were played, but a great human was necessary to interpret his music, and Karajan was the person to show us how Mozart himself had meant it to sound.

The next day, still enchanted by Karajan's great concert, I was thrown back to reality by Heinz's question, "Tell me, Eva, why are your troops killing the helpless people in Vietnam?"

How embarrassing to be identified with the ongoing mass slaughters in that tiny country! "Our government says it's done for 'our national security.'"

"And you folks believe that nonsense?"

"Half the nation does. I, of course, belong to the other half."

In the four weeks of my vacation this pattern remained the same, flowers, long hugs, tears, *Danziger Goldwasser*, roaring laughter and next day the Vietnam question. Only the cities and the persons changed.

In East Berlin I was in Golly's arms — Golly, my father's former sales manager, a Jewess he had twice rescued from the Nazis' grip.

In 1939, Hitler presumed to annex our Free State of Danzig to Germany and assaulted Poland. The German troops occupied Danzig and other eastern European countries, calling them "the liberated eastern territory." To justify this euphemistic term, the Nazis had to restrict their usual harsh treatment by making allowances and avoiding notice.

Frequently we discussed how we could protect ourselves from the new rules of this German Reich we suddenly belonged to. "This is 'liberated eastern territory,'" my mother said. "They'd respect that." She turned to my father. "Besides, you're an 'Honorary Citizen.'" We all knew he'd been honored, because he had accepted the guardianship of several orphans before the war. "Now this status could be handy."

One morning in 1940 a civilian man of about twenty entered the retail outlet of my parent's company, asking to speak with the boss. He was led into my father's office. I sat with my back to its open sliding window and was able to listen to the conversation.

"You have a Jewish employee at your company, Golly Cohn," the visitor said with a sharp voice. "You have to fire her."

I thought my father would throw out this brazen kid on the spot, but he answered, "Whoever has to be fired I alone decide."

"But she's Jewish," the visitor said.

"This conversation is finished," my father said.

The man left the office and disappeared, obviously exercising restraint.

My father immediately told Golly to stay away from the store for two days. She did, and the danger was put aside.

Two years later, in 1943, when food shortages became imminent, big headlines in the media announced that Jews would be sent to the Ukraine, Europe's bread basket. My Jewish godfather and his wife were already gone and we hoped to visit them in the Ukraine after the war's end.

"None of our family is moving to the Ukraine," Golly told us. "We're going to stick it out here."

"In case of immediate danger you go upstairs to our apartment and wait it out there," my father told her.

Golly's sharp eyes quickly evaluated every stranger who entered the store. One day a middle-aged man in an SS uniform walked in and let his eyes linger on her longer than necessary. He asked to speak to the store's owner.

Golly, anticipating danger, picked up the phone and dialed my father's extension number. "A man is on the way to you. He stared long at me."

"Go upstairs right away," my father said.

While the uniformed man entered my father's office, Golly ran to my parent's apartment on the second floor.

The Nazis never caught her. She hid in different places until the end of the war, when Soviet bombers destroyed Danzig and Russian soldiers burst into the cellars, where the population was hiding. Like all other females — my mother included — she was the victim of mass-rape. My mother had immediately committed suicide, while Golly had regained her balance. With hundreds of thousands of other Germans she — as well as my father — was shoved into one of the many stock cars with standing room only and shipped to Berlin. My father disappeared at that time. Months later I received a message from a lawyer in a small North German town, saying that my father had died. Through a network of refugees and their contacts Golly had found me in Wilhelmshaven, West Germany.

Now, twenty-four years later, I stepped out of the train in East Berlin and went through a tension-filled check for my entrance into the communist world. The uniformed young man in his booth let his inquiring eyes wander from my passport picture to my face back and forth several times. I had to tell him whom I visited, why and how long. Also, why I, an American citizen, spoke German so well. I knew the East Germans were highly suspicious of West German refugees. Yet my American citizenship mollified my threatening presence, and he pounded his rubber stamps into my passport and let me go.

And a few steps away from the checkpoint stood my friend Golly. We hugged for a long time — I dwarfed by her big stature. She'd brought me pink carnations. Later, after the tears, talks and *Danziger Goldwasser*, we strolled through communist Berlin without being bothered by anyone.

"How's life in East Germany?" I asked.

"Exactly like under the Nazis. Only I'm not persecuted as a Jewess anymore."

The sun shone brightly, and at a military barracks some uniformed soldiers, neat and clean, leaned out the window, their hats off in the warm afternoon, bored and eager for a chat. We stopped and joked and flirted with them as if we were young and unmarried.

Until Golly pointed to me and said to the soldiers, "My friend just arrived from America."

Abruptly, the smiles disappeared, the soldiers stood up, closed the windows and disappeared. That lone word "America" had re-created the notorious barrier.

Golly never questioned me about Vietnam but only said, "Too bad, your country's good reputation has gone down the drain."

I sighed. "Here in Europe I'm seen as an American, responsible for Vietnam. In America I'm a German, responsible for the Holocaust."

Golly put her arm around my shoulder. "I didn't mean to hurt you. You are my dear friend. And your father saved my life several times."

I kissed her cheek.

"Are you going to Danzig?" she asked.

"No," I replied. "Into that rubble? It would be traumatic to see the total destruction of our beautiful city."

Not ready to see more friends, I longed to submerge myself in the depth and beauty of the most magnificent place in the world, the Cathedral of Cologne. The train station bordered on the front plaza of the cathedral, and it took only a few steps to make the transformation from bustling modern life into the calm eternity of the cathedral's other world. One ought to be alone there to experience the impact on one's senses. The aroma of incense surrounded me while the majestic nave soared up into infinity. Someone practiced the organ, Bach's *Toccata and Fugue in D-minor,* and the music swept me up heavenward. Even the holy water I touched became a magic potion on my fingertips and forehead. If I missed anything in California it was the Cathedral of Cologne.

Now I was ready to go to Geneva, Switzerland, where my buddy, Anne Fenton, lived. The train took me through squeaky-clean villages to the grandiose mountains whose natural beauty resulted in places of extraordinary scenery. I was reminded of Chile and how it was called "the Switzerland of South America."

At Geneva's railway station Anne stood there, tall, tan and terrific, greeting me with a bouquet of red roses. Yet because we had no common nostalgia, there were no tears, and because Anne didn't know Danzig's great liqueur, she served good French wine which for sure had as much loosening effect as *Danziger Goldwasser.*

We were sitting on the terrace of her apartment and talking as we had in the old times in Palo Alto. As for Vietnam, she, always proud of America, told me how she had endured many accusative remarks about the hair-raising war. "A Swiss neighbor once asked me, 'After bawling out the Germans all the time, aren't you ashamed of your own country now?' Can you imagine such a rude person, Eva?"

"The way she said it was terribly rude," I answered. "But do you know anybody in Europe who condones the Vietnam slaughter?"

"You think our involvement with Vietnam is a mistake?"

"Mildly said. Here in Europe I've heard only critical remarks about it. Some even call it a genocidal war."

Anne sighed. "After his fiasco at the Bay of Pigs, Kennedy wanted to prove his strength by winning in Vietnam."

"Two years ago," I said, "when 20,000 antiwar demonstrators marched on the Pentagon, we hoped they would achieve something. Instead, the bombing escalated. Some people even went to jail for resisting the massacre. I felt so upset I could have strangled the entire Pentagon staff."

Anne poured more wine. "World War II pulled America together and Vietnam tore it apart."

There was a long silence, during which I calmed myself, aided by Anne's French wine. Finally I asked her, "Tell me how you like it here in Geneva."

A pensive shadow fell over her deep-tanned face. "It's definitely interesting. The Swiss people are a bit reserved, but they have a fine democracy." Her face lightened up. "Then the great mountains! I feel exalted just by looking at them. Then the skiing..."

"How about your French?"

"Ooph! It's a torture!" She raised her wine glass. "Now it's your turn. Did you find Germany changed?"

"And how! I left when it was a shambles. Now, they've cleaned up and rebuilt everything. It's as if there'd never been a war. And also, they are the front runners for a United Europe."

"I know. I'll give them an A for that and also for their educational system."

I smiled. "Praise from you is worth a mound of gold. But one thing is strange about the teaching of history in German schools. There's a gap of twelve years in the textbooks, from 1933 to 1945, from Hitler's seizure of power to his end. History teachers are obliged to leave out that period."

"What do they say if the students ask about those years?"

"They say, 'You'll get that next year.'"

Anne shook her head. "They can't cope with the Nazi times yet."

"Obviously. Yet at the same time they're paying enormous amounts of money to Israel. I just read in Berlin that as an act of atonement West Germany has paid 25 billion dollars to Israel so far, plus ten billion dollars to Holocaust survivors." For a lighter tone I changed the subject. "There's something else they have learned. They are polite and friendly now! They don't snarl at you anymore. Apparently they have learned good manners from the British and the Americans."

"I think my kids have learned their good manners from the Swiss," Anne joked as her three children, 14, 12 and 7, walked in from school and properly greeted me with a kiss. They were indeed well-behaved, spoke French with each other and were a delight. Doug, a successful business man, was out of town.

After dinner we planned the next day. "Let's drive into France," Anne suggested. "Take your passport along. I'll take you to Lake Annecy. It's good swimming there."

Crossing the border, we drove south through rolling hills, the Alps on our left, until Anne stopped. "From here we can see Mont Blanc, the highest point in Europe."

We got out and stood before the majestic, snow-capped mountain. "Almost 16,000 feet high," Anne said, pride in her voice.

I thought: a dwarf, compared to the Andes' Aconcagua with its almost 23,000 feet. Nostalgia threatened to well up. With force I suppressed it. "It's beautiful," I said.

Deep-blue Lake Annecy was surrounded by lovely green hills, overgrown with vineyards. Sailboats cruised in the sunshine, and I suddenly felt as though I were in California. We took off the clothes we wore over our swimsuits and from a small pier dove into the comfortably warm lake. Anne, former swim instructor, took off with a powerful free style, leaving me with my poor breast strokes way behind.

Later we lay on the pier, drying off in the summer sun. "In all these years we've never been swimming together," I said.

"Times change. Even I do. Listen to this: I've joined an institution which I have admired for some time. The United Nations in Geneva."

"Wow! What are you doing there?"

"I work for women's rights. I'm President of the NGO Committee on The Status on Women."

Surprised, I raised myself on my elbows. "I thought you surrendered to your husband in earnest. Letting him make the money and catering to his wishes. What happened to my Anne and her suburban dream?"

"The dream turned to dust while facing a different culture. The kids are in school, Doug often is out of town, and the *au pair* takes care of the house. My dream now is to learn French well enough to be of real service to the United Nations."

I smiled down at her. "Incredible. I never thought you'd get out of your nest. What does Doug say to this?"

"He tries to ridicule me, but he can't stop me. I've got more freedom than you think, Eva." She got up and dove into the lake again. I followed her, realizing how much a change of cultures had transformed this family.

When the swimsuits had dried on our sun-drenched bodies we drove back to Geneva, headquarters of the United Nations, that union with the most advanced political ideals in the world, of which Anne now was part.

Entering Anne's apartment in the evening, we saw Claudette, the *au pair*, glued to the TV. "Something great is going on in America!" she announced. "A concert at Woodstock. A half-million people are there!"

On the screen half-naked young people rolled in the mud of sloping hills, stirred up by rock-and-roll music and long-haired singers whose words I didn't understand.

Anne, always sensing my linguistic limitations, explained, "They're singing of peace and love."

The constant rain at Woodstock worsened the quagmire, although the sometimes totally naked people seemed not a bit disturbed.

"Do you hear it, Eva?" Anne asked. "Bob Dylan's song? 'Everybody must get stoned.' On Marijuana and LSD."

Claudette sat mesmerized by the aired chaos. She rocked with the music, surely longing to be with the frenzied crowd.

Suddenly guitars and synthesizers were subdued, a blow-up of a singer rapped out at us and I even understood him. "We're going to avoid what my father and his father did... they worked hard until they were 65, got a gold watch, lay down and died...we'll escape this crap...here we are... creatures from the dust of exploded stars...fighting against this slaughter in Vietnam...we have the right to live a different lifestyle...free from materialism...music is our escape..."

With full sound the instrumental music flooded into the living room and this time it created such a nostalgia in me that I thought I couldn't wait the few days until I would be home in America with all her pleasures, madness and contradictions.

Uprooted

Two days later our plane landed in San Diego. Manfred picked me up at the airport. "I missed you a lot," he said, pressing me hard against his chest.

"I missed you too," I replied, feeling the tears come.

I had only carry-on bags, and hand-in-hand we walked to the parking lot.

Arriving home I found my dream house seemed different to me. Physically little had changed, but as always during weeks of absence, memory had played tricks on far-away images. The children were still at school, the house was quiet and it was good to repossess all the rooms, the furniture, the incredible view of the warships in the bay and the on-roaring airplanes, drowning out our words and threatening to swallow us under their enormous wings.

Finally, after dinner, we sat down with a glass of wine before the window to the bay. The city lights across the bay sparkled, creating dubious nostalgic feelings in me. I told Manfred about my European encounters, until he said, "I too have news for you."

Surprised I looked at him.

"You know that the Nixon Administration has removed funds from all ocean research and General Dynamics must close its Marine Technology Center."

Oh God, he's lost his job, I thought, tumbling down from my heights.

"Before I could be laid off," he continued, "I searched around for jobs in ocean mining. There's nothing in this country. Yet the Brazilian government is going ahead with it and hired a firm in Washington to do the job. They need experts there. I applied for the job."

I had a foreboding of being uprooted, dragged away and thrown into another strange spot. "Washington or Brazil," I mumbled, suddenly tired, "I don't care. All I want is to stay here."

"Of course, I'd move alone, in case I'm accepted. You and the kids would stay. I might have to work in Brazil a lot, and so you'd be better off here in San Diego."

As for me, I was completely exhausted and all I wanted was to go to bed and sleep. Tomorrow everything would look better. Manfred was chasing his ocean-mining rainbow and I couldn't stop him. Yet hearing it the second time was not as painful as the first time, I thought. I'll talk more about it, until I take the whole thing for granted. "What's the next step?"

"To tell them I accept."

I've already half accepted it, I thought. *The rest will come tomorrow.*

Manfred did accept the job. It turned out he would have to move to Washington DC in three weeks. I'd be alone again. A feeling of being superfluous flooded over me, but I said nothing, not wanting to bother him during his difficult time of looking for an extraordinary job.

"First let me see how it goes in Washington," he said. "Then, if it's good and you want to move, come." As simple as that.

I bought him a small Portuguese dictionary for Brazil, and he packed and left.

Next day he called me. "Everything seems to be okay here. Nice office, interesting people. We've started the project for Brazil, but it will take at least two months before we go down there. By the way, there was a big war-protest demonstration going on here. Over 600,000 people rallied before the White House and the Pentagon. That would have been something for you, right?"

"In thought I'm belatedly with them."

"I'm sure you are. Everything okay at home?"

"Nothing has changed since yesterday, Manfred. I just miss you."

"I miss you too." We hung up.

I stayed seated next to the telephone, trying to make sense of my feelings. I was alone again and angry. Why was he so far away? Couldn't he have found a job in California? Engineers were always appreciated. But he didn't want to be "just" an engineer. He wanted to be an ocean mining researcher, a very noble idea — definitely far from my own world of music, but nevertheless the right thing for him. And then, traveling in Europe, I'd been away for four long weeks myself! So it really wasn't fair to complain. I was going to manage! I got up to get ready for a private piano lesson.

I was in the middle of teaching in the living room when the doorbell rang. I opened the door to a policeman who was bringing Wernher home. "I caught your son in a burglary," he said.

I went into shock. Speechless, I noticed that my piano student packed her music and fled the scene. My brain began to work again. "Please come in, sir," I said.

"There's no need to discuss more, Ma'am. He's already booked. You'll hear from my supervisor." He left.

Wernher walked in, his expression contrite. We sat down in the living room. "What's this about?" I asked.

He wiggled in his chair. "You see, Paul said to me he was going to show me something. We went to this warehouse and he showed me how to open the lock with a pocket knife. We went in and there was only electrical stuff. He took some cable and batteries and I took some light bulbs."

He looked contrite, but I wasn't sure if it was real or faked. I was even less sure how to handle the situation. *Oh, Manfred, where are you, when I need you?*

I didn't know what to do with him. "I'll tell Dad," I said, feeling miserable because of my incapacity. "He'll be delighted. Go to your room now." The dumbest sentences I'd spoken in a long time.

Visibly relieved, he got up and went downstairs to his room.

An hour later a police officer called and told me he had informed the high school principal and I should talk with him. In order to get this off Wernher's record he should get group therapy for youngsters from a psychologist who worked for the police department.

I decided not to tell Manfred, not wanting to burden him with problems he couldn't do anything about. So I called the psychologist and enrolled Wernher for group therapy. Yet I had the very disturbing feeling Wernher would be glad to have escaped a stronger punishment than psychotherapy, which probably wouldn't touch him at all. Hopeless, I shrugged my shoulders.

Manfred had been one month in Washington when he called. "We've got snow here! I had almost forgotten what snow could do to the environment. It's like a fairy tale."

Manfred had become romantic? This wasn't the way he expressed himself. What was behind it?

The answer followed immediately. "At work everything is fine. How do you feel about moving back here with the kids?"

I felt as if a heavy load was suddenly thrown on my shoulders. For a moment I was speechless. But then, I had expected this, so why not answer his demand the way I was supposed to react? "Okay. I'll come," I said in despair.

We talked more, but my brain didn't register it. I thought I knew what I had to do. I turned off my feelings, informed the children, remained untouched when they protested and put the house on the market. No emotions interfered.

Reluctantly, we began to strike our tents in San Diego. I gave notice to the university that I wouldn't come back next semester.

In all this turmoil I had forgotten to take Bach's *Toccatas* to the university to Xerox them for my harpsichord class. Since it took only ten minutes to reach my house I rushed home to get the sheet music.

When I entered I heard the telephone ring. Should I answer? No time! *Let the person babble to the answering machine!* But the machine wasn't on and the phone rang insistently. I gave in and picked it up.

"This is Jack Reed from Global Marine. May I talk to Manfred Krutein?"

"Sorry, he's working in Washington D.C."

"Is this Mrs. Krutein?"

"Yes." Nervously I looked at my wristwatch. I shouldn't have answered the phone at all.

But now Jack Reed's voice sounded like a harbinger's call, solemn and important as he spoke. "The Los Angeles office of Global Marine wants him for a big ocean mining project. Do you think he would be interested?"

Lightning and thunder hit me at once. An ocean mining job here in California — we wouldn't have to move to the East Coast!

"I can give you Manfred's phone number," I said, not wanting to lose my prospective rescuer. "Here's his number." I gave it to him. "If you want to call him, please do!" I urged.

"I'll call him right now."

I hung up and heard my heart pound so loud I had to take a breath, before I could rush to my car to return to the university. Would it be something Manfred would accept? Don't talk to the dean before you hear Manfred's answer, I told myself.

His reply came next morning. "It sounds like a huge ocean mining job. Of course I accepted it. So Brazil is out. I'll finish here in December and start with Global Marine in Los Angeles in January."

I jumped for joy and danced around in the kitchen. We'd stay in California! In the afternoon I greeted each child with exuberance, shouting to them about our good luck.

Ronnie accepted the news with her usual calm. "Congratulations, Mom. But after New Year I'm moving in with my friends anyway."

Our realtor called to say that she had an offer on our house, but instead, I took it off the market and made plans for redecorating the living room for Manfred's return.

The return became an occasion. Manfred had bought a new VW in Washington and wanted to drive it home to San Diego. "Fly up here and we drive back together. Fly to New York, I pick you up and we spend a few days there. Then I'll show you Washington and we drive cross-country to San Diego. We should be home before Christmas."

Since Ronnie planned to move out only after the new year

began, I had a wonderful substitute at home. I left for New York without concern.

New York, New York! At Kennedy Airport we fell into each other's arms, and I sighed from my deepest heart. No longer alone! We climbed into Manfred's new light-blue Volkswagen Bug and drove towards glittering and pulsing New York.

Out and back into New York's night-splendor! Manhattan's myriad of lights made us forget about sleep. As we walked on 42nd Street we saw, not far away, a small crowd of people, laughing and shouting. There was a fist fight in the street, a scene I hadn't seen since my childhood in Danzig.

Manfred put his arm around my shoulders. "Let's go to the hotel now." His urgency sent a shiver down my spine. We drove to the hotel and hastily went to our room, rushing into a wonderful embrace which made me feel I had arrived in heaven.

On our last day we visited friends in Staten Island, left shortly before midnight and took the ferry back to New York. Quietly we stood with others at the ferry's bow, watching the approach of Manhattan.

There was no wind or noise from the ship's engine, the ferry seemed to stand still, exposing illuminated Manhattan in the distance. And now a miracle happened before our eyes: Manhattan, beautifully lit, slowly and steadily grew. "I know it's an illusion, but it's like a mirage," I whispered to Manfred. As the twinkling island became an immensity, we were dwarfed by the spectacle and finally swallowed up by the metropolis.

In contrast to New York's magic, Washington, D.C., spoiled by rain, appeared to be a wash-house. Richly rewarded by the lovely Shenandoah National Park, we drove along the Appalachians to Huntsville, Alabama, where we parked at the Marshall Space Flight Center.

We had written to Wernher von Braun, who was still the head of NASA, asking if we could tour the center although we would be without his godson. Von Braun wrote back:

Unfortunately, during the days of your staying in

Huntsville I have to appear before Congress to testify on the urgent need for a bigger budget. But I will place at your disposal a German scientist, Dr. Merkel, to show you around. Greetings to you and my godson, Wernher.

Wernher von Braun.

Short, middle-aged and bespectacled, Dr. Merkel treated us like royalty. "Welcome to Rocket City," he greeted us with a smile. He'd show us everything of interest, he added, and we should tell him what else we wanted to see. We'd never dreamed of getting such treatment.

In the big hall where the space ships were assembled we entered the living spaces of a mock capsule. Merkel pointed to a corner from which belts hung down. "This is a sleeping corner with a harness. The astronaut would be in an upright position and in order not to float off he would be held by the harness."

All of a sudden I felt dizzy. "The space ship is moving!" I shouted.

Then I heard Merkel chuckle. "You have an excellent imagination. Nothing moves here, so there's no reason to get seasick."

He led us to the huge training pool whose tall walls were transparent like an aquarium. "The astronauts practice here under water — reducing gravity. That's as close as we can come to weightlessness on earth."

Here, where spaceflight wasn't only exciting science fiction but hard reality, I felt boundlessly exalted to be at the birthplace of spaceships, the symbol of our and our children's future. If I myself couldn't fly into space, at least I'd been at the fountain of the noblest human effort.

Days later in Odessa, Texas, I dutifully called the parents of my harpsichord student in San Diego and got an unexpected response. "We've been waiting for your call for days," the lady said. "Please come and visit us."

Surprised by her warmth, we drove to their house, a typical southern mansion with columns in front and surrounded by lush trees. The exuberant hosts urged us to stay overnight, hoping I could play the harpsichord for their Sunday service in the morning. I couldn't reject their request, and so I played the harpsichord and the organ alternately for the Baptist service.

I had performed in churches hundreds of times, but I'd never had such a touching experience. The minister, a dignified, gray-haired giant, approached me. "You played to the glory of God," he uttered, tears in his eyes. "Let me thank you in His name."

A dozen members followed him, each of them saying, "Thank you and I'll pray for you. That you should always be happy."

I was so touched I could have hugged the entire congregation, yet all I could say was, "Thank you!"

From my student's parents we experienced so much Texan hospitality and warmth that we stayed another day before we left for California.

The wonderful intimate days of Christmas and New Year were over, Ronnie moved out, and Manfred drove to Los Angeles for his new job at Global Marine, Inc. Alas, it meant that we had to live separately again. So he rented a downtown hotel room, two blocks from his company, and flew back to us in San Diego each Wednesday night and weekends.

Continuing my teaching and waiting for Manfred to decide on our next location, I felt like I was living in limbo.

One Wednesday night he told me, "Put the house on the market again. I like my job, and you should prepare to move. I've started looking for nice areas. It seems Pacific Palisades is a good location."

I went into shock, seeing and hearing everything through a glass wall without any emotions. Surely, I'd have to give notice to the university. In two months the semester was over. I could leave any time then. Sometimes it was good not to have a contract. But where in the world was Pacific Palisades?

Secrecy

Manfred's Diary. Los Angeles, Jan. 20, 1970

OH GOD ALMIGHTY! Eve, yesterday something happened that drastically changed my life. It was as if a bomb exploded in front of me, knocking me down and leaving me in deep shock. Unfortunately, I won't be able to talk to you about it for the next months or maybe even years.

To soften the frustration of my forced silence I was thinking about an alternative to communicating with you. The only way I could do that — as I see right now — is by writing this diary which I can give you later, possibly in several years when everything is over. This will help me bear the burden of my secret life when you see me go to the office, apparently developing ocean mining from eight to five.

What happened on that day?

In the morning Curtis Crooke, Vice President of Global Marine, called me into his office. Two other men were there, Chief Naval Architect John Graham, a wiry, chain-smoking, articulate man, and the personnel manager, Jack Reed, who once called you for my phone number in Washington to offer me this job and whom you call "the harbinger of good news."

We began discussing how an ocean mining project could be handled. Yet the way the three led the discussion was strange. I told them I couldn't follow their ideas because they seemed to be keeping certain facts from me.

Their reaction was very strange. They whispered to each other, nodded, and Reed left the room. Shortly after that he returned and handed me a type-written declaration, which referred to an important project, one the government was involved with and whose data and actions were the property of Global Marine and had to be kept secret.

I found the requirements acceptable and nodded my OK to Curtis. Before I signed he pointed out that I was under no pressure to sign, but if I did I could not talk to my wife, relatives or friends about the project. It had to be completely secret and I might have to lie if necessary. I signed and so did the three others as witnesses.

Curtis smiled thinly and finally, in his usual subdued voice, disclosed the project. Under the pretense of ocean mining we would raise a sunken Russian submarine — an operation never before attempted. I was shocked to my bones. The Soviets, he said, had lost the sub two years ago and didn't know where it had sunk. Our Navy had found it through an undersea surveillance system, a technique called acoustical holography. The government, with one of its goals to undermine communism, had selected Global Marine because of its ocean engineering expertise and its ability to use the cover of ocean mining. The company had hired me because of my work in ocean mining and my WW II missions on German submarines. My future in ocean mining had become a spy project!

When I suggested that a massive ship would have to be designed and be outfitted with a mammoth claw, John Graham, veiled in blue smoke, explained that the ship was already on the drawing board. The Russian sub was of the Golf-II class, had three nuclear-tipped missiles and a top-secret naval code room and was lying on the ocean floor at a depth of 16,500 feet, where cameras had taken 6,000 shots of it. Since Soviet subs continuously cruised along our West Coast, ready to shoot their missiles, the government wanted to find out how dangerous our situation was.

"Manfred, you are one of the first people pulled into this project," Curtis said. "Because you are an ocean mining expert who can tell the government if the top secret operation can be done under the cover of ocean mining or not."

"What a job!" were my only words.

Overwhelmed by the prospect of becoming involved in international espionage I asked if I could sleep on it. My wish was granted.

What a sudden change of life! This was the highest political involvement, the most secret spying on the Soviet military colossus. What would happen in the next years? I was still awake at midnight. If only I could tell Global Marine how much I hated submarines after my missions on German subs in the Atlantic! For years I had nightmares about depth charges blowing me up, and swore never again to deal with submarines. Lying in bed I heard your deep breathing at my side and regretted that I couldn't talk to you about the new direction in my life. I'd have to be silent and maybe even lie to you. Was it really worth it? After much pondering I fell asleep.

When I woke up next morning I knew this: I used to hoped WW II would be the last war, but lost this hope when the two superpowers began to threaten each other and the Soviets built the Iron Curtain through Europe. Exploiting the Russian sub would mean peeking through a spy hole in the Curtain. I went to Curtis' office and told him I would join the project.

Manfred's Diary. January 24, 1970
On flight, returning from Washington D.C.

On this trip I entered the Great Game of Intelligence. What an adventure! In Los Angeles my bosses made sure I took my report on the future of ocean mining with me and all the pictures and articles I had collected over many years' time. Curtis Crooke, cautious as always, warned me not to leave anything in the hotel room or my rental car.

I'd never known what pressured me to collect so many data and pictures of ocean mining concepts, plans and information. Private conglomerates had worked on them, kept them hush-hush, but finally disseminated some information to show off how much effort they spent on their ocean mining task.

The minute the jet landed at Dulles airport. I rented a Ford and drove to a hotel downtown. I never let go of my briefcase containing the report, and even in the dining room I kept myself alert to any prospective thief who would snatch it away from under the table. Once in bed, I slept with the briefcase under my comforter. Despite all this fuss I slept well.

Both my alarm clock and the room service woke me at 6 a.m. As directed, I drove westward on the freeway, exited and parked in front of the building of the United Research Center. It looked like hundreds of other office structures. Precisely at 7:30 I entered the building.

Inside I checked in with the receptionist who in turn announced my arrival via phone. A minute later two gentlemen entered the lobby. Both about 5'6", 30ish and immaculately dressed, they looked like clones; even their body movements appeared synchronous like marching soldiers. They introduced themselves as John and Tom and asked me for my ID, checked it and returned it to me. They ushered me to the elevator, and the three of us stepped into the cage. Surprise: Instead of level lights showing the floor numbers going up, the panel stayed dark and I felt that we were going down. My guess was: three levels.

The elevator door opened to a small room with a clean-shaven guard sitting at a table who demanded my ID. I showed it to him. He picked up the phone and announced, "Manfred has come in." Surnames seemed obsolete here.

We sat down on a bench opposite the guard. After only a few seconds a buzzer sounded and another door slid to the side, giving way to the sight of an electric four-seater car with a driver in the front. I was told to sit next to the driver, and my two bodyguards sat down in the rear seats to protect and/or to watch me.

For quite a while I had the feeling I was a pawn in a spy plot. Now we were whirring through a long tunnel that stretched way below Washington's daylight.

I turned back to my bodyguards, asking where we were going.

They didn't answer.

After a drive of not more than two minutes we stopped in front of a sliding door. We entered another waiting room where the guard checked my ID again and announced my arrival. We stepped into an elevator and rode up several stories where I was led to a conference room.

Dominated by a huge screen, the room had comfortable armchairs around a long table and huge potted plants next to the window. A minute later five impeccably dressed men entered, each carrying a bundle of papers. My bodyguards left.

"Here comes our U-boat captain!" a man with broad, powerful shoulders joked, stretching out his hand to me. He introduced himself as Burt. I asked him how he knew I'd been on U-boats. He chuckled and said they had to check out my history before giving me clearance for this job. They congratulated me on having accepted the job for the project and welcomed me.

The other four men presented themselves by their first names, which, of course, I could attach to the individuals only gradually. All shook hands with me with obvious cordiality, telling me they used only first names here. "Even those change sometimes," said a man with diabolical black eyebrows, who introduced himself as Hank.

We sat down around the long table. Broad-shouldered Burt sat across from me. He asked me to tell the group about my World War II experiences. I realized these men were doing everything to make me feel comfortable, conveying to me that I was among good friends. They all were scientists and engineers.

After several cups of coffee the official meeting started. David, a wiry and bespectacled man, seemed to be the leader. All of them had their papers in front of them. When I was going to hand David my typed report on the future of ocean mining he warded it off. "We already have a copy of it, Manfred."

I thought he was mistaken. How could they have a copy of my report which I had worked on till yesterday?

David guessed my confusion. "While you were writing your report in L.A. in the daytime, our agent took it out at night, copied the new pages and sent them to us via telex. Also those you finished yesterday. So if you refer to any specific page we already have it before us."

So, my reports had been copied and read. Surely, I was in the middle of a mystery. And now I had to discuss with the scientific staff whether or not the cover of ocean mining was the best camouflage for the planned raising of the sunken Soviet sub. During the before-noon hours I explained in detail how ocean mining procedures looked to the observer and how obsessive the different private companies were about keeping their technical plans secret. But we also investigated alternate cover scenarios like "Mohole," a project to drill into the Earth's crust down to the molten lava. They asked intelligent questions with a perseverance that was astounding. Every hour we recessed for another cup of coffee or a pit stop. Then the discussion went on again until we went to the cafeteria for lunch. The afternoon meeting went on until 7 p.m. By then I was dead tired and went to bed right after dinner.

The next day I followed another standard procedure to maintain secrecy. After registering at another hotel under a fictitious name I drove, following the ordered route, parked the car off the highway, was picked up by another vehicle and finally ended up in a wooded area.

Today's meeting brought agents from higher positions to the

meeting. After I'd given my report they asked me question after question about details until hours later the highest decision-making person, named Edgar, stated in his deep voice that the project would be continued under the cover of a private ocean mining operation. Details would be discussed the next day. I drove to the hotel and after eating a hot dog and a bratwurst from a vendor on the street I went to my room and hit the hay. After three hours of intensive discussions the next day I was excused.

Now I'm looking at the thousand lights of Los Angeles below me. Soon I'll be home, holding you in my arms, Eve. I don't have to lie to you and can tell you the truth: that I discussed ocean mining plans in the capital with The Customer who doesn't want to be named at this time.

On the weekend, when I picked Manfred up from the San Diego Airport, I told him that our house was on the market now.

Plunging into the driver's seat, he just said, "Great!" and drove along the quay where several ships were moored. "There's a nice house for rent in Pacific Palisades. Come with me tomorrow and see it. You can fly back anytime."

A good idea! So I asked Ronnie to stay overnight with the children and flew with Manfred to Los Angeles, or as I finally learned to say, "L.A." From the airport we drove to Sunset Boulevard, which led right to Pacific Palisades.

Known to be smogless because of the ocean breezes, Pacific Palisades represented a rare spot in the greater Los Angeles area. I was overwhelmed by its direct location on the ocean, the green rolling hills and the beautiful homes. Feeling humble, I asked myself: *How do I deserve to live here?*

"The millionaires live on top of the hills," Manfred explained. "Governor Reagan is one of them."

"Where do mere mortals live?"

"By the bluff, looking at the ocean from a lower level."

We drove to Arbramar Street which ended at the steep bluff. From there we could overlook the beaches below. Our prospective rental house lay only one block away. In its front yard grew some sturdy shrubs and a lone palm tree.

"It's small but cute," I said to Manfred. "Good enough while we're looking for a house to buy."

"With only two children —"

"— one who had his first shave and one her first date —"

"— we don't need much space anyway," he concluded.

"The backyard is okay. And the birds are singing," I said, completing the agreement.

I flew back to San Diego the same evening.

Our house in San Diego sold within two weeks. Manfred flew to Washington again.

Manfred's Diary. February, 1970

Now I'm very busy, developing and designing the overall cover story for our project. Hundreds of small details have to be thought over carefully.

Our President said, "Manfred you've got a hell of a job! Everything depends on the efficiency of the cover. If it breaks, we can close shop. Remember, if you want to discuss something with me see me right away, my door is always open for you."

For the overall cover story: Fortunately, the Soviet submarine lay North of Hawaii, 16,500 ft deep, the same depth where manganese nodules could be found that were considered economical. The salvage gear depth range could be the same as for private mining operations. Most engineering teams working on mining equipment designed only prototype equipment to save money. Since our salvage vessel must be huge I told everybody that our management had already decided to build the vessel for the full-size gear. That was the reason, I said, to keep the name of The Customer still hidden from the public.

I planned what to say to the ocean mining engineers from other conglomerates whom I would meet at the next International Conference. That would be an important moment. I participated in all design meetings with our management in order to be able to always find the relevant explanations to cover the submarine salvage. However, the main attitude of talking about the project should be:

Not a single word about technical concepts or details.

Never mention the words "ocean mining."

Let them assume that we are in the same business as

they are.

Only general phrases such as "Our jobs are mostly running on time."

On technical drawings: Avoid all words that could arouse suspicion. Replace "filter room" with "nodule storage room."

I planned to discuss everything with Brad who was my counterpart in this group. I'm happy about my work.

Manfred's Diary. Los Angeles, March 28, 1970

I'm very much enjoying my work with Global Marine, the firm that developed the concept of drilling in the ocean from ships instead of artificial islands that cost a lot of money. John Graham was the naval architect who designed the first drilling vessels. The engineers developed the method of keeping the deep-drilling vessel, CUSS-I, in one place without anchors.

More young engineers joined the team and worked under Graham's direction on the ship and the salvage components. The lines of the vessel were designed, the derrick, the substructure for it, the lift-pipe and hundreds of other components began to show up on drawings I viewed just to stay informed.

Because of all this increased activity we had to move. It simply was too difficult to keep the salvage project under cover as long as we operated in the same office with the engineers from the oil drilling project. To shut out unbriefed personnel we had to hold meetings behind closed doors, which was unusual and could make the non-initiated suspicious. So under the pretext of needing more space Global Marine rented the sixth floor of the eleven-story concrete block building on Sepulveda Avenue, which bore the letters HUGHES on its top.

The fifth floor was occupied by an insurance firm, unattached to Global Marine, but was often used by The Customer for secret purposes. The employees of the insurance firm and those of Global Marine used the same elevator, but never talked to each other, pretending to other passengers to be strangers. Those in the back of the elevator could give stealthy winks to the entering collaborators.

Inside the offices there was intensive teamwork between the two groups. Global Marine had a stairway built from the fifth to the sixth floor, connecting the two offices. Every evening the stairway was hidden behind movable closets that kept it invisible to the cleaning personnel. All documents, notes and photographs were tightly locked up in safes, nothing left on desks. Secret documents were given out only with signed receipts. The windows were permanently covered by shutters, so no one could peek in from the outside and nosy KGB agents wouldn't be able to recognize individuals they already knew from former projects. In the evening employees left the offices at different, but strictly-scheduled times. Another trick that showed The Customer's ability to keep a project secret.

In April I received my Bachelor of Art's degree with honors. The event was simply ignored by the family; Manfred was in L.A. and the children were out saying goodbye to their friends. So I "celebrated" my long-desired diploma with a Coke and potato chips and stared at a TV show of which I perceived nothing.

Suddenly the program was interrupted by news of the flight of Apollo 13 to the moon. The astronauts had radioed, "Houston, we have a problem." This obvious understatement kept me glued to the TV set.

"Over 200,000 miles from Earth and 45,000 miles from the moon an oxygen unit has exploded in their spacecraft," the anchorman reported. "This has cut off the electrical power and is threatening the crew's survival in space."

For most of the night and next day I followed the rescue attempts. My admiration of the Apollo program for its boldness and ingenuity now turned to almost worship of this know-how, of the cooperation and the discipline of the astronauts in space and the ground controllers in Houston.

Finally, the safe return of the Apollo 13 crew released me from the tension I experienced during their space odyssey. It also filled me with gratefulness for belonging to a country that ventured into space and possessed a vision of the future.

Shortly after this I said farewell to my colleagues at Cal Western University and the School of Performing Arts, and we moved to Pacific Palisades, to the cute two-bedroom bungalow I'd seen before. Since we wanted a third bedroom and I needed a studio we decided to convert the garage into a multi-purpose room. We covered the cement floor with wall-to-wall carpeting and hung curtains on the three windows. To make it a bedroom we added a convertible sofa, which at night turned into a double bed. And to make it into a studio I added my instruments, which included the baby grand and the upright piano, the harpsichord and the new clavichord with its whispery sound, which music-whiz Manfred had built shortly after he finished the harpsichord.

I lost no time in making social connections. The neighbors turned out to be open and friendly. I searched for a Buddhist temple, but there was none in the Palisades. So we joined one of the most liberal church groups, a Unitarian Fellowship with its built-in friends.

With the recommendation of Dr. Teutsch, my department chairman at Cal Western in San Diego, I called Dr. Robert Haas, the director of UCLA's extension program, who invited me for lunch.

The short, jolly gentleman showed his warm interest. "You aren't the only harpsichordist in the Palisades. You should contact Susanne Shapiro." He pulled out a small notebook and gave me her telephone number. I called her the same day, and she invited me over.

Her house was located at the town's higher level. I rang the doorbell, and a lady, short, slim and dark-haired like myself, opened the door. "Hello," she said with a warm smile. "That's Eva, isn't it? Come on in."

She led me into her living room which was crowded with keyboard instruments. "Welcome to the Palisades," she said. "Let's sit down and talk. How about a cup of coffee?"

"I'd love one."

We sat down. The coffee was ready on a side table.

"Tell me about yourself, then I'll follow," she said, pouring the coffee.

When her turn came, she leaned forward and spoke with agitation. "We are German Jews. My family foresaw the escalated persecutions and left for England, just before the war when the borders were hermetically sealed."

I sighed. "I'm happy for you. I wish all Jews had left in time.

My Godfather who was Jewish didn't make it and disappeared forever."

The political situation cleared between us, we turned to the field in music we cherished the most: the Baroque Period. She let me try out her various instruments, two harpsichords, a clavichord, a fortepiano and, way at the end of her interests, a piano. "I hardly use it," Susanne admitted. "It would spoil my touch for the harpsichord."

Our morning encounter was delightful from the very beginning. We clicked, played for each other and talked shop for hours. We also shared the same opinion on the Vietnam war.

"They are planning an anti-war protest march with candles here in the Palisades," she said. "I'm going to join them."

"Please let me know when it's on," I urged. "I want to join too."

Yet when the march happened, I had a 24-hour flu and was unable to get out of bed. I would regret this missed opportunity forever!

Meanwhile, Susanne announced her lecture recital at nearby Santa Monica College. This was an opportunity to show my new friend's talent to Manfred.

But he declined, because he was chasing his rainbow, and flew to Houston, Texas for an ocean mining conference.

I sighed. This ocean mining job took a lot of his time, but after all, that's what he loved to do. So I went alone.

The college's large music hall was filled up to the last seat, and I was lucky I found an empty one in the back. People talked in an undertone or were reading the program. With delight I saw a Bach Toccata, Scarlatti Sonatas and pieces of the French Baroque announced. What a treat!

Up on the stage stood Susanne's two-manual harpsichord. It looked like a small, brown baby grand, its wing open. Susanne's appearance on the stage changed the audience's murmuring into applause. She looked good in her long, gold-brocade dress that gave the evening a festive atmosphere.

She bowed, sat down at the bench, concentrated a few seconds and then raised her small hands to the lower of the two keyboards and began her concert with a Scarlatti sonata.

The silvery sound of harpsichords is always a surprise for the ear, because listeners expect the familiar sounds of the piano; even I experienced the delightful shock of hearing the silvery tinkling.

She played with a secure technique and elaborate ornaments, and between the pieces she got up and explained the instrument and the different compositions with charm and humor. I thoroughly admired her. Joining in the applause, a thought hit me. *Can't I do what she is doing?* I asked myself. *Yes, I can,* my self-confidence answered. And instantly, Susanne became my role model.

Beyond that, I wanted a Master's degree. From the catalogues I received from different colleges and universities I chose Cal State Northridge because of the reputation of its music program and its location near Pacific Palisades. Having passed the various tests for acceptance with flying colors, I began to take classes with a euphoria seldom experienced before. Not only was studying fun, but the opportunity to go to college at the age of fifty was a gift — not exactly from heaven — but from America! I was grateful beyond words.

Manfred's Diary. Los Angeles, April 1970

I can now fully appreciate my decision in Chile to take the huge step of immigrating to America. I had participated in several interesting projects: mining; ocean mining; being on the team of the research submarine in San Diego; studying the ocean environment at Scripps Institute of Oceanography; applying for my own patents. And now this simply fantastic salvage project!

At last I could return something to our new homeland. I could contribute by helping to break the Soviet obsession with secrecy. What a wonderful spirit of cooperation between The Customer, Global Marine and the many engineers of other firms who were included in the briefing! The cover was accepted by all of them and strictly observed — a good feeling for me.

I had to travel with vice-president Curtis Crooke and chain-smoking John Graham to several companies from which we had to buy components, such as the huge hydraulic cylinders we needed for pulling out the claw and the submarine after shaking it loose from the sea floor. My role as "Manager Ocean Mining Technology" was to show that we were in the ocean mining business. When these engineers heard about our request they said, "You don't know what you're asking for, to deliver something that doesn't exist yet. We must design devices that require a factor of ten above today's technology. Impossible."

We negotiated back and forth, ending up with the message: "Just do it. We'll pay all costs. We think you're the top company in this field. If you don't develop it, your competitor will." And they accepted the demand.

I admire the work ethic, so typical of America. All those work hours filled with pure work; individual initiative shown everywhere; cooperation and coordination between teams and individuals; willingness to work overtime — all this leading to efficiency.

So different from Chile, where individuals were excellent but team spirit was lacking. In Germany workers obeyed blindly — another way of achieving excellence.

As for me, I prefer the American way.

Unperturbed by Manfred's frequent absences, I plunged myself into graduate studies with an eagerness I'd never had before in any school. Did I take time away from my hours with Manfred? No way. He often flew to New York, Pennsylvania, Texas and other places and stayed away for two or three days. Sometimes I picked him up at LAX, and sometimes he left his car at the airport.

One night at the airport, Manfred greeted me, exuberant as always.

"How was New York?" I asked.

"Interesting as usual. Lots of talks."

As we drove into our driveway at home, our neighbors, Marilyn and Jim, stood in their front yard, obviously out to get some fresh air.

"Hi, Manfred," Marilyn greeted him. "Back from your trip?"

"Alive and well."

"Where were you this time?"

"New York."

"How was the weather?"

"Beautiful."

Marilyn stepped a bit closer. "That's strange. I talked to my sister in New York today. She said it has been pouring rain for days."

Manfred chuckled. "I was in the hotel all the time, didn't see much of the weather. Thought it was good. Good night."

We entered the house, and I asked, "That's all you saw of New York? Just the hotel? Poor Manfred."

"Like yourself. You get out of the house only for classes, right?"

I was too tired to worry about my indoor existence or the weather in New York.

Manfred's Diary. Los Angeles, August 31, 1970

The neighbor almost caught me lying. I have to be more careful with everything I say. After all, I'm involved in international espionage. Of course, I wasn't in New York at all. I was in San Diego for a discussion about the building of the barge on which the claw, designed to grab the Soviet sub, will be built. I had arrived at LAX from San Diego shortly before the plane from New York came in, had waited and joined the New York passengers, as if I had come from New York too. An easy deception.

Still, I have this uneasy fear I may never be able to tell you, Eve. Then, on other days, I think I'm going to burst if I don't tell you about the submarine.

By and large, things are going ahead, the barge will be built in San Diego, and the construction of the salvage ship will be assigned to the Sun Shipbuilding and Dry Dock Company in Chester, Pennsylvania. If I didn't have such an interesting job — spying on a Soviet sub — I'd like to be in Chester, building that great ship.

After Labor Day a new school year started for Wernher and Irmie. To help with the bills I accepted several private piano students, whom I could teach at my home studio. Manfred went out for a sea trial of the drill vessel GLOMAR II, returning home only on the weekend.

"What's a sea trial?" I asked at a rare leisurely lunch out on the back terrace.

"Trying out the equipment for ocean mining."

"It's still Chinese to me."

"We simply let the strobelights and the cameras down to see where the most nodules are."

Couldn't be simpler!

Yet studying wasn't always simple. I was aware of my fear of libraries; no one had ever explained to me what the system was and how to find my way around the labyrinth. But early in the game I had to do research in it, and when I went astray in the maze, I couldn't hold my tears back.

At this moment a cynical voice from long ago echoed in my head: "Eva, are you feeling sorry for yourself?"

Immediately, the tears stopped and I realized how childish my behavior was. I went to the librarian and asked her to explain the library system to me. Once I understood it, I loved this orderly book world and was eager to help other students who came in as helpless as I had been.

Manfred's Diary. September 18, 1970

Eve, your intensive studies at the college couldn't have come at a better time. You're so absorbed in them you hardly ask me questions. You're content with whatever vague remarks I make. I don't even have to lie to you.

I have to be present on the sea trials of the drilling ship GLOMAR II near Catalina Island for a few days. But it's another story when it comes to explaining to you that I have to work in Hawaii for months to coordinate between the GLOMAR II and The Customer as Global Marine's representative on the ocean mining project.

There were some points not quite obvious from the pictorial record of the parts of the Soviet sub that had to be clarified. It was decided to move one of Global Marine's drill ships, the GLOMAR II, to the location and verify these data. A complete data acquisition system had to be designed, built and installed. This will keep lots of people busy and especially me, as I seek explanations to give to the outside world, keeping them in the dark, but giving the impression that we have to test parts of our system in prototype-scale.

Today, Manfred came home earlier than usual. I left my textbooks and greeted him. "What's going on?" I joked. "The ocean miners let you go home early?"

He put his briefcase down and went into the kitchen. "What's for dinner tonight? But first let's have a drink." He poured two glasses of Mountain Rhine wine. "Let's sit down and enjoy it."

I was alarmed. His behavior was absolutely strange. We sat down in the living room. I was all ears.

"I have to fly to Washington tomorrow," he began.

I shrugged. "What else is new?"

"I'll come back the next day. But then I have to fly to Hawaii."

"To Paradise? Congratulations! How many days?"

He took a sip of wine before he said, "At least three months."

A shock hit me. He in Hawaii and we alone in the Palisades? No way. "I'll go with you."

He turned red. "Impossible! I have to work there! This is not a vacation."

"You work wherever you want to. But I'll be with you."

"And the children?"

"They'll come along." I saw no further problems. "They could go to school over there."

He put his half-emptied glass on the coffee table with a clang. "Do you know how expensive that would be?"

He's getting to me on my frugal side! I thought. "Being together in Hawaii would be worthwhile for all of us," I said.

Stubborn as both of us were, we cut our debate short. I got up to prepare dinner.

Manfred's Diary. October 6, 1970
On flight to Washington

What an awful mess! Eva seems adamant about coming along to Hawaii with the kids. How should I present this problem to The Customer? Yesterday I should have said NO to her! I was just a coward. But that was yesterday. Today I'll persuade The Customer that taking the entire family to Hawaii would look more leisurely and provide more cover for the operation than if I went alone. So be it!

I'm definitely going to Hawaii! I repeatedly told myself to build up my self-esteem. *I'll have to cancel music history classes and take them next semester, but in Hawaii I can practice the piano for my Master's recital wherever we stay. And if there's only one piano on all the islands, I'll track it down and practice on that! As to the expenses of our flying to Honolulu, I'll put the furnished house up for rent. That would cover the price of the tickets.*

Manfred's Diary. Washington, D.C., same day

David and his team explained my task in Hawaii in detail. For my office I'll have to rent an apartment in downtown Honolulu to be close to RCA Telecommunications. I'll carry a beeper so RCA can reach me when I'm away from my office-apartment. I'll have to pick up telegrams from the GLOMAR II, which now is on her way to Hawaii.

The codes for deciding if the telegram had a secret message or not were the following: If the address read "Manfred Krutein, ocean mining engineer," no decoding was necessary. If it said "M. Krutein, ocean mining engineer," it must be decoded. In any case I had to call the agent at his hotel in Honolulu, suggesting we have a beer together or play cards, according to the time of day. The two of us would discuss in what restaurant we'd meet. Each time in a different one, of course. Whatever developed, I'd always be on call. We discussed many possible scenarios and David made sure I understood everything.

Only then I threw the bomb, declaring my family wanted to accompany me to Hawaii. David parried, saying I couldn't combine my family pleasure with our secret work. "Manfred, you're the placard we're holding up high for the world to see that we're doing ocean mining."

We argued back and forth. "I just by myself would look more suspicious than with a wife and children around," I said. "And if people heard my German accent, they wouldn't think this guy was working on a suspicious project. These two points will be important cover aspects."

David didn't give up. "You wouldn't have time to take your family around the island."

"That wouldn't be a problem, because Eva is very independent."

"By the way, Manfred, how do you keep written messages out of your wife's sight?"

"I never leave things lying around, and Eva isn't the snooping type; we respect each other's privacy."

"Has she ever asked you about your work?"

"No. She has her mind set on getting her Master's Degree as fast as possible." Again I emphasized, "My family would be excellent for a cover. Nobody would think that our project was suspicious."

David finally collected his papers, turned to his staff and declared they would discuss the matter over lunch without me around.

In the cafeteria we ate separately, and only Albert, a naval architect with a PhD, sat with me. Afterwards we all met again in the now familiar conference room. David announced their decision. You and the children could go with me on one condition. None of you should ever meet any of the agents. Nor should you be allowed to answer the telephone. If I had meetings with our agents at my office-apartment, you and the children would have to leave, even if it were at midnight. And another point, I should talk German with the family as much as possible. That would be an important aspect of our cover.

I think, you won't mind all that, Eve. Right or wrong?

It was well after midnight when Manfred came home. He tiptoed in, but when he saw me awake, he sat down on my side of the bed. "You won, Little Bear. You and the children can stay with me in Hawaii. And the company will pay for your trip."

"Yay!" I threw my arms around his neck. "Was it hard to persuade them?"

"Well, yes, in a way. Listen, I have to leave for Hawaii tomorrow. You follow me as soon as you have everything arranged."

Tomorrow came, and a lot had to be done. I'd have to notify Wernher's and Irmie's high school about our temporary move to

Hawaii. And in the middle of the semester I had to cancel classes I was taking. Hawaii was calling!

Susanne Shapiro called. "Could you substitute for me in December?"

Light-heartedly I replied, "Of course, I'll be back by then." It was October now.

A lady whose home was damaged by fire was happy to find our furnished house. She rented it for the next two months. All went as expected, and a week after Manfred's departure the three of us flew to Honolulu.

Hawaii's Fragrance

On the five-and-a-half-hour flight to the Hawaiian Islands the children experienced the wonder of time difference, as we competed with the sun on our westward race.

At Hawaii's noontime we strained our eyes, watching the islands pass by below us until the aircraft descended on Oahu. Impatiently I anticipated my first deep breath of the famous Hawaiian scent. Yet as I stepped off the plane in Honolulu a puff of hot humid air choked me — tropical climate! How would I survive the humidity? But the tropical tradewinds fanned such a lovely fragrance into my face that I felt this was the unique reception Hawaii offered its visitors.

And Manfred waved from afar! I collected my two youngsters and the flight bags and walked into his arms. He had brought three garlands of intensely perfumed, white flowers and hung them around our necks. "Aloha!" he said. "All newcomers to Hawaii get these leis as a welcome sign."

"How beautiful! What's the name of these flowers?"

"Plumeria."

Many of our co-passengers were treated the same way by those who picked them up. More Orientals than we'd ever seen milled around. Wide-eyed, we stared at the exotic environment which we had seen on TV many times.

Sitting next to Manfred in his leased Toyota I pointed to a small, black box hooked on his trouser belt.

"That's a beeper. RCA Telecommunications beeps me when a wire from the ship has come in."

He took us to Waikiki and its Tradewinds Apartments, two blocks from Waikiki Beach, where he had rented a one-bedroom flat in the penthouse. The double bed seemed good enough for Manfred and myself. Otherwise the apartment was his office, complete with a file cabinet with padlocks on every drawer.

"The two of you," Manfred said to the children, "sleep in the living room. One on the sofa, the other one on the floor in a sleeping bag. You can take turns every week."

"What do we do with the leis?" I asked.

"Wear them. At night you put them in the fridge." He turned to the telephone. "By the way, you may use the phone for making calls, but you are not allowed to answer the phone when it rings."

I was baffled. "Why not?"

"Our 'Customer' doesn't want to be identified at this point. So just don't answer the phone."

I said, "Okay," but I felt distrusted beyond reason.

The apartment was just about right for one person. Now I had to squeeze the belongings of four into the few available drawers. It reminded me of my flight from the Russians at war's end, where we had to make do with a minimum of space and things. It had worked then and would work now, particularly here, in so-called Paradise.

Paradise! Surely, I could see it from the balcony. I stepped onto it — and saw only a parking lot and some palm trees. The wrong side of paradise! Well, there would be other ways to see Honolulu.

Returning to the living room, I looked for my family and discovered them in the spacious shower room where Manfred showed the kids how the faucets worked.

"How do we get around the island?" I asked Manfred.

"I'll have very little time to take you around," he replied, stepping back into the bedroom. "You have to rent a car for yourself. It's expensive, but after all, your trip and your stay are free."

"And our house in the Palisades is rented. That pays for the rented car."

I began to make plans. First I called Ralph Harding, Verne's father, whom I hadn't seen since the Buddhist teachers' conference in Sacramento.

"Aloha!" Ralph's soft voice said. "Come over to see us. How about tomorrow? As you know, we live in Kailua. That's on the other side of Oahu. Have lunch with us. Bring your swim suits."

I told Manfred about the invitation.

"Sorry, I won't be able to go with you," he said. "I have to be close to RCA downtown."

Disappointed, I faced the makeshift kitchen. In contrast to the spacious shower room the kitchen niche in the living room consisted only of one electric hotplate and a tiny sink. At least there was a tea kettle.

I turned to Manfred. "What does RCA have to do with ocean mining?" .

"It accepts the messages from the ship and immediately calls me on the beeper. I'm on call twenty-four hours a day."

We quickly unpacked and went for a short walk around the block. The evening was hot and humid. The sidewalks were crowded and the heavy-traffic noise was irritating. I saw Wernher and Irmie shuffle like sleep-walkers. It was only 8 p.m. in Hawaii, but for our bodies it was 11 p.m. Jet lag forced us back to the office-apartment and our diverse sleeping arrangements. The hum of cars and trucks rolled through the night like ocean surf...

On my way to a car rental place next morning I noticed the cooler temperature in the air.

"Winter has begun today," the car dealer said as he handed me the key to the Honda Civic and a map of Oahu.

"You call this winter? It's great!" I replied.

I studied the map. Oahu was the shape of a crooked pentagon and had two mountain ranges and a very convenient highway that ringed the island. It seemed that we could circle the whole place in one sweep and get a good view of the coastline. We'd do that tomorrow.

Yet this morning I yearned to swim in the Hawaiian waters. Manfred had gone to work — wherever that was — and I took the jubilant children to nearby Ala Moana Beach.

Lots of people were lying on the sand. As I scanned the coast line with its high-rise buildings toward the east I fixed my eyes on the great crater. Far away from me, on the other end of Waikiki, Diamond Head stood quiet and imperturbable, a symbol of steadfastness and eternity. How often had I seen its image on pictures of Hawaii, but to see the brown rock face-to-face over a crowded coast was a mystical experience for me. *The extinct volcano and I — once and for all we both are one*! And then I discovered its injury, the scar on its stony mass, cutting from left to right on its upper body. Instinctively I looked down at the twenty-five-year-old scar on my thigh and back to the crater, and strongly felt we were one.

With this feeling of oneness I turned to the ocean. Its water felt warm and silky, not rough and cold like the water in California. The same ocean, but warmed by a tropical sun. Even Wernher, not exactly a water rat, liked it. Irmie, as usual, didn't say much, but her freckled face was beaming.

It didn't take long until I hit a coral reef. The sharp edge broke the skin of my ankle, and it began bleeding. *Probably only a matter of minutes before it stops,* I thought.

Right after our morning swim we started out to Kailua — only a short hop across the pentagon's slipped fifth corner. Soon we drove down the Pali Highway to Kailua.

Trying to show off my language skills, I said, "Pali means cliff."

"How do you know Hawaiian, Mom?" Irmie asked.

"I just looked up the word in the tiny Hawaiian dictionary Dad gave me. So somewhere there'll be a bluff like at home in Pacific Palisades."

So far we had seen only lush greenery on both sides of the highway. Coming from desert-like California I couldn't appreciate enough the richness of the green trees, shrubs and grass that competed with each other in abundance and color variations. When the road submerged into two successive tunnels we drove on with full lights. Emerging from the underworld we arrived at the Pali Lookout and were almost blown away by the gale. We literally leaned against the "wall" the trade winds created against the vertical cliffs. Despite the effort to stand tall we enjoyed the wide view with its three dimensions: The lush-green coastal plain way below us, the deep-blue ocean behind it and the shimmering sky above.

"How can anything be so beautiful?" Irmie asked. I pressed

her hand in confirmation.

Wernher had given up trying to stabilize his tripod and camera. "I can't shoot in this wind." His shoulder-long hair waved around his head. We soon left the look-out.

Twenty minutes later we arrived in Kailua and drove to the Harding's one-story house, which was almost hidden by yellow hibiscus, purple wisteria and white plumeria, all competing with narcotic scents. In this house Urs had spent nine months of her high school days eight years ago.

The friendly, white-haired giant himself opened the door, followed by a tiny Japanese lady, his wife Mitsi. His 6′5″ vs. her 4′8″ — *how do they ever make love?* rushed through my brain. Well, somehow they had managed, producing four children.

As they welcomed us in, Ralph looked down at my foot. "What's the matter with your ankle? It's bleeding."

Embarrassed I looked down. A thin rivulet oozed from the skin. "I hit a coral reef."

Ralph seemed concerned. "That's very bad. It takes days if not weeks to heal."

"Weeks?" I asked, terrified.

"By brushing the coral you got particles of it into your wound that prevents it from healing normally. Let's at least put a bandage on it." He went to another room and returned with a Bandaid. "Change it as long as the wound is open. Now let's have a cool drink inside."

We walked into the dining room, sat down at the table and began to eat.

I turned to our tiny hostess. "Your mahi-mahi chowder is delicious, Mitsi. What exactly is mahi-mahi?"

"Dolphin. I'm glad you like it."

"It's Japanese, isn't it?"

Mitsi smiled. "Actually Chinese. It's so much easier to prepare than Japanese meals and cheaper." She served a huge plate full of fresh fruit: Sliced pineapples, papaya, mangoes, kiwis and coconuts.

In the course of the meal we discussed Honolulu's high schools, and Ralph gave me the addresses of Roosevelt High and

McKinley High.

"I need something too, a piano," I said. "I have to practice at least three to four hours a day."

"Every church has one. Ask the Unitarian Church on Pali Highway."

After lunch Ralph took us to an empty beach. "The tourists haven't discovered it yet," he explained.

The water was warm and silky, just like on Ala Moana Beach. "There are no coral reefs here," Ralph assured me. We swam this way and that. "You came at the right time," Ralph said as he was within earshot. "Next week is Aloha week. Everyone wears Hawaiian clothes then. If you don't own any, buy some. It's fun and you won't look like tourists who don't know what's going on."

After the swim we said goodbye to Ralph and drove back to Honolulu.

"Let's hunt for Hawaiian clothes right away," I said. At the Ala Moana shopping center with its more than 150 stores, including familiar Sears & Roebuck, we discovered a pool crammed with iridescent Japanese carp, wiggling and racing for space, food and a chance to breathe.

At the escalator the sign saying "Caution: Persons With Barefeet Please Use Staircase" delighted not only rebellious Wernher but also me, since we loved walking barefoot and took it as another sign of Hawaii's carefree atmosphere. Eventually we bought some colorful, long, loose-fitting mu'u mu'us made of original hand-screened fabric for Irmie and myself and Hawaiian shirts for Wernher and Manfred.

Back at the apartment, we surprised Manfred with the Hawaiian shirts. "Good idea, thank you," Manfred said as he tried out his new shirt. "By the way, I have a meeting here at my office early in the morning. The three of you have to be out of here by seven. Is that okay?"

I grimaced. "That's okay. Your 'Customer' pays for our trip and room. We'll be out by seven."

I packed sandwiches for lunch, fruits and some soda cans, and exactly five minutes before 7 a.m. we left, appropriately Hawaiian-dressed. Everyone else seemed to be asleep. From the elevator at the other end of the corridor emerged a tall, thin man, clad in a Hawaiian shirt, his ears protruding over a golf cap, shading half his face. I assumed he was Manfred's secret Customer, and he might guess we were Manfred's family, making room for him. Fleetingly, we just looked at each other without greeting.

Downstairs we climbed into our Honda. "Up to Ala Moana Beach!" I said. "Ralph told me that Ala Moana means 'on the route to the ocean.' The park, the beach and our street have that name and also the shopping center across the street, where we bought our Hawaiian clothes last night."

The beach was empty at this hour. Diamond Head beckoned, and I smiled back at it. Although we had little time for swimming and I had to be very careful not to hit a coral reef again, we still enjoyed the soothing water. Then we quickly changed and drove first to McKinley High and then to Roosevelt High School. At McKinley they were having recess, and teachers and students, most of them Orientals and clad in Hawaiian outfits, milled around the courtyard. It turned out that McKinley offered courses in photography which Wernher wanted, and Roosevelt had German classes which Irmie preferred. Both children would start school the following day.

Then we drove up on Pali Highway and stopped by the Unitarian Church in search of a piano. Parking in the front yard of the unobtrusive church building, I went into the office. A short, plump lady in a colorful mu'u mu'u rose from her desk. "May I help you?"

I told her I was a Unitarian from the mainland and needed to practice the piano for my Master's recital.

She smiled. "I'm Florence. If you want to play the piano, please come as often as you like. We Hawaiians love music." She led me to the next room which had a brown upright piano next to the wall. I opened the lid and played a few scales and chords. It was even in tune, what more could I wish?

"Oh, how well you play! Are you coming tomorrow to play for me?"

I was jubilant. "Yes, I will." From the first moment I liked this friendly lady with her black mop of hair and dark eyes, apparently a real Hawaiian.

Continuing our exploration trip, we drove north between lush, green mountains and the palm tree-lined white beach. Palms here in Hawaii seemed to take on a different meaning than in southern California. There the stately trees formed lanes like statues for passing-through royalty. Here in Hawaii they grew curved, arching every-which-way, wild, abundant, jungle-like, awakening my deep-seated desire for wilderness. What a joy to see palm trees in their natural creative power!

Wernher's shouting brought me back to reality. "Mom, stop! It's Sunset Beach!"

The fabled big-surf mecca spread out its white sand and offered a smashing view of the pounding surf. I stopped the car.

"At this time the waves are highest!' Wernher shouted. Camera in one hand, dragging his tripod along with the other, he ran toward the water to shoot the incredible scenery. Huge waves, twenty to thirty feet high, approached like dark, threatening monsters, but decayed into white foam before they could reach us. Many surfers were trying to ride the big rolls, using them as vehicles of joy, but were ultimately overwhelmed and wiped out by the surf's power. In the azure sky white clouds moved fast, leaving only fleeting images of fairy-tale castles or snow creatures.

Reluctantly we left Sunset Beach and drove south on Kamehameha Highway with its bamboo and endless fields of sugar cane and pineapples stretched out on both sides. We even stopped for samples of pineapples at the Dole plantation. Picked here only when ripe, they were sweeter than any we had ever eaten before.

Wernher cleaned his juice-dripping mouth with his hand. "What a word for a highway: Kamehameha!"

"The name of five Hawaiian kings," I said, collecting our paper plates. "This morning I learned a long name for a little fish: *humuhumunukunukuapuaa*."

"Mom!" Irmie shouted. "How do you remember this?"

"By breaking it up: humu-humu-nuku-nuku-a-pu-a-a."

We got up from the table.

"What's next?" Irmie asked.

"Pearl Harbor."

"Ah!" Wernher said. "The attack on the Navy ships. Shame on the Japanese!"

"Not on all Japanese," I said. "Only on that old emperor and his cronies. All soldiers in the world must obey."

"But they attacked our ships without warning!"

"That's how most wars get started. Wars are evil with or without warnings."

At last we arrived at Pearl Harbor. A regular Navy shuttle took us to the Arizona Memorial. The striking white monument seemed to float on the water, and only later we saw the protruding tower and several deck items of the sunken remains of the battleship USS ARIZONA.

Entering the monument I marveled at its modern design, but was quite surprised when I saw other visitors tiptoeing and whispering to each other. For a moment an elderly lady with a big straw hat stood next to me, and I decided to talk to her. "May I ask you," I said under my breath, "why people are whispering here?"

She turned her big brown eyes to me. "This is a giant tomb. More than 1100 sailors and Marines lie entombed under our feet."

War memories, long banned from my consciousness, came back, step by step; walking home through burning streets, dead bodies on the road, drunken enemy soldiers mass-raping women, the ensuing suicides of the victims... *Stop! I want to get away from the memories of war! Hawaii is such an enraptured place, it's easy to feel an eon away from the world's suffering. That's all I want here, to forget the wars, the pressures of every day and the worries of tomorrow.*

I managed to wait until Wernher pulled himself away from the memorial. The shuttle took us back, we climbed into the Honda and returned to Honolulu.

Arriving at the Tradewinds in the afternoon, I placed a call in the lobby to our apartment to find out if we were allowed to enter yet. We were.

Tired from the long drive and the usual endless search for a parking spot, we took the elevator up to the penthouse.

Manfred stood at the door and greeted us. "Sorry I had to keep you out for so long."

We walked in, took soft drinks from the fridge and grabbed left-over potato chips from the table. Manfred also removed three ashtrays, filled with cigarette stubs. *So there were more than the one with the golf cap,* I thought, when I fell on my bed. *Well, peace be with their ashes!*

Manfred's Diary. Honolulu, October 14, 1970

Eve, I was anxious about you and the kids leaving early enough, so you wouldn't encounter my visitors for the all-day meeting. You had just left when I heard a knock at the door. Shock: had Eva forgotten something and was returning? Relief: it was Jim, our middleman with the protruding ears, which fit him so well, as if he could hear more this way. He told me he had just seen my family in the hallway. I closed the window, pulled down the shades and turned on the radio to create some background noise to make any neighbor's potential listening difficult. Eleven more men, in singles or twos and at different intervals, entered my living room; the GLOMAR II's captain, government reps, scientists and technicians, some of whom would sail with the GLOMAR II to the site where the sunken Soviet submarine had been in its two-year-long sleep. While the technicians checked the room for electronic bugs I locked the door of my "safehouse." Half my visitors sat down on sofa and chairs, and the rest sat on the carpet.

Jim distributed sheets with the agenda. Everyone knew the ship's trip would depend on the outcome of this meeting. Jim's ability to moderate the talks, giving each of us a chance to speak up, led to a satisfactory brainstorming session. I could see that The Customer's people had plenty experience in planning secret actions. They addressed all possible scenarios and potential reactions that might occur during the GLOMAR II's mission.

Jim threw bones of contention into the brainstorming session. "The Soviets have thousands of spies around our country."

We discussed what would happen if the Soviets put a ship alongside the GLOMAR II and kept it there for spying purposes.

"They could try," he said, "to ask for medical help for a sick crew member as they have done on two previous occasions in order to come aboard American ships. They know all kinds of tricks. They once tried to entangle a rope in the propellers of one of our ships." No possible trick was excluded, no detail neglected.

We discussed the different steps of the GLOMAR II's mission. The former drilling ship, working in relatively shallow ocean waters, had been converted to one that could work in the extreme depths of the Pacific. Two more propellers had been added for remaining at the precise point above the sunken submarine. Moreover, our ship was in lock with a satellite to keep its exact location in the immense and ever-shifting Pacific. With the help of the derrick, long steel pipes would be assembled, one after the other, about 300 in total, to reach the depth of 16,500 feet. The lowest pipe would contain a special camera, encased in a cylinder with strobe lights on its sides and would be operated from the ship to take shots of the Soviet submarine. Daily schedules were worked out and improvements debated. Possible mishaps were anticipated and remedies suggested. The hours passed like minutes.

In the heat of discussion we got thirsty. The numerous soda drinks in the fridge now came in handy.

Jim told the others that I had a triple role to play in this mission. First, the one of an ocean-mining expert to tell the world we were mining the ocean for minerals. I had to continue to present reports about ocean mining and attend ocean conferences all over the world. My second role was that of a communications specialist in Honolulu, preparing and making sure the radio communications from the ship to me and then to The Customer and back again would be safe and reliable. I had to forward scrambled messages to Jim. My third role was that of a coordinator, with responsibility for hotel rooms, rental cars, meeting rooms for officials from Washington D.C., and the performance of dozens of other little jobs.

Jolly Captain Dawson of the Glomar II asked if I provided movies for the crew. I assured him that yesterday I had sent ten films to the ship. The crew wouldn't die of boredom.

At noon we heard the expected knock at the door: A caterer delivered sandwiches, potato chips and soft drinks, and we relaxed and talked about the weather, beaches and ballgames.

After half an hour we resumed our discussion. Problems about security came up. "Manfred, has anybody ever asked you questions about why you are here?" Jim asked. "Or were you aware of the same people around you several times, checking up on your actions?"

No, not at all, I answered. People seemed to think our family was thoroughly enjoying Hawaii.

"Just remember," Jim said. "If you see the same person twice, start getting concerned. If you see him three times, you know you've got something. We always have to be on the lookout for people who are spying for the Soviets."

When the meeting was over my visitors left the apartment in groups of two or three during the next ten minutes. Before Captain Dawson of the GLOMAR II left he said, "I'd like to invite your family for dinner on board tomorrow. That will look pretty harmless to the public and the media."

I thanked him and assured him that you, Eve, and the kids would enjoy that.

When the gang was gone, I opened the shades and windows, turned off the radio, took out a can of beer and slumped onto the sofa.

Hawaii's Treasures

Early in the morning I woke up the children — Irmie on the sofa, Wernher in the sleeping bag on the floor — to take them to their respective schools and myself to the Unitarian Church for piano practice. I dropped off the kids and drove straight to the Unitarian Church.

Chubby little Florence greeted me like a long-awaited sister, kissed me and then took me to the piano. "Go ahead, dear. Play as long as you want." The telephone rang in her office, and she went to answer it.

Long ago I had made up a schedule for practicing and decided to stick to that sequence. Scales and arpeggios first, then right away to Scarlatti, Bach and Beethoven. Composers of later periods were out of the question, because at the recital I was going to use three different keyboard instruments, clavichord, harpsichord and piano with the emphasis on compositions for the respective instruments and their periods. I'd use both harpsichord and clavichord — Manfred-built — and proudly I was going to demonstrate my ingenious husband's achievements at the public performance I had to give for my Master's degree.

After one and a half hours of uninterrupted practicing I got up and stretched.

In no time Florence appeared with two glasses, filled with guava juice. "Here, drink this. You deserve it."

Her language was a good mixture of English and Hawaiian, and sometimes I had to ask her for the meaning of an Hawaiian word, like "A *wahine* said to me —"

"Wa-hi-ne?"

"Oh, a woman. That's a word you might want to learn so you wouldn't walk into the wrong restroom."

"And what's 'men'?"

"*Kane*."

"Wa-hi-ne and ka-ne," I practiced.

We laughed, had instant rapport, and I relaxed in her presence. We told each other the trivia of the day without fear of being ridiculed for it. *The easy-going way of the Hawaiians — I could stay here forever!*

I stopped practicing after two more hours and said goodbye to Florence.

"What are you cooking for dinner?" she asked.

"Tonight we're invited for dinner on the GLOMAR II."

She kissed me goodbye. "Have fun!"

In the evening we drove on traffic-packed Ala Moana Boulevard to the Honolulu Harbor, which was crowded with fishing boats, freighters and catamarans. The clock on the square Aloha Tower showed seven.

At Pier 8 Manfred stopped and parked the car before the black-painted GLOMAR II, which stood out from the other ships because of her derrick, the tower-like framework that protruded from the center, pointing at the sky.

"What's that thing for?" Wernher asked, shooting it with his still camera.

"The derrick?" Manfred asked. "On its peak they hang up the pipes and let them down through the hole underneath into the water."

"What for?"

"Sucking up manganese nodules from the ocean floor."

We walked up the gangway. As we stepped on deck a pudgy, jolly man stood there to receive us. "Welcome to the GLOMAR II." Manfred introduced us to Captain Dawson, who shook hands with each of us and then led us past oil barrels and rusty equipment to the dining area, where all the tables were occupied by the crew except for the table with the captain and us. It was noisy and the air was thick with cigarette smoke.

To our surprise we were served German food. *"Sauerbraten!"* I said to Manfred. "The last thing I expected on an American oil-drilling ship in Hawaii." To Captain Dawson I said, "You have an excellent cook."

The cook was summoned and appeared, short and pudgy like his boss and round-faced.

"Your *sauerbraten* was delicious," I said to him. "Where did you learn to make it?"

"Thank you, Madam. I was with the Army in Germany and got to know German food. It's good to have different cuisines. Keeps the crew from boredom all those weeks at sea." He thanked us again for the compliment and left.

"How long will you be offshore?" I asked the captain.

"About three weeks. We've got enough food and water, fuel and oil. We're ready to sail tomorrow morning."

We wished all of them good luck and left.

At 9:30 p.m. Ala Moana Boulevard was as packed as in the afternoon. Yet the scenery was enhanced by colorful Japanese lanterns, swaying in the hands of those celebrating Aloha Week. The crowns of palm trees were spotlighted, and on various buildings lit torches flickered in the ever-present wind, which wafted the perfume of frangipani through the air.

When the children were sound asleep, Manfred and I celebrated life in our own way. Under pale moonlight we embraced, feeling on fire from head to foot. The moment of ecstasy, usually so short, seemed to stretch in the fragrances of Hawaii, and afterwards we felt Hawaii had led us to the fields of bliss.

Today was the beginning of Aloha Week! From our balcony I watched the parade of King Kamehameha and his lei-decorated entourage move along Ala Moana Boulevard, accompanied by a drummer and weird-sounding wind-instruments. With longing I stared east, but Diamond Head was hidden behind high-rise buildings. It began to drizzle, and I left the balcony,

Thanks to my conversations with Florence my Hawaiian vocabulary was gradually increasing. To me the language sounded melodious because of its heavy use of the five vowels, which were loosely held together by only eight consonants. Whenever I happened to be present when native Hawaiians talked to each other I could hear the rich sound of their words —

ideal for singing. I could hear them in shopping malls or on the radio.

Yet their music was mixed with western musical characteristics, based on the European major and minor scales — a disappointment for me. Hawaiian music easily became kitsch, particularly when the electric "Hawaiian guitar" was used. This was laid on a table, and a musician, armed with a movable metal bar, slid it up the strings, producing a howling sound the singer tried to imitate. Yet those cultural adulterations were probably unavoidable.

Even rainbows behaved differently in Hawaii. On the mainland they domed in the distance, where their ends faded into nowhere. Stepping out to our balcony to check if the drizzle had stopped, I saw a rainbow not only close by but its one end reached down into the parking lot beneath me, exactly between Manfred's green Toyota and a purple VW.

Feeling the urge to touch it and making it mine, I took the elevator down and ran to the parking lot. I easily reached our Toyota and the VW, but to my dismay I couldn't see or touch the rainbow. Disillusioned, I went up again and onto the balcony: The rainbow was still shining between the two cars. No touch, no possession, just a longing look.

Disappointed, I went to pick up the children from their schools. I scanned the horde of teenagers leaving the school building. Some girls seated themselves on the low stone fence in front of the school and began to smoke. Finally Irmie appeared and climbed into the car.

Wernher kept watching the smokers. "What are they smoking? Pot?"

"Sure," Irmie answered. "Nobody minds it here."

He sighed. "Lucky Hawaiians."

Passing by the striking modern architecture of the State Capitol, we waved a hello to the big idealized statue of King Kamehameha outside, whose heroic chest now during Aloha Week was overflowing with leis of fragrant flowers.

Shortly after Aloha week was over, Ralph Harding called one

afternoon to invite us to see a Chinese temple. On time as always, the friendly giant picked up the children and me and drove to the temple.

The Chinese Hsu Yin Temple was as colorfully decorated as it possibly could be, compared to the subdued decorations in Japanese temples. New to me were the occasional dog or cat strolling through the temple as if it were their home. "Animals are living beings like us," Ralph explained. "Buddhists accept them as equals." My animal-loving heart was deeply touched.

There was another feature special to this temple: Several black-and-white prints covered the temple walls, telling the Buddha's life story. I had learned long ago that the Buddha's eighty years on earth and his personality as such were not sacred and that only his teachings were worshipped in the temples. Nevertheless, the pictures on the walls were fascinating.

Ralph pointed to a drawing of a king's castle and told us, "In southern Nepal, in the foothills of the Himalayas, a son was born to the king and his queen in a spring about 500 years before the Common Era." Ralph, who had avoided saying "before Christ" let his hand wander to the next picture with the baby placed on silk brocades, surrounded by his parents and several wise men. "He was given the name of Siddhartha, which means 'accomplishment of the goal.' The king asked the wise men about his son's future. They answered, 'If he remains in the palace and pursues a worldly life, he will become a monarch. However, if he renounces his home, wealth and position and wanders forth as a holy man, he will become a completely enlightened buddha and satisfy all beings.'"

Ralph stepped from one picture to the next, telling the story as we followed him. "The king decided to do everything in his power to shelter the prince from the real world and surrounded him with luxury and pleasures, musicians and beautiful women who entertained him. The concepts of old age, illness and death were unknown to him. When he reached the age of sixteen, a bride was given to him, a royal wedding held, and a year later a son was born to them.

"When Siddhartha was in his late twenties, he demanded that his charioteer, named Chandaka, take him to a particular garden outside the palace. There they encountered an old man, sick people and a funeral. Siddhartha asked Chandaka who these people were and learned from him that old age, illness and death await all of us."

We followed Ralph, spellbound.

"On other outings the prince encountered a mendicant with upright bearing and a radiant face. Chandaka explained, 'This is a holy man who has renounced worldly pleasure and entered a life of homelessness. He has no possessions but wanders from place to place, begging his daily food.' Siddhartha returned to the palace but it dawned on him that the mendicant's path might be his own in the future. One night, after a drunken orgy with beautiful women, he woke up and saw with disgust the sleeping women around him in repulsive positions in puddles of wine and leftovers. He renounced his former life and walked out of the palace forever." Ralph stopped, smiled and seemed to think he had talked enough.

"Why did you stop, Ralph?" I asked. With a look at my children's wide-open eyes I added, "We'd like to hear more."

Smiling, Ralph pointed to the next picture. "Siddhartha exchanged his silk robe for a hunter's simple clothes, gave his gold and jewel ornaments to Chandaka and sent him back to the palace. From now on he was homeless like the other wandering mendicants."

I was moved by the thought that homelessness was considered a virtue. When Lilo and I were homeless after our flight from the Soviets in WW II, I was desperate to find a place to stay. But after all, I wasn't a saint.

"Siddhartha listened to other holy men, learned to meditate and for the next six years, lived an ascetic life to the extreme. He almost died of hunger and exhaustion. People helped and fed him, and he regained his strength. On a full-moon day, when he was thirty-five, he sat beneath a tree. He attained enlightenment and so became a buddha."

Ralph turned to me. "I suppose you learned the Four Noble Truths long ago." I nodded. "From now on the Buddha kept teaching his followers who grew in numbers and positions. When he was eighty he fell sick of food poisoning..."

My favorite part was coming, and I told it myself; "When the Buddha was dying he saw his favorite follower, Ananda, weeping, and said, 'Ananda, didn't I teach you detachment from what we hold dear? What is born will die. But the Dharma, the Teaching, will remain.'"

Ralph smiled. "That's the end of the story." He ushered us to the temple door where a young boy was standing in front of a box with oranges. The youngster took out four and gave one to each of us.

"It's a common way in this temple to send visitors off with a gift," Ralph explained.

We left the temple. Ralph ushered us into a small restaurant across the street that announced, "Delicious Hawaiian Food." The room had only four small, round tables; two were taken. We sat down.

"I want you to try *poi*," Ralph said, ordering it. "It's made from boiled taro roots and wrapped in ti leaves, which the early Hawaiians considered sacred."

The chubby Hawaiian waitress soon brought two plates full of brownish heaps on big green leaves. Ralph began to eat his mound with great appetite. Cautiously the children and I tasted a bit from the second plate.

"Ugh!" Wernher cried.

Irmie had tears in her eyes, but with good manners swallowed the strange paste. I followed her example but without tears.

Ralph laughed and laughed. "I believe you don't want more of it? See, that's why I was cautious, ordering only two plates."

Having finished his *poi* with great appetite, Ralph took the children back to the Tradewind Apartments and me to the Unitarian Church for my piano practice.

Eventually I realized that I couldn't use the Unitarian Church only for practicing and ignore its main goal of gathering and educating people, and so on Sunday I pulled myself together and attended the service. There was little I disliked more than going to church on Sunday mornings, which I equated with conservatism and philistinism. Yet my effort was richly rewarded.

Out of the all-white congregation of about 100 people at least five approached me and, with great Aloha spirit, said they'd heard me play the piano and would like to invite me and my family over for dinner. Delighted, I accepted. My calendar for the next week was almost full; only Tuesday was open.

"Would you like to attend our new Venture Group on Tuesday nights?" A young man with blond hair hanging to his shoulders asked me.

"What do you do there?" I asked.

"Talk openly about our problems," he replied.

How fun! Of course, I accepted.

Later when I told Manfred, he said, "Once in a while I'll go with you to dinner parties. But I'm neither interested in the Venture Group nor do I have time for things like that."

"I'll go and tell you about it," I said.

I absorbed Hawaii, I breathed Hawaii and I was intimately involved with Hawaii. Tranquilizers were long forgotten; I slept well without them. Firmly I adhered to my daily piano practice in the morning and to swimming with the children at Ala Moana Beach in the afternoon. I always kept Diamond Head in my field of vision, smiling at it, visually caressing its 25-million-year-old scar that was visible even over miles of distance.

Hawaii's Magic and Dangers

Manfred's Diary. Honolulu, October 23, 1970

Still recovering from yesterday's adventure, I'll record it for your and my future, Eve.

After the GLOMAR II left Honolulu I thought I'd have some peace and quiet for a change. It would take the ship a week to arrive in the Northern Pacific, where it would work above the site of the sunken Soviet submarine. Yet yesterday morning Jim called me for an immediate meeting at my office-apartment. He arrived ten minutes later, his usually gangling posture stiff and tense. He grabbed two chairs and slapped them next to the refrigerator, whose humming was loud enough to discourage any hidden microphone. I turned the radio on and checked if the windows were closed. We slumped on the chairs.

In spite of all our precautions Jim spoke under his breath. He said additional data had to be conveyed to the GLOMAR II. The message must be brought aboard the ship. The data were being flown by jet from the East Coast to Honolulu and would be in our hands tomorrow. It was very important for the Glomar II to find the right spot on the ocean and it was absolutely necessary to get the papers to the vessel as fast as possible. Besides, heavy weather conditions were expected soon, meaning trouble for the GLOMAR II which needed good weather and calm seas. No time must be lost.

I got up, unlocked the lower drawer of the file cabinet and took out the nautical charts. They showed where the ship was located at every moment, and, checking my wrist watch, I pointed to the spot of the moment: 200 miles north of the Hawaiian Islands.

We discussed how to deliver the papers. To use a fast motor boat from the Navy was impossible for cover reasons; the Navy would never be involved in our so-called private operation. To fly an airplane to the ship and drop the package of data with a parachute was too risky; the package could fall in the ocean. Meanwhile, GLOMAR II had been ordered to stop immediately and to wait for further instructions.

A challenge! How about a helicopter? I asked. I'd find out if it could fly that far. Jim agreed and left with the speed of an arrow.

I put the chairs back, took the phone book out and called the airport. During the next ten minutes, several numbers of helicopter facilities were given to me, and I conveyed my question to each of them: Did they have a pilot who could fly at least 200 uninterrupted miles in a row and back? "No, sir," was the usual answer. Helicopters flew only from one Hawaiian island to the other.

After another negative response a glimmer of hope appeared. The source said there was a pilot who owned a private company, Eric Hatcher. He might be able to fly that far.

I reached Hatcher via telephone. After a short but hopeful conversation I went to meet him at his helicopter business. A white chopper stood next to a barracks like a greeting host. I went inside the barracks and found a tall, blond, Scandinavian-type man in his thirties sitting at his desk, huge charts in front of him. Eric Hatcher. We shook hands, and he told me that he was already studying the charts for our flight. He told me he'd flown for years with the Navy. He called the chopper "my good pal Jenny," which could take him over a good part of the Pacific. Its range was 200 miles, which meant 100 miles to the ship and 100 miles back. Disillusioned, I said the ship was already 200 miles away.

Hatcher knit his brows, pondering something. Suddenly his face lit up. He had an idea, he said. It was quite risky, but he thought it could be done. He could take me and an extra tank with fuel and fly 200 miles north to the ship, land on it and pump the extra fuel into the chopper's tank. He'd leave the empty tank on the ship and then fly back to Hawaii. But the ship must be there, he emphasized, not more than 200 miles north of Kauai, and it must wait for us. It would be a precision flight and again, it was risky. If we didn't meet the ship when the gas ran out we'd have to "get out" and swim. Just like on my WW II submarine missions, I thought. Win or else. "Sounds great," I said. We discussed the costs and I accepted the deal.

I definitely was aware of the risk in case we didn't find the ship in the vast ocean, but I had taken so many risks in my life I could add another. I told you, Eve, that I'd leave with the helicopter at five a.m. and would be home late at night. You shouldn't worry about me and you could answer the phone for a change.

In the meantime Jim was busy making sure our flight would be safe. He had contacted the Navy, which assured him our helicopter would be observed by radar and our position would always be known. A rescue team would be ready at all times to pick us up, if necessary.

Jim met me at my parked Toyota and handed me three items: a long, sealed cylinder with the important documents inside, a mail bag for the GLOMAR crew and a small red rubber raft with a radar-reflective surface. He said, in case we had to go down into the sea, we could throw the raft into the water, it would pump itself up, and we could stay in it until we were rescued. The rubber raft was lightweight; still, it gave me a feeling of security. Jim said he'd be with the Navy and follow our flight on the radar screen.

At 5 a.m. Hatcher was already waiting for me at the airport. He insisted on demonstrating a possible "get out," which was relatively easy, considering the smallness of the craft: open the small door, throw the rubber raft in the water, jump and swim to the raft. Didn't sound too hard.

At last I climbed into the chopper and found that half of Hatcher's seat and half of mine were taken by the dirty, stinking extra gas tank, an indispensable monster.

As the blades began to turn and the noise quickly became hellish, the helicopter lifted off and took a course to Kauai. The rotor above us spluttered like coins in a turning clothes dryer, loud enough to make one deaf. Conversations were impossible, but in time I realized that by shouting at the top of my lungs I could make myself heard.

We were flying over the blue sea of the Pacific between the Hawaiian islands with Kauai ahead of us. A short while later we were over the island itself. We headed in the direction of its capital Lihue and landed on a meadow. Only then I saw a small service station for helicopters. A limping Hawaiian in his fifties appeared from nowhere, shook hands with us and then filled the chopper's tank. Hatcher started the engine again and flew toward the northeast coast. For a few moments I saw the dramatically steep, vertical, green cliffs of the Na Pali coast, which rose to 3,000 feet, a sight of unheard-of beauty.

From then on we flew straight to the north, with only a small compass, heading for a tiny ship in the immensity of the Pacific Ocean. The sky radiated a deep azure, undisturbed by clouds or fog. There was nothing visible but the grayish-blue water with its many different shades, depending on the local wind gusts and the angle of the sun reflected in it. The waves were small and without any white foam. After a while I became used to the rotor's deafening noise, finding it almost tranquilizing. No ship, no airplane, not even jet condensation trails could be seen. We were alone in a world without humans. But below us in the water there were whales, dolphins, and hundreds of species of fish which had been there for millions of years.

My eyes scanned the instrument panel. Shock! The fuel gauge's needle was approaching zero! If we didn't meet the ship within a few minutes we might as well "get out and swim" in the ocean.

Then I heard Hatcher shout, "Watch out for the ship! Look east. I'll look west." As intensely as I could I scanned the blue vastness but saw only the empty ocean around us. Suddenly I spotted a tiny dark point in the distance which rapidly grew to a ship of toy size. It became larger and larger and suddenly we were right above the GLOMAR II. We saw the crew on deck waving to us, the heli platform was clear for us to land. The chopper hovered above it and gently lowered itself, whipping up a gust of wind. Hatcher stopped the engine and the hellish noise died. A great silence enveloped us, and it took a few moments before we realized that people were talking to us. The captain and the government reps approached us to shake hands and welcome us with champagne. I handed the data cylinder over to Captain Dawson. In order to comply with the rule that every transfer of secret data had to be documented he signed the receipt I had prepared. Then I delivered the bag with mail, newspapers and magazines for the crew members, and in return we were treated to a good lunch: filet mignon, green beans and potatoes, followed by a huge serving of chocolate ice cream.

I asked Captain Dawson, who sat across the table, if his crew had watched the ten movies I had delivered to the ship.

With a deploring smile he replied that they'd watched none, because I'd failed to deliver the popcorn. Without it they wouldn't watch movies. What an inexcusable oversight! So as soon as the ship got back to Honolulu I had to make it my first priority to deliver movie food.

Soon after, Hatcher went back to the platform to pump the extra fuel into the chopper's tank, leaving the empty barrel behind. Dawson and the crew gave us a hearty farewell and good-luck wishes for a safe return flight.

Without the extra tank between us we now sat comfortably. Hatcher started the engine, and the blades began their deafening splutter again. Lifting off we saw the ship below us sink deeper and deeper, shrinking again to toy size. I saw the water stir up behind the ship in white lines as the propeller started to work: Glomar II was already sailing north.

We flew south and I fell asleep. When I awoke Hatcher pointed to the gray clouds over Kauai, indicating rain and a difficult flight. Indeed, the nearer we came to the island the denser the clouds became. We had to ascend to 3,000 feet to make sure we didn't hit the now invisible mountains. The gas gauge's needle again was close to zero. Persistently we scanned the cloud cover to find out if we were above Kauai or not. We also had to find a spot to get down. Suddenly we saw a small opening in the clouds.

"I can see Lihue!" yelled Hatcher. "Ain't we lucky!" He managed to fly through the narrow cloud opening and landed beside the helicopter gas station. As in the morning the lame attendant appeared from nowhere and helped Hatcher with the pumping.

I looked around and found a telephone. For a minute I stepped out of my role as a spy, being only a husband. I called you. You seemed relieved, told me a man had called every fifteen minutes to ask if I were back. Jim, of course.

I called Jim and said we were on Kauai, filling up. Thirty minutes later we arrived at Honolulu's airport, where Jim was waiting for us. I passed over the rubber raft to him. He told me, while we were close to Kauai he could no longer see us on the radar screen and had worried.

At home, after telling a bit about the flight, I had to unwind and watch TV with the family, pretending this had been an ordinary chopper flight like hundreds of them that occurred every day between the islands.

Having explored much of Oahu, I had saved Diamond Head for later. I was told that entering the crater was off-limits to civilians, since it housed the control center for all aircraft entering and departing the air space. *But I must see my crater's inner self!* So I called Ralph for help.

"Of course the control center doesn't want tourists around," he said. "But I'll see if I can get you in. By the way, how's the coral injury on your ankle?"

I sighed. "Still open."

"It takes weeks to heal."

The next afternoon dear, helpful Ralph picked up the children and me to drive to Diamond Head. To get in seemed easier than I thought. Ralph, an electronics technician for the Federal Aviation Administration, said a few words to the guard, who then let us pass through the tunnel.

A moment later we stepped on the deepest part of the crater. Ignoring the barracks with its high antennas, I took in the green walls around us up to the rim and bent down to feel the crater's rocky bottom. It was given to me: whatever I touched with my hand, spiritually became mine forever. So much of Hawaii was already mine, and every day I acquired more.

We'd been on the Islands for more than two weeks, but I hadn't contacted Reverend Fujitani yet, whom I had met in Sacramento eight years ago. So I called him. Before I could explain to him who I was he said, "Welcome to Hawaii, Mrs. Krutein." *Surprise, he remembered! And what formality to call me by my last name! But the Japanese are known for that.*

"How long will you be in Honolulu?" he asked.

"Two more months. My husband even longer."

"May we invite you and your husband for lunch whenever it's convenient for you?"

We agreed on Thursday noon at a Japanese restaurant. Fujitani had said "*we* invite you" and so I was looking forward to meeting his wife.

Glad that Manfred could come with me for a change, we made it to the crowded restaurant. Manfred and I seemed to be the only "whites." *How I hate that incorrect term! Our skin is beige, not white.*

As the hostess led us to a table in a corner, I immediately recognized Rev. Fujitani's handsome, inscrutable face. He got up and introduced us to the delicate lady at the table, "Mrs. Tanaka." *Not his wife? Who else then?* He didn't explain.

Mrs. Tanaka flashed a warm smile. "Glad to meet you, Mr. and Mrs. Krutein. Welcome to Hawaii."

We looked up the Japanese and English listings in the menu, hardly knowing what they meant. Fujitani explained and at last suggested food I had never heard of and ordered for us all.

Manfred quickly became the center of attention as he told our hosts about his ocean mining project while I unobtrusively observed our new Japanese friends. Or would they, reserved and formal as they were, not call us "friends" as the Californians did a minute after meeting people? Positively prejudiced toward the Japanese, I decided I very much liked those Asian faces.

A waitress brought the salad, artistically arranged on the plate with the lettuce leaves' different shades of green.

Before we could begin to eat, Manfred's beeper began to emit its high-pitched signal. Abruptly he got up, said, "Excuse me, please," and rushed to a phone booth.

Fujitani turned to me. "Please tell us about your studies of Buddhism."

I told them about my mother's admiration for Japan, the many German translations of books about Buddhism, the Obon Festival in Palo Alto and my regular organ-playing at the Buddhist temple there.

Manfred hurried back to us, remained standing and told us, "Sorry, I have to leave you. I must pick up a cable from the RCA center. It can't wait."

"Where will you eat lunch then?" I asked.

"Somewhere I'll get something." He said goodbye and left.

"That's how we live," I said with a sad smile. "He's on call twenty-four hours a day, coordinating the ocean-mining project. So far he hasn't had time to enjoy Hawaii at all."

"Yet he looks like he's enjoying his job," Fujitani said.

"He certainly is."

The entrees were served and I had the visual pleasure and the taste of cucumbers filled with crab meat, rice wrapped in bamboo leaves and seaweed and sushi with countless different fillings. Small bottles of hot sake seemed inevitable on Japanese tables, and we observed the old-fashioned custom of raising the tiny sake cups and using first names.

"I'm Edith," "I'm Yoshi," "I'm Eva."

The conversation turned to Yoshi's Buddhist Temple on Pali Highway, the main road to Kailua, on which we had driven so many times without seeing the temple.

"We have a very active congregation," he told me. "Edith is our religious education director. We invite you to attend service on Sunday."

"I'll certainly be there."

Manfred's Diary. Honolulu, October 31, 1970

Leaving the Japanese luncheon I drove to RCA and picked up the cable. The message told about some difficulties with parts of the ocean mining equipment. Above all, the cable was addressed to "M. Krutein, ocean mining engineer – the "M." instead of "Manfred" telling me it had to be decoded. Immediately I called Jim and we agreed to meet in a coffee shop in the Ala Moana Shopping Center.

Within five minutes I entered the cafeteria and saw him sitting alone at a small table. I forced myself to a leisurely pace, pretended (for our invisible enemy) to be surprised at seeing Jim there and joined him. We exchanged a hearty handshake.

The waitress brought menus. We held them straight up, pretending to study them. Stealthily I pulled the cable from the inside of my long sleeve and, hidden behind the menus, passed it over to Jim and then pointed to an entry in his menu, asking him if he'd like to try it. He cautiously slipped the cable under his own long sleeve, chuckled and said he wanted just a cup of coffee. The coffee was served, my job was over and I led him into a conversation about German food, the Hawaiian weather and other trivialities.

Suddenly Jim looked at his wrist watch. "Oh my! I have a

golf game at two! See you!" He got up and left.

Remembering Eve and the Japanese now eating lunch, I picked up the menu again and at last ordered a meatloaf with green beans and mashed potatoes to satisfy my rumbling stomach.

Sunday came, and Manfred drove us all to the temple. My dislike of attending a Sunday morning service was replaced by my desire to plunge into the Japanese community.

As we entered the large temple with its sparse, but tasteful decorations, about two hundred black-haired people were already seated. I inhaled the incense, whose slim column of smoke rose from a bowl in front of the altar. The gong sounded outside, indicating the beginning of the service. Rev. Fujitani entered, clad in a black robe with long, wide sleeves and a golden stole around the shoulders. He sat down on a chair, his profile toward us, hit the large metal bowl, whose pitch was indefinable, and began chanting in a monotone. *I know all the details of the service. I feel at home.*

The big surprise came when Yoshi Fujitani stepped to the pulpit to begin his sermon. Remembering his unusual speech in Sacramento eight years ago, I was ready for another modern interpretation of Buddhism.

Instead he opened his sermon with, "This week I had the pleasure of again meeting a German woman who indulges in Buddhism and lends her musical abilities to the Buddhist Sunday service on the mainland. We renewed our friendship and I hope she will be active at our temple as long as she is here in Hawaii."

I sat, thunderstruck, as if my clothes had been ripped off, not daring to look around.

"Wow!" Manfred whispered to me. I swallowed hard.

The sermon went on about Buddhism and modern-life problems, but I didn't hear much of it, still in a state of shock from being publicly announced. The service ended with the congregation's chanting of Japanese syllables.

Outside, Edith Tanaka approached us and introduced lots of people to us, whose names I didn't understand. They greeted us with bows and polite smiles, but none of them referred to their priest's public introduction of me; maybe they didn't put the two things together.

On our way home Manfred's beeper went off and he drove to the next gas station to place a phone call. He returned to the car. "I'm very sorry, but you have to go to the beach without me. I have a meeting in our apartment. Please get your swim stuff and leave as soon as possible."

My disappointment grew into anger. "Not even on Sundays do they leave you alone! You can tell them I disapprove of their way of doing business!"

"You must understand, Bear, this is a very expensive project. No eight-to-five days and no Sunday leisure. But you wanted to be in Hawaii." *Dammit, he's right!* I thought.

Back in the apartment, I hastily gathered our beach stuff. "When can we come back?"

He shrugged his shoulders. "I really don't know. Call every hour after four."

The telephone rang. Manfred answered it. "Thank you very much, Reverend." He turned to me, holding the receiver away from his ear. "Rev. Fujitani invites us for dinner." He spoke into the shell again. "At seven? By then, I hope I'll be through with work." He jotted the address down.

The children and I were already at the door.

"Remember, Little Bear, call me after four."

We left and, having to kill more time, drove to a nearby beach which was free of coral reefs. It sprawled right in front of the pink Royal Hawaiian Hotel. Diamond Head, looming in the east, but now closer to us, appeared more somber today. *I know I'm transferring my dark mood to the volcano,* I thought. *I hope the ocean waves will wash off my gloom.* I followed the children into the mild surf.

Turning back, I saw clouds racing in from the west. The trade winds chased them at lightning-speed over Honolulu until they burst and poured the heaviest rain I'd ever seen over beach and swimmers. My hairdo was ruined.

"Rain is fun!" Irmie shouted.

Wernher raced out of the water. "My camera!"

The rain became so intense we couldn't see more than half a block away. Our clothes, covered by the now wet towels, were drenched, but Wernher's camera, stuck in a watertight bag, was still dry. From the corner of my eye I saw him secretly pet it; his camera was his life.

Soaked with warm rain, we stood aghast, then the rain suddenly stopped as if turned off by a hand on the faucet. At the same time the sun reappeared. Now what? Get into the wet clothes? Sit in the car until dry? After all, our apartment was taboo at this time.

I looked around and saw people acting as if there had been no rain at all. They were swimming or hanging up their wet wardrobe on the hotel fence or they just strolled in their drenched clothes, apparently expecting the sun to dry them out.

"That seems to be the Hawaiian way to fight rain," I said, resigned. So we hung up our clothes on a fence and plunged into the ocean again.

In fact, when we finally left the water we found our clothes dry. Strolling along the beach in the warm wind, we felt our swimsuits drying on our bodies. My hair was dry, but it hung straight down like the unshorn mane of a horse. *Would Yoshi Fujitani ever mention in a sermon a person who looked like that?* I thought. *Maybe he would,* the answer came from within, *because he had publicized my studies of Buddhism, not my looks.*

When shortly before 7 p.m. Manfred still was busy, we had no choice but to make our appearance at the Fujitanis' house with wrinkled clothes and hanging hair — also barefoot, because we left our sandals outside, next to the residents' shoes. Luckily, Manfred appeared only a few minutes after us — well dressed and appropriately in his socks.

The Fujitani's two-story house was a disappointment to me. Being old and unimaginative, it contained no special Japanese furniture or decorations, but at least had an upright piano in one corner. It could have been anybody's home in the world.

Yet Yoshi's wife, Tomi, turned out to be as petite and charming as so many of the other Japanese ladies. When I explained our shabby appearance she took me by the hand and led me upstairs to her dressing-room, took a bolero jacket from her closet that would cover my crumpled dress, tied a blue band around my hair and put a yellow hibiscus on top of it. With this transformation she had made me feel comfortable.

In the living room Yoshi introduced his children to us, twenty-year-old daughter Maya, a heavy-set young woman, as sweet as her mother, and sixteen-year-old Steve, thin, sloppy and long-haired as Wernher and most American teenagers. Both boys clicked immediately: Steve was a big surfer and Wernher one who photographed them.

During dinner Maya and her mother were mainly confined to the kitchen, cooking rice and numerous vegetables and serving them. Meanwhile Yoshi, the master of the house, using chopsticks and soy sauce, cooked the chopped meat and veggies in an electric wok on the dining table before he put the food on our plates.

At one point I said to him, "I almost fainted when you announced me from the pulpit this morning."

Undaunted, he replied, "I have to let my congregation know about newcomers." Period. That was it.

Observing Maya, a thought hit me. *Here was a perfect friend for our Ronnie, same age, same sweetness. Ronnie should be with us! Thanksgiving lay ahead, a good reason for a family gathering.*

Arriving back at the Tradewinds, I told Manfred of my plan to get Ronnie to Hawaii.

He seemed to ponder it and at last said, "Not a bad idea. And good timing. My boss from Global Marine, Curtis Crooke, is coming in from L.A. tomorrow. I'll talk to him about Ronnie."

Next evening he told me, "I talked to Curtis. He immediately said: 'Of course, let her come. We'll pay for it.'" With Manfred's next paycheck a second check was enclosed for Ronnie's flight to Hawaii.

After the Fujitanis cooked dinner for us we were officially declared a part of their circle of friends, and Japanese hospitality filled our calendar up to the bursting point. The respective hosts didn't only invite us for dinner, but combined it with attending a Koto concert, a Japanese movie or a torchlight ceremony. Too bad Manfred could attend only some of these events.

Manfred's Diary
Honolulu, November 2, 1970

Again my "safehouse" was the scene of a hastily called meeting. Five of the thirty agents in Honolulu dropped in at the appropriate time intervals, scheduled by Jim and timed up to the second. First of all Jim himself, whose golf cap and protruding ears revealed him from afar. And an old friend from Los Angeles among the others — Hank with the diabolical black eyebrows. We heartily shook hands. The three others, although not looking like brothers, nevertheless resembled each other in clothes, posture and attitude. After two of them had rechecked my office-apartment for electronic bugs, Jim opened the meeting.

Our current problem, he said, was to find out how much the Soviets knew about our secret operation. The cables from the GLOMAR II said Soviet ships had followed them to the north and stayed next to them. Without even trying to hide the Soviets had filmed all the activities on the ship. They took pictures of the crane when it was moved to transport parts. They shot the winches when they were pulled on deck and when the crew lowered the "drill pipe." Luckily they couldn't see the recording equipment as it was lowered to the sea floor.

Jim stubbed out his half-smoked cigarette and continued. We couldn't go to Moscow to find out how much they knew, he said. But we could test the possibility of their suspicion here in town. If the Soviets suspected something, it was our duty to stop our enterprise. We could not lift the sub when the Soviets knew about our plans. They'd do anything to stop us, even use military action.

He turned to me and outlined my next job. We should try to kill two birds with one stone. One, to transport certain documents from the GLOMAR II and two, to test for any possible Soviet spies in Honolulu. I should rent a truck that was covered and had two doors in the rear — no other type of truck could do the job. And we needed two more station wagons with tinted windows. His own was the third. I should rent two for one day only. I said it might be difficult to find such a truck here in Hawaii. Jim said it had to be a closed one. An open truck would not be used for important secret material. Jim lit another cigarette, and I waited for further revelations.

The GLOMAR II was leaving from the north on November 10 and would arrive here about a week later. By that time I had to get those vehicles to the GLOMAR and carry the boxes with the documents from the ship to the truck. At an exact time I'd start driving toward Ala Moana Boulevard with one of our station wagons before and two behind me. Eight agents would be in each station wagon for my protection.

"That's twenty-four agents for my protection! But protection from what?" I asked.

"A possible attack by Soviet spies," Jim replied. Recently, he continued, the KGB had tried to attack such a closed truck with documents in it by staging a mock car crash at an intersection in Washington, D.C. They bumped into the rear of the truck so that the impact forced the doors open. When the truck driver stopped to call the police, several KGB spies removed the boxes and carried them away. The truck driver stood helpless and saw his highly classified cargo being snatched away. This time it would be different. We'd be prepared to catch those bastards.

"Shouldn't I take out life insurance?" I asked half-jokingly.

Jim replied, the truck driver he'd talked about wasn't hurt at all. And I would be protected by twenty-four agents. But that wasn't all, Jim added. We'd give those bastards another chance to try to steal the boxes with the documents. I should stop at Koa's restaurant and park there.

I interrupted. "Koa's parking lot is always full."

Jim was adamant. The moment I turned into the parking lot, he continued, another car would pull out and leave. The same for the station wagons. I should leave the car and enter the restaurant. We'd meet there and have a beer and tell jokes. If the Soviets knew we were interested in their lost submarine, this would be a chance to steal the documents. If they tried to break in the truck there would be enough agents to catch them."

I'm part of a James Bond plot, I mused.

Jim said our agents in their apartments along Ala Moana Boulevard would be filming the cars before and behind our parade. Then I had to take the loop in Ala Moana Park. If the agents saw the same cars following me on that senseless loop they'd take care of them.

I looked at Jim. He raised his eyebrows and said urgently,

"Manfred, that's the moment to find out if we continue or stop the raising of the sub."

I nodded. But Jim wasn't through yet. He kept developing the plot. After the loop I would keep driving to the Ilikai Hotel and park on the third floor of the garage. Just as I arrived another car would leave and I'd take the spot. Then I'd walk to the up-elevator, see Hank there and hand him the car keys. End of job.

With growing astonishment I listened. What an undertaking! Better not to think about my safety. I would do my job as I had done it in the U-boat in the mine-infested and radar-hunted Atlantic during the war.

At dusk on a mild evening, Florence, my friend from the Unitarian Church, picked me up in her old Ford for a moonlight party at the beach, organized by the Tuesday night Venture group. When we climbed into the car, I noticed the big, covered platter on Florence's backseat. "What's in there?" I asked.

"Poo-poo," she replied.

"Whaaaat?"

"Hors d'oeuvres," she translated. "*Pupu* in Hawaiian. It will take you a while to learn all the common Hawaiian words, won't it?"

"Maybe. Meanwhile I'm in love with the pleasant, peaceful life in Hawaii," I said.

"How's your coral wound?"

"Finally okay. It took six weeks to heal."

The moonlight party at the beach turned out to be as much fun as the Tuesday nights with the Venture group, where the ten participants freely talked about their problems and always ended up with laughter. Tonight there was only laughter and no problems. Many of us went swimming, while the full moon's light reflected in the small waves like tossed silver coins.

The night was mild and the sweet scent of Hawaii fanned around me in the eternal wind. A feeling of utmost well-being spread through me and a certainty took place in my conscience: *I was born here, I have never been anywhere else, I belong here and I'll never leave these islands.*

Notwithstanding my profound love for Hawaii we had to labor through the move from the Tradewinds Apartments to the Ilikai Hotel across the street. The apartments were to be converted into condominiums, and at the Ilikai we'd have a larger place on the tenth floor.

The four of us pushed shopping carts full of our belongings to the room 1041 at the hotel. The breathtaking view from the balcony onto the ocean made us all thankful for the move.

Yet an unpleasant experience dampened our enthusiasm a bit. A group of fat Hawaiian singers howled below our balcony every evening for at least forty-five minutes. So we closed our windows and turned the air-conditioner on to shut out the noise.

"Why are the Hawaiians so fat?" I asked Manfred as I turned away from the windows. "Where are the slim, notorious girls who pursue male tourists?"

Manfred grinned. "Only *tourist* girls do that. Once I was going up in the elevator with one of those females. On the sixth floor she winked and said, 'I'm in 622.'"

"I hope she waited in vain."

"She sure did, my love," he said and kissed me.

Manfred's Diary. Honolulu, November 18, 1970

Yesterday at dawn, the GLOMAR II arrived in Honolulu Harbor and tied up at the pier. The bright, sunny morning seemed more appropriate for swimming and sunbathing than for an espionage scenario. Leisurely I drove my Toyota to the pier and parked it behind the covered truck and the station wagons I had placed there the day before. The James Bond plot could begin.

The gangway was out and I stepped on deck. A "sailor" with diabolical black eyebrows passed by, wishing me a good morning. I recognized Hank; disguised as a sailor, he was watching the immediate surroundings. As I entered the mess hall, Jim and my protection team sat at a long table with mugs of coffee. They signaled me to join them. As they put a steaming cup before me, I quickly counted them: twenty-two. So besides Hank another agent must be snooping around.

I checked my wristwatch, 9:46. In exactly six minutes they'd begin to carry the boxes to the truck. Only now I noticed the four large cardboard boxes in a corner.

Jim told me, while the guys were loading, I should stand at the bulwark for a minute and casually look around. Then walk to my truck and make sure everything was properly stowed away. At 10:02 I should get the engine started and leave. At 10:07 I'd enter the restaurant's parking lot.

"Yes, sir," I replied, suddenly feeling I was back in the German Navy again. I slowly sipped my coffee. Watching my twenty-two protectors, the thought of imminent danger entered my consciousness. How could they help me if a gunfight broke out? I had no weapon, wouldn't want to carry one in the first place — America against the KGB and I'm in the middle of it!

The huge clock on the wall showed 9:52, and two by two the agents lifted the four boxes and carried them out of the mess hall. As directed I went out and leaned on the bulwark for thirty seconds, then stepped on land and went straight to the truck. Seeing the four boxes well-stashed away, I closed the two doors, climbed in the driver's seat and started the engine.

10:02. One station wagon pushed in front of me, I followed it, seeing the two others behind me.

10:07. Approaching the restaurant at the corner of Ala Moana Boulevard, my forerunner turned into its small parking lot. No empty spot. He drove on.

Suddenly a small Opel pulled out just in front of me and I drove into its place. So far it had worked as plotted. In the rear mirror I saw the other two station wagons pass by and park.

I got out, locked the car and stepped into the crowded restaurant. Through the screen of cigarette smoke I saw that every table was taken. Suddenly a young couple got up to leave and I took their table. Were they part of our deal too?

Jim and two of his men entered.

"Hello!" I waved to them.

Waiters brought two more chairs. Jim placed four breakfast orders, told jokes and coaxed us into kidding and laughing. "After all," he said, "we're celebrating the safe return of the GLOMAR II!"

I pricked up my ears. Did I hear gunfire in the parking lot? After all, we were giving prospective Soviet spies a chance to steal the boxes with the documents. Don't be silly, I scolded myself. If they knew we'd been above their lost submarine, they'd use this moment to get the data. We had enough agents in the parking lot to catch the spies stationed here in Hawaii.

10:40. Jim paid the breakfast bill, and we left for the parking lot. No gunfire, nothing unusual. Next step: Checking to see if cars were following us. With one station wagon in front of me and two others behind me, I turned right on Ala Moana Boulevard. From their apartments agents were now filming our parade and our prospective pursuers.

The dullness of the procession made me nervous. Was it the lull before the storm? At intersections I looked in all directions, struggling with my fear of a staged car crash. Carefully I turned into the loop within Ala Moana Park and then passed the same apartments again. Had the agents discovered that we were followed? The radio was silent.

Now I had to continue along the boulevard to the Ilikai and park on the third level. As I arrived at that crowded floor, another car pulled out in front of me and I took its place. A well-oiled operation.

Next step: take the ascending elevator. The door opened and I joined four strangers and, leaning against the back door was Hank with the diabolical eyebrows. I placed myself in front of him, leisurely put my arms behind me, the truck key in my right fist. When I felt Hank's hand touch mine, I released the key to him. The elevator stopped at several levels, letting people in and out, until at the tenth floor I stepped out of the cage and away from the adventure.

Immensely relieved, I felt my mood changing into roguish joy. Everything had worked beyond my expectations. And it seemed to prove that the Soviets didn't know of our operation. The four boxes would now be transported to the Navy and flown to Washington D.C. for analysis. And with the new data the big recovery ship could now be built in Pennsylvania.

Hawaii There and Then

Thanksgiving was approaching and with it the time of Ronnie's arrival in Honolulu. There she was, a slim, young woman in a long, almost-Hawaiian dress, her brown hair freshly permed, her doe-eyes beaming. Big hugs and kisses.

"I can't believe I'm in Hawaii!" she said over and over again, her voice subdued. She put her arm around my shoulders; it was great to walk with her this way.

Passing a flower stand, we inhaled the exotic aroma of plumeria, pikake, orchids and took in the colors of scent-less anthuriums and birds of paradise.

"Sure, I'm in the tropics!" Ronnie rejoiced.

"You are in paradise," I reminded her.

At the Ilikai Hotel a big crowd was pushing, trying to enter. A film crew was shooting in the lobby. We struggled through the throng of cameramen, electricians and other movie personnel to the elevators, zoomed up to the tenth floor and entered our apartment.

Ronnie looked around. "Wow! How large!" Then she smiled. "A living-cum-bedroom?"

"Wait," I answered, pulling the Japanese sliding door through the room, creating two separate chambers.

The phone rang. Manfred answered it, while Ronnie unpacked her flight bag and Wernher and Irmie went to check the refrigerator for goodies.

Manfred turned to me. "Now that's something. Reverend Fujitani wants you to be interviewed at the Japanese radio station." I took the receiver and heard Yoshi's cool voice repeating the inquiry.

"Interviewing me about what?"

"About your studies of Buddhism and whatever else you want

to reveal."

He also invited us for Thanksgiving. I felt a shadow rushing through me. I told him that we already had accepted an invitation from the Hardings. He then asked us to come on Sunday after Thanksgiving.

I told the family about the news.

"Hawaii!" Ronnie rejoiced. "A film shoot, a radio interview, a dinner invitation, all within 15 minutes! Is this your life here in Hawaii?"

I chuckled. "Just about."

On Thanksgiving Day we drove to Kailua to celebrate with the Hardings. Instead of zipping through Pali Highway we took a sideloop, driving through the lush vegetation of mature trees that formed a canopy overhead, all draped with hanging vines and wound around with philodendrons.

Ronnie, in the co-pilot's seat, said, "Ah, this really is paradise!" A minute later, "What's the name of that tree with hanging aerial roots?"

"Banyan tree," I said, proud to know this at least.

"And that one with the huge leaves?"

"Banana tree."

Past a bamboo grove the road ran into Pali Highway again, and minutes later we drove through Kailua and stopped before the Harding's house.

They must have seen the car park, because the friendly giant opened the door, a bit stooped as if not to bump against the door frame. We introduced Ronnie to him and Mitsi and were ushered into the living room. After a short talk Mitsi invited us to the dining room.

The table groaned under the weight of Mitsi's culinary goodies. We took samples of roast pig, fish steamed in *ti* leaves, macadamia nut waffles, stuffed pastries, *poi*, coconut pudding, papayas, mangoes, pineapples, guavas and bananas — the different fragrances blending with the colors of the decorations of orchids, anthuriums and plumeria. Intoxicating Mai Tai drinks for the adults and sweet guava juice for the children.

"I haven't eaten so much on all the Thanksgivings of my

life," Ronnie said.

I chuckled. "Getting fat was a must for Hawaiian royalty."

"That's why they are dying out," Wernher said.

Before Sunday we took Ronnie on a tour of Oahu. Under the influence of her soft nature — which she obviously hadn't inherited from me — there was so much harmony between her two younger siblings that we wished she could stay longer. She now was twenty, majoring in Spanish and German, had good grades and a boyfriend who was a psychologist.

On this Sunday she became good friends with Maya Fujitani, who was of Ronnie's age and also in college. As a matter of fact, Yoshi had planned their encounter by inviting us to lunch.

On the porch six pairs of sandals stood orderly near the door, so besides the Fujitani family we'd find two guests inside. We left our sandals outside and walked into the house. We found Edith Tanaka there and met her diminutive husband. Sushi and tiny sandwiches and green tea and juice were served, while we chatted away.

One question had been going around in my mind lately, and I decided to ask the Fujitanis and the Tanakas, "All of you were born in the States. How do you feel, American or Japanese?"

"Hawaiian!" the four said in unison.

"Neither American nor Japanese would express what we really are," Yoshi answered. "We were born in Hawaii and we belong here."

I smiled. *They feel what I feel, being born here and belonging here.* But I didn't say it.

Steve's voice came from the back. "Maya, let's close all the curtains! Wernher and I want to show you something."

Maya and Steve darkened the windows while Wernher put a projector on the upright piano and we all settled before a white wall, which would serve as a screen. Film operator Wernher began to let the movie run. Beach and ocean and suddenly a bold surfer riding a wave.

"Steve!" Tomi cried, half afraid, half admiring her son.

Steve mastered another monster that churned in at a threatening height. But the greatest thrill he gave us was when he rode a tube that didn't seem to end. His following wipe-out was a relief for us and we applauded heartily.

"Watch this!" Wernher called, stopping the applause.

On a high wave appeared a man without a board, riding a huge wave, approaching us...

"Manfred!" I cried, watching him being wiped out. I grabbed his hand, relieved that he had survived. "When was that?" I asked him.

"One rare afternoon when I had the time to accompany the boys to the beach."

"You never told me," I said.

"Wernher was going to surprise you."

Yoshi turned to Wernher. "What's your next project?"

"Shooting the big surf meet at Sunset Beach next week."

"Don't you get caught by the waves," Yoshi said.

In the meantime Maya had pulled the curtains back, and daylight flooded in.

This time Yoshi turned to me. "You've practiced the piano for weeks now. Let's hear what you have accomplished." He opened the lid of the upright piano.

First I was shocked. *Asking me to play without a warning! But why not try out one piece before this audience? Bach's Italian Concerto, the first movement maybe.* I sat down at the piano and began to play. The instrument was in tune, and I enjoyed playing the memorized movement. When I finished, the crowd applauded. For a change, I was satisfied with my playing.

"You are a good musician," Edith Tanaka said. "I'll mention it during our interview."

The interview! I almost had forgotten about it. We discussed day, time and location.

When the time for our departure came we thanked the Fujitanis for their great hospitality. Out on the porch we put on our shoes and walked to Manfred's car.

The interview at the Japanese radio station was taped without preparation, glamour or any guidelines. In the radio station's small recording room Edith and I had a fifteen-minute casual conversation about Germany, Chile, the U.S., Buddhism and my music. I received a copy of the tape, and we listened to the interview when it was aired next Sunday morning. Manfred and the children said they were proud of me, and I tossed the tape into my suitcase.

A day before Ronnie's return to California we were waiting for Maya who was going to take us to a hula show. "I hope Wernher will be back soon from Sunset Beach," I said.

Suddenly, the door opened with a bang and Wernher rushed in, crying. "What's the matter?" I asked.

"My Beaulieu fell in the water!" he sobbed.

His Super 8 movie camera! "My God! How did it happen?"

"I stuck the tripod in the sand and was shooting the surf competition. All of a sudden a huge wave came in and washed over us and toppled the camera. I retrieved it, but it's totally wet and ruined." He cried louder, and I took him in my arms. His camera was his baby! But I was at a loss how to console him.

Then Ronnie's soothing voice resounded. "Don't cry, Wernher. Tomorrow I'll take the camera home to California and get it fixed." Wernher stopped crying, fetched a towel and began to dry the Beaulieu.

A knock at the door and Maya walked in, clad in a blue, long and wide mu'u mu'u. We told her about Wernher's misfortune. She expressed her sympathy as if the camera were human, and Wernher's sobbing subsided.

"Time to go to the show," Maya announced. She hesitated. "Wernher, the Kodak Hula Show is designed especially for camera fans. Since your camera is out of order, would you make do with mine? Film is in it."

His eyes lit up. "Thanks a million! Let me pay for the film."

Lovely Maya! She was a problem-solver like her father.

She drove us through Waikiki to Kapiolani Park. Near the ocean stretched a plot of grass, surrounded by swaying palm trees, all of it feigning a stage. We sat down on a row of amphitheater-style benches.

As the show began, five corpulent Hawaiian ladies, dressed in mu'u mu'us of different colors and wide-brimmed straw hats, filed in and arranged themselves in the background. They immediately began to pluck their ukuleles and howled, as we had heard them every evening below our hotel windows. A dozen slim dancers moved onto the grassy stage, barefooted and neatly clad in green or red skirts, made of *ti* leaves, and bras and leis of matching colors. Half a dozen more dancers entered the grass stage, wearing long cotton gowns with a train.

"The ukulele and the gowns both are foreign intruders into our culture," Maya said to me under her breath. "The ukulele came from Portugal and the gowns from the Victorian era." In thought I added, *And the howling comes from the wolves.*

Wernher happily shot scene after scene, which indeed were a rich source for color photography.

After the show Maya assembled us around her and said, "You just saw the contemporary hula dances. Now I want to show you the old Hawaiian dances, the authentic ones."

"You mean they exist side-by-side?" I asked.

"It's a kind of revival of early Hawaii," Maya replied. "You'll see and hear the difference."

She drove us north through elegant neighborhoods and along golf courses to the Manoa Campus of the University of Hawaii. She parked and led us to a flat edifice, which inside looked like a gymnasium. At present it was filled with dancing natives.

"Now watch how the early Hawaiians performed," Maya said.

From the moment we entered I was fascinated by one man's chanting to his own drum beating. His sparing use of notes — the first three of the pentatonic scale — reminded me of the American Indians' chanting. To provide rhythm the one-man band used only a coconut drum. His words obviously conveyed meaning to the dancers. Barefoot, wrapped in green *ti* leaves, they moved to the chanting with careful steps and swinging hips, which oddly enough didn't seem erotic.

Maya bent over to us. "The early Hawaiians had no written language. But they were eager to express their history with dances. So they gave every motion a distinct meaning. The rules were so strict that when a dancer made a single mistake during the performance she was killed immediately."

I shuddered with horror.

Maya pointed to four men who also were wrapped with *ti* leaves or ferns. They carried long spears and faced the dancers. "Those guards made sure no girl who made a mistake in the dance stayed alive."

I wished she hadn't told us this. It took away from the mysticism of the performance. Horror squeezed me like a vice. Only gradually I was able to shake away the thoughts of the past's violence. *Only the present count*s, I told myself. *Only Hawaii now, the enchanted island I belong to.*

"Thank you for showing us this," Ronnie said to Maya. "I'll remember it for a long time." Her last day in Hawaii was coming to an end. We would have loved to have her stay longer, but job, college and boyfriend were waiting for her return — no matter in what order. She left us behind on an enchanted island where one easily forgets the mainland and time itself.

Coming back from the airport, I checked our mail. Among Christmas brochures and catalogues I found a letter from my friend Susanne Shapiro. "....I'm going to Europe on a concert tour on December 2. Could you substitute for me on December 3 and 5? That's my piano class at the university."

I went into shock. *Return to the mainland? Don't I belong here in Hawaii?* Slowly I remembered I had promised Susanne to fill in for her, but then I hadn't known that I would never leave the Islands...

I gave my head a knock. *Wake up! The Hawaiian dream is coming to an end! Face reality: you promised Susanne to help her out. I must go now!* I also knew I would take Hawaii with me because it was within me forever, no matter where I lived.

It was hard for me to say goodbye to all my friends. I had this painful feeling I was lying. Innermost I was adamant I belonged to Hawaii and would never leave it, but now I was talking about "going home to the mainland."

Manfred put his arm around my shoulder. "I hope I won't be here for too long."

"You'll come back," our good friend Ralph said.

"We'll wait for your return," my good friend Florence said.

"You can love Hawaii, but don't attach yourself to it," my favorite Buddhist priest said.

With a heavy heart I left Oahu with the children and flew to the evergreen, circular island of Kauai. During the morning rain we visited friends of the Fujitanis, and by midday we sailed on the Wailua River along blossoming jungle-like greenery toward the Fern Grotto. The misty, fern-choked cavern was filled with a trickling waterfall and huge ferns, tall as trees, dripping warm raindrops — as the entire island seemed soaked in moisture.

In the Fern Grotto we heard of Hawaii's fire goddess Pele, whom Manfred always called "the only American goddess." The young, half-naked Hawaiian seaman initiated us into the mysticism. "Pele tried first to make a home here on Kauai for herself and her lover, the king of Kauai."

I easily pictured the seaman himself as Pele's sweetheart.

"But, after several unsuccessful attempts to dig a dry pit where she could start her fire, she moved south to the other islands and lives now on the Big Island, in the crater of the volcano Kilauea."

The young Hawaiian's tale had enraptured me like Bach's or Mozart's music. Mythology meant art to me just as much as operas or great novels, and I was readily awed by its ideas and the imagination of the believers.

To some extent we were searching for Pele's new lover as we flew to the Big Island in the late afternoon. Arriving in Kona, we stood speechless before a blood-red sunset contrasted with a perfect rainbow.

"Pele's way of greeting us," I said.

When the heavenly firework was extinguished I rented a car and chose a motel — in time to avoid being drenched in a tropical rainstorm that hammered on the motel roof.

Next morning the sky emptied out its water reservoir of the millennium. Noise and invisibility scared Irmie so much she started crying.

"Pray to Pele to stop!" Wernher scoffed.

Consequently, either Pele or whoever else controlled the rains showed consideration and cut the water flow in half.

While braving the rain that came down in sheets we fleetingly saw and heard the mighty Akaka Fall drop more than 400 feet down a fern-draped cliff. Even a rainbow appeared in the spray. *Pele's work?*

As abruptly as always in Hawaii the rain stopped when we arrived at Black Sand Beach. We got out and walked barefoot on the black sand. We experienced one of the wonderful sensations on these islands. Our soles were massaged by the coarse sand grains as if heavenly forces had gathered to give us pleasure and a feeling of unending well-being — all that by concentrating on our soles.

"I could walk here forever!" said Wernher. I had never agreed with him so whole-heartedly. To our delight the sun now tore the clouds apart and brightly shone on the road to the active volcano Kilauea, which had "mildly" erupted a few weeks ago. We drove as near to the rim as possible and stepped on the lava, still warm from the last eruption.

"The heat goes through my shoes!" Wernher cried.

"What's the awful smell in the air?" Irmie asked.

"Sulphur, of course," Wernher snarled.

From an overlook we could see deep down into the still steaming crater — Pele's present home. Stark, desolate, eerie. Here I said goodbye to the land and its beauty, to the fiery goddess and her descendants. I thanked Hawaii for being and for enhancing us with her inexhaustible fountain of timelessness.

At Kona's airport the jet to Los Angeles was waiting for us. The children rushed up the stairs to the plane while I followed reluctantly. On top of the steps I turned around to look at my beloved land one last time. *Why is leave-taking so painful?* I asked myself. *'Because you are attached to it,' I heard my teachers' voice. 'You can love Hawaii. Wanting to have it forever is greed.' Who was saying that? Did I?*

"Please come in, madam," the stewardess urged me on.

I entered the plane, and shortly it took off, carrying us back to the mainland.

Pacific Palisades

Coming home from teaching Suzanne's piano class I found Wernher in tears. "My Beaulieu is gone," he sobbed. "The saltwater has destroyed the electronics."

On the dining room table lay the corpse of the Super 8 movie camera, bleak, hollowed and useless.

"I saved only the lenses," Wernher said.

"Better than nothing," I said, immediately aware of my poor choice of a phrase. I knew how he felt, but I couldn't find words to console him. It was late and I went to bed.

When the tears came I suddenly understood that I identified Wernher's frustration with my own, being unable to go back to Hawaii. The feeling was the same as years ago, when I so badly wanted to go back to Chile. That nostalgia had ended, and so might that for Hawaii. *Remember Lilo's psychology textbook?* "Nostalgia is maladjustment." *Remember Yoshi Fujitani?* "You can love Hawaii, but don't be attached to it."

Enough of that! Resolutely I dried my tears, blew my nose, turned to my sleeping side and slipped into the dream world.

Manfred's Diary
Honolulu, December 6, 1970

I worry about what the Soviets really know about our secret project. Did we get the right answer when we invited the Soviets to break into the truck which carried our data? There had been no action from the possible spies in Hawaii. And I was relieved when the coded and cabled messages from the Glomar II said: "No longer Soviet observers aside." Also, when the Glomar II made a camouflage trip westwards from Hawaii to a region where rich and economic nodules could be found on the ocean floor, no Soviet ships appeared. So we can continue our efforts to lift the sub and call our employer "The Customer."

Yet our Customer's name was still kept secret. In my opinion the time to reveal the name of our Customer should be now. Eva and the kids have returned to California and I'm now waiting for two things: First, the revelation of the fictitious Customer's name; second, to be relieved of my duties as a cable carrier and billeting officer in Hawaii.

December 7, 1970

Early in the morning, I received a phone call from our Los Angeles office. Jack Reed, our personnel manager, Eva's "harbinger of good news," was on the line. He said representatives from Global Marine and the Customer's company had now decided to disclose the name. Curious, I asked what the name was. Jack said he didn't know. We had to wait till tomorrow. I had to organize a party for thirty people at the Ilikai Hotel for tomorrow morning, preferably at the penthouse. I jotted everything down. By tonight we needed twelve rooms for two or three days for the top people of our participating companies. He, Jack, would give me the names in the afternoon. Then he needed ten rooms for the management of the Customer. They were all flying to Hawaii today but would arrive in Honolulu at different times. I should reserve sixteen cars at Hertz for them. All under the name of Global Marine.

"Invite the press of Hawaii," Jack said. "Three or five of the largest companies may send reporters. Arrange the catering for thirty people with drinks and hors d'oeuvres. Don't forget the champagne! The party should begin tomorrow at 11 a.m. The announcement certainly will hit the public like a bomb." He chuckled. "If we had names of the Soviet spies in Hawaii, we would invite them too. Other private companies are not invited, repeat, are not invited." No radio stations were to be invited, he said. But an elevated stage, lectern and microphones were needed.

I asked about Jim.

"No. We don't want him in that crowd." We hung up.

I had mixed feelings about Jack's call. This secrecy was going too far. Since The Customer would hardly reveal itself but instead invent some person to whom they could "entrust" the project—why not tell Jack or me? Well, one camouflage after the other, that was my life now.

The task of organizing the party kept me busy for half the day until I called Jack and told him everything was prepared. Again, no mention of the Customer's name. Tomorrow, the new twist of the circus would be enacted.

December 8, 1970

The large room of the Ilikai's penthouse with its high ceiling was ready long before the first guests showed up. Jack Reed, the harbinger, was the first to enter — as always. He looked pleased as he glanced over the white-decked tables and the buffet in the back.

Jack was followed by our boss Curtis Crooke, vice-president of Global Marine, as short as Jack was tall. Usually informal and in sport shirts, today Curtis was wearing a tie and jacket. He seemed satisfied as well. "Good job, Manfred. So far things seem to be in order. Yesterday, when I had to announce this event, I thought, how will Manfred manage all this in such a short time? But then I told myself, 'Why do we have a former U-boat captain in Hawaii? He can do anything.'"

I smiled politely, although I was tired of this joke, which I'd had to deal with since I came to America. Once I complained to a colleague about this, "On the U-boat I was twenty-two, an ensign and did the job of a 3rd watch officer. Why always give me the rank of captain?" The colleague had grinned, saying, "People see you now and you don't look like a twenty-two-year old ensign. You are the image of a successful U-boat captain." *Quatsch,* baloney. But I resigned myself to it.

By II a.m. representatives of Global Marine and managers of the private companies involved in the secret raising of the sub were seated at the tables. I directed the press reporters to their places in the back and asked them to take pictures only when the announcement began.

Soon Curtis Crooke walked to the stage and adjusted the microphone. "Aloha, gentlemen!" He welcomed them and expressed his pleasure in their long-time cooperation. "Last but not least this has been made possible by our ocean-mining expert Manfred Krutein." I rose to applause. Thank God he didn't mention the U-boat captain.

"Until now," Curtis continued, "there's been a reluctance to tell the world who the Customer for this private venture is. But now, our Customer has decided to lift the curtain and indicate who is behind our secret project. Mr. Holliday, please come up here and lift the veil of secrecy."

Mr. Holliday, a distinguished-looking, gray-haired gentleman stepped up on the stage, thanked Curtis and presented the new lie to the world. "It was a pleasure for me and my colleagues from the Howard Hughes Tool Company in Houston, Texas, to work with you and all the other directors of the companies which contributed to this project. Now the moment has come when our boss, Mr. Howard Hughes, has decided to show the world that he personally provided the finances for the unique task of mining manganese nodules from the sea-bed."

What a masterful stroke, to have lured the famous billionaire Howard Hughes into the scheme and to now use him as a smoke screen to cover up the underground activities in the Pacific Ocean. With a straight face I watched the reactions of surprise at the announcement. Mr. Holliday continued praising and thanking various directors, but I no longer listened. The second act of the comedy had begun and the audience applauded the play. I announced the buffet-style lunch, and everyone got up to sample the Ilikai's delicacies.

I observed the reporters rush out. I sat down at a nearby table, where five representatives from several companies involved in the project were seated, and listened to their remarks.

"This strange guy Howard Hughes....a courageous pilot, flying planes at record speeds....built the Spruce Goose out of plywood....put film stars on ice for future films which were never realized....bought all the silver mines of this country to get control over the silver market....now spends his money on ocean mining...."

"How can he do that? He lies half-dead in a pitch-dark cubicle....doesn't allow anybody to touch or see him....communicates only with slips of paper to his guards....his fingernails three inches long....he's got bedsores all over his body....he's practically dead...."

Soon the newspapers will be full of stories about him, I thought. And the hoax will go on.

Back in my university classes in Pacific Palisades, I tried to shoo away the memories of Hawaii as I had so successfully done with those of Chile.

There was only a week left before the Christmas school break, and it was time to look for a job before the next semester resumed. I applied at various universities and colleges to teach piano, music appreciation and theory. It didn't take me long to find out that there was no shortage of college music instructors. *No need for my skills and knowledge, no hope there will ever be a need. Too many of us highly educated teachers. It's like going begging from house to house.* "Apply personally," one well-intended counseler had told me. "You're outgoing and friendly. That helps." So I went and offered my skills to the chairmen of music departments — *like a prostitute on Hollywood Boulevard.* As soon as I got to this metaphor, I stopped applying in person. *Just sit at home, put ads into local newspapers and get private piano students. No begging anymore, no rejections.*

During this time one bright light shone in the darkness: Manfred was coming home! Jack Reed, as usual, played the harbinger of good news and replaced Manfred in Hawaii. Manfred was told that from now on he had to represent Global Marine and its big ocean mining project at international conferences on offshore sciences all over the world. So he'd be home only sporadically. I sighed. *What else is left for me than to accept the inevitable? I just wonder where he'll go next.*

Manfred's Diary. March 13, 1971
In flight: Paris to Los Angeles

It's midnight, and we are flying over the Atlantic. The days at the Oceanexpo 1971 in Bordeaux, France were a welcome break before we returned to Paris. "We" means Paul Reeve, the executive from Hughes Tool Company in Houston, Texas, and I, representing Global Marine. The purpose of our trip was twofold: First, to demonstrate that Hughes Tool Company and Global Marine are together in the ocean mining business, and second, to learn what the other consortia are doing in ocean mining development.

Bald-headed Paul and I had met in New York, flown together to Paris and taken a train to Bordeaux. Being in France again revived all the good memories I had of this country. My fascination with the French culture had begun early in life. Even as a youngster I had admired the French, and in high school studied French to perfection. Unfortunately, I'm no longer perfect in French; Spanish, English and German are constantly interfering.

In the past I had seen the chateaux in the south, attended the Opéra and the Opéra Comique in Paris, listened to concerts and visited the Louvre — I only regretted that all this happened during the war when we Germans were the hated occupiers. Now, twenty-six years after the war, I had returned to the country of my admiration.

The Oceanexpo conference was held in a huge complex near the ocean, with thirty-two different flags flapping in the cold wind. In the spacious conference room we listened to papers being read in French and English. In between readings we visited the table where coffee and juice were served, met colleagues from American companies, who were as silent as we in disclosing details of their research.

On the first day of the conference we observed a strange group, a Chinese delegation of uniformed engineers, who, released from their isolated country, were on their first excursion into the Free World. They looked bewildered and unsure how to behave. They stood huddled together in groups of eight or ten like a football team, apparently discussing what to do next. Then they split into smaller groups, walked to the exhibits and asked intelligent questions in French or English and took notes. Just for the fun of it I approached one of the small groups, spoke to a bespectacled man and tried to move him away from his colleagues. Immediately, three Chinese joined us, preventing their colleague from talking to a stranger alone. Years ago, I had seen similar behavior by Soviet scientists abroad.

Paul was happy to be in France with someone who spoke French. He suggested we see a musical at the local theater but soon learned that the performance was sold out. Paul was ready to resign himself to his fate until I talked to the theater manager on the phone and explained to him that I had an important executive from the USA with me, who was dying to see a French musical. The manager immediately made his own box available to us. The manager's friendly gesture impressed us more than the musical itself, which suffered from provinciality.

The conference lasted three days. Then we rode the train

back to Paris, where we stayed at the Ritz, and next morning I took Paul to the airport. I stayed behind and impatiently saw him off.

I now had two days for myself and an emotional return to Saint Nazaire, where I had worked during 1943 as technical manager of the submarine pen. A train took me to the Atlantic coast, to the harbor town of St. Nazaire. I hired a taxi and had the driver take me around to all the places I remembered. At the old U-boat bunker I paid him off and continued on foot. As I approached the huge open doors I vividly imagined the dozen submarines which had come in for repair. I heard the crackling of the blow-torches, the hammering, the horn-blowing and smelled the burnt oil and the dry rot of the algae on the boat hulls, all going on in the glare of flood lights.

Yet when I entered I saw nothing in the darkness. Total silence lay over the empty bays, and I smelled only decay. I found the place where I once had my office. Empty. The doors and windows had been removed, even the light switches were missing and electrical cables had been ripped out. A weird place, dead and desecrated. Only the two nails on which I had hung the repair schedule of the day remained.

I returned to Paris, quickly bought a small bottle of Soir de Paris for, you, Eva, the same perfume I had brought you from Paris twenty-six years ago, took the night jet and flew over the city's thousand lights on my way home to California.

Manfred was home! And what a nice idea to bring me Soir de Paris! What memories that exquisite scent evoked in me! And as it had been in WW II, thirty years ago, he came and left again. Barely home from Europe, he had to fly to Washington, D.C. Again I was alone with Wernher and Irmie. Ronnie now lived with her boyfriend, Peter, in San Diego. *Oh God, why can't I live a normal life, together with my husband? Dear God, are you listening?* No answer.

The Big Deception, Jail and Ascent

Meanwhile, everywhere car stickers displayed the motto of the time, "America, love it or leave it."

"We leave it," Peter told me on the phone.

Ronnie was on the phone too, telling me she and Peter wanted to live in Germany for a year. She had received her Bachelor's degree in Spanish and German and Peter his Master's in psychology. She was fluent in German, but he was not.

Now taking them to the airport, I gave Ronnie our friends' addresses in Germany. This would give them a point to start from. Germany was a small, civilized country and many of our old friends would be within reach. Reluctantly and with melancholy I let Ronnie go.

Both were approaching the jetway as Ronnie stepped back to me and said, "Mom, you'll get a letter from me tomorrow." Then she entered the jetway and disappeared with Peter into the plane.

The next day was Saturday. I was going to cut a story out of the newspaper but couldn't find the scissors. Damn, the kids had taken them and not replaced them. Wernher wasn't home. I asked Irmie.

"I didn't take them," she said. "Probably Wernher. He fumbles around with his cameras and stuff."

I went to his room. His bed was unmade, and his clothes were scattered all over the floor. I looked at his desk, opened the drawer — and saw a syringe! A sharp physical pain cut through my body. Wernher was shooting drugs! I was devastated. Clasping the syringe in my hand, I dragged myself to Irmie's room.

"Mom!" she shrieked. "What's the matter? You look awful!"

Then she looked at my hand.

"I just found this in Wernher's room," I stammered.

"Do you think Wernher is shooting stuff?" Her voice was calm as if nothing had happened. I nodded.

She shook her head. "Wernher would never do that."

I was still trembling. "Why not?"

"He's way too busy with his photography. Only kids who have no interests use drugs."

Her cool words told me that she meant what she was saying, and that prevented me from breaking into tears. In my distress I remembered our friendly pharmacist. I rushed to the car and drove to the pharmacy.

Mr. Goldman, a bespectacled gentleman in a white coat, heard my plea. He took the syringe and carefully squeezed the fluid until drops came out. With my hand clasping the counter, I held my breath.

"Is your son working with stereos or cameras?" he asked, still focusing on the drops.

"Yes," I stammered. "With cameras."

Mr. Goldman turned to me. "It's oil," he said with emphasis.

For a moment I closed my eyes and felt the tears of relief come and swallowed hard. I wished I could hug this man and cry on his shoulder. Instead I tried to smile and thanked him.

Back in the car, I slumped over the steering wheel and let out a sigh of relief. Under a sprinkling rain I drove home and related the pharmacist's information to Irmie. She said simply, "I told you so."

Manfred wasn't home to cry on his shoulder. So, I made a cup of tea and buried myself in music books.

When I heard the mail slot flap I rose to pick up the letters. One of them was Ronnie's. Six hand-written pages!

Dear Mom and Dad,

I have to tell you about a terrible experience I've gone through, and why I haven't been able to visit you during the past six months.

One Saturday six months ago Peter and I, together with two friends, went camping in Arizona's Yuma Desert.

We swam in the Colorado River, hiked through the desert and had a good time. Sunday at midnight we left Yuma to drive back. I have to admit that we were all smoking pot, and Peter was speeding. Near El Centro we were stopped by a cop. He shone his flashlight into our car.

"Hide the jar with the pot!" Peter whispered. I quickly put the spice jar under my armpit. The cop made us get out and searched the car. Inconspicuously I threw the jar into the bushes. I couldn't believe what was happening and wished it wasn't true. The cop found half a joint in the car and arrested and handcuffed us all! Can you believe it? He told us to get in his police car, and I realized how clumsy I was with my hands tied behind me.

At the police station in El Centro they took the handcuffs off and fingerprinted us. Peter and our two friends were taken into the male section of the jail while a policewoman escorted me into a room, where I was told to undress. She watched me and it was terribly embarrassing. I felt like crying but I didn't, because I was afraid she would yell at me. She gave me an overall that looked like a potato sack to put on, as well as a pair of sandals. She took my purse, found an envelope with marijuana and threw it in a trash can. Then she led me down a hallway and unlocked a cell with six bunks, where five Mexican women were asleep. It was 3 a.m. and very hot. It was a nightmare! I climbed in the sixth bed, but couldn't sleep. Some machine was going all night long, and the air smelled bad.

At 7 a.m. bells rang. Breakfast time. We went to the eating hall, lined up and got a tray with pancakes and one cup with sugar instead of syrup, a tiny apple, black coffee and water. We sat at long tables. Since we weren't allowed to talk, I whispered to the woman next to me, asking her what else to expect. She whispered back, "You have the right to two phone calls. Demand them."

"Quiet over there!" a woman guard screamed.

After breakfast, when we passed by the guard, I asked her to allow me to make my phone calls. She pulled me out of the line and escorted me to the room where I had changed. She allowed me to take fifteen cents from my purse, and then she took me to the pay phone.

I was just dialing the number of my boss in San Diego as someone tapped on my shoulder. I turned around and saw this civilian man. "I'm the bail-bondsman," he said. "I'm getting you out."

I was so bewildered that I couldn't say a word. The woman guard took me to the changing room, returned my clothes to me and told me to change.

When I returned to the hall, the bondsman escorted me out of the jail and said, "I've already paid for you." He took me to the next building, where his office was located. Surprised and relieved I saw Peter and our two friends sitting there! The bondsman said, "I paid $50 for each of you. You owe me that plus ten percent." We paid with our credit cards and were released.

Now it was Monday, around 10 a.m. We returned to the spot where we'd left our car, but it had been towed away. A slip on a nearby tree gave us the address, we walked to the place, had to pay $150 for the towing and then we drove home.

A month later we were arraigned, pleaded guilty and went through a group-therapy program and were put on probation for six months. Once a month we had to see a probation officer in El Centro and report what we were doing. About our grades in college, our work and what money we were making. Eventually our police records were expunged.

Mom and Dad, I'm sorry to have to tell you this. But I'll never be that careless again, smoking pot or letting someone else under the influence drive. Now you know why I haven't come to the Palisades to see you for months because I had to drive to El Centro every four weeks. But now it's over.

I love you both, Ronnie.

The letter sank into my lap, and I let the tears run. I felt devastated. *My gentle daughter had been in jail and we hadn't known about it. Will this destroy her future? Ah, nonsense! She's out now and has learned a hard lesson. Considerate as usual, she told us when it was over, hadn't asked for any help. Yet what will Manfred say?*

When Manfred came home from Washington, Wernher was out shooting, and Irmie babysitting, and so we ate dinner alone. I showed Manfred the letter.

"Oh shit!" he shouted. "Our daughter in jail!" He put the letter down. "Why do we hear this only now?"

"She wanted to struggle through it herself," I said, trying to calm him down.

His face was red with rage. "Her jail time will stay on the records forever!"

"No, they won't! See here? She said the police records were expunged."

He ate with fury — I watched him with concern.

After eating silently he said, "It's actually ridiculous to make smoking pot illegal. After all, alcohol is legal, why not pot?"

"I agree. But as long as one deals in illegal activities one has to bear the consequences."

"You sound very Americanized."

"I am American," I said.

He looked at me and smiled thinly. "Good to hear! By the way, yesterday, there was a huge protest march in Washington because of the My Lai massacre and the devastation by Agent Orange in Vietnam. More than half a million protesters were supposed to be in the streets."

"I wish I'd been there." I put my hand on his. "I'm so glad you're back. Often I want to talk to you and you're gone."

He took my hand to his lips and kissed it. "You don't know how much I miss you when I'm out of town. If all these meetings could be held here it would be so much better. Unfortunately I have no control over them."

We spent the evening quietly, while my thoughts flew to Ronnie in Europe, wishing her a good time there.

Next morning at the breakfast table Manfred reached for the

newspaper and began to thumb through the pages. "Hey! Look who's coming to Malibu!" He pointed to a headline.

"DR. WERNHER VON BRAUN, HONORED GUEST AT PEPPERDINE UNIVERSITY'S INAUGURATION OF ITS MALIBU CAMPUS."

"How glamorous!" I said. "Where the movie stars have their beach homes."

"Malibu is a quasi extension of Pacific Palisades," Manfred said. "Last time we went to Alabama to see von Braun's work. Now he's coming to us."

When our Wernher came home I told him the news.

"Are we going to see him?" he asked.

"Of course," I replied. "It's only twelve minutes from here." His face lit up.

I too was looking forward to seeing von Braun again. With his Saturn 5 he'd put a man on the moon. What was next — besides inaugurating a new university campus? More spaceflights? To Mars?

On the day of von Braun's speech in Malibu we sat on hard folding chairs on the flat ground of the future campus, our backs toward the ocean, our eyes on the row of VIPs. It was windy, and thick clouds hung low as we listened to von Braun's talk about NASA's accomplishments. There was no mention of going to Mars; instead he stressed the need for more emphasis on science in education.

After his talk a crowd of admirers surrounded him, we being part of it. To our immense joy he singled us out. "The Krutein family! Where's my godson?"

The godson pushed forward and greeted his idol. We managed to shove close enough to greet our "hope in space." He dedicated a few minutes to our family and introduced us to the vice-presidents, deans and other dignitaries of Pepperdine University. Our encounter with von Braun lasted only a short time before he was whisked away by his staff.

"I'm disappointed," I said as we drove beside the movie stars' beach homes on our way back to the Palisades. "All we got was an introduction to the Pepperdine people."

"That alone is worth a piece of gold," Manfred replied. "Aren't you looking for a job? Now there will be a new campus and you were introduced to all the important people at Pepperdine."

"Are you saying I should apply at the new campus? There isn't a single building there, only trailers."

"The buildings will follow. Find out when they accept applications."

When I awoke the next morning I was more than ready to drive to the non-existent Malibu campus and apply for a job. Twelve minutes later I was wandering about the five trailers until I finally saw a small sign on one: "Dr. Harns, Dean."

I entered the trailer. Smartly dressed and European-looking, Dr. Harns rose from his chair to greet me with such cordiality that I thought he mistook me for someone else. We shook hands, he asked me to sit down and called to the secretary for two cups of coffee and opened the conversation with, "How's Wernher?"

Bewildered, I asked myself why he was interested in our son until it dawned on me that he meant the rocket scientist. "Busy as usual," I answered. "Traveling around and giving speeches." Then I told him about my desire to teach music here.

Harns leaned back in his chair. "It might sound strange, but we intend to start classes even before the buildings are ready. We are looking for suitable locations."

I threw out the bait. "How about my home? I live in Pacific Palisades."

Visibly surprised, he took the bait. "Would you be willing to teach for us at your home?"

Although overwhelmed, I tried to hide my own surprise. "Yes, I would."

We agreed that I should teach piano, harpsichord, music theory and appreciation for the university in my home. I thanked Harns for the interview and left.

I was about to jump and run and sing but forced myself to stride like a university instructor and drive home with dignity.

When Manfred came home in the evening, he went into our bedroom-cum-studio to change clothes. As he was about to put a T-shirt on I told him about my new job. "Since the campus isn't ready yet, I'll teach them here at home."

He stopped, held the T-shirt in his fist. "Are you out of your mind? You want to teach university students here in the garage?"

"It's not a garage! It's a studio!" I shouted.

"But we sleep in it!"

"Not when I teach. Our bed becomes a sofa every morning."

He looked as if he'd hit me with his damned T-shirt. "How the university accepts that I don't understand."

Feeling secure at my new job, I shrugged. "It's the teacher that counts."

Abruptly he yanked his shirt on. "Well, let's see if anyone will enroll."

When the semester started, the enrollment turned out to be enormous, under the circumstances. I had thirty-five students for all the offered music classes and had to make very sure the vestiges of our bedroom habitation were removed from the "class room" before the first students arrived. I had left all of Wernher's photography on the walls, and soon the students asked for the prices and bought some of them.

When Manfred heard that he jeered. "Why don't you also sell coffee and donuts?"

"If you'd be the waiter, I would."

"Thank God, I'm going to San Diego instead. I have to attend the launch of a barge."

As usual I was dealing with my rivals — ships. This time it was a barge. *What the hell's a barge?* But I wasn't in the mood to ask for and listen to any description he might give. I had to concentrate on my upcoming Master recital.

Manfred's Diary. San Diego, January 15, 1972.

I'm sitting on the sunny terrace of the 100-year-old Hotel Del Coronado with its wide view on the ocean, and recalling the events of the day, which have brought information, pleasure and satisfaction to me, a rare combination.

I arrived early at the National Steel & Shipbuilding Co. of San Diego. What a rare opportunity to stroll around a shipyard again! Building ships had been my training and my first career.

Creating my own shipyard, the "Jade-Werft," from scratch in Germany was a dream come true, although that huge effort after a lost war had almost cost me my health. Nevertheless, strolling around today between half-built ships, with cranes transporting steel plates, machinery or complete sections of a ship to the launching pads made me happy. I smelled the sea water, the odor of burnt steel, and heard the din of riveting and welding. Talking to the engineers and workers about ships in general and the new barge in detail thrilled me.

We are now heavily into the construction of the secret vehicles for our project. It needs the cooperation of many companies to design and build the equipment to lift the submarine into the huge salvage ship, whose construction has already begun on the East Coast. In Redwood City the gigantic claw will be built that will grapple and lift the sub from the seafloor in the unheard-of depth of 16,500 feet.

To build the claw a barge was needed in which the claw could be constructed in utmost secrecy. And here it was: A kind of floating dock with tall walls and a domed roof, resembling a gigantic aircraft hangar. It was longer than a football field — exactly 324 feet long.

My attendance at the launch made it believable that the barge really was "ocean mining equipment" — one of the many occasions I have to attend to reinforce the ocean mining cover again and again.

The ark-like barge stood on the large dry-dock, waiting for the ceremony. The white letters HMB-1, short for Hughes Marine Barge One, shone on the black hull. After Paul Reeve, my companion in Bordeaux, gave a brief talk, Mrs. Holliday, wife of a Hughes Tool's executive, had the honor of christening the monster. She climbed up to the platform beside the black hull and broke the traditional champagne bottle on the striker plate, splashing sparkling liquid across the HMB-1's bow. Applause came from all sides and the barge slid down into the water. Soon it would be towed to the facility in Redwood City.

Most of us drove over to the Hotel Del Coronado for lunch. Even from far away one can see the shining white of its structure with its many small, wooden towers. Built in the 1800s, its windows are old-fashioned, tall and narrow. The inside is old-fashioned and elegant. I sat with executives of Hughes Tool Co. of Houston. Champagne flowed, exquisite food was served and the conversation was lively.

When the time came for the out-of-towners to drive to the airport they walked to the cashier and got their checkbooks and credit cards out to pay for their overnight stay and the luncheon. It seemed the ancient hotel had not advanced to accepting checks or credit cards from other states and asked for cash. No one carried enough. The hotel guests, fearing they would miss their plane, turned to shouting. The manager was summoned and asked the bystanders, "Is any local person willing to lay out the money and write a check for these people?" Knowing the unhappy guests, I stepped forward and wrote a huge check, covering all of their expenses. I hope I'll be reimbursed within three days at least.

One day later: I received the money through Western Union with a nice thank-you note.

Master Recital

Pacific Palisades, February 15, 1972

Dear Alicia,

I'm glad to read that you received the printed program of my public Master recital on the very day I was giving it at Cal State University of Northridge.

Manfred had taken care of his "babies," the harpsichord and clavichord he had built from kits, so I could play all pieces on the instruments for which they were written. Time and again he had tuned the harpsichord which gets so easily out of tune, and had adjusted the various mechanical devices so the sound would be clear and silvery.

Although I knew my pieces well, my nerves were stretched to the breaking point. Can you imagine this: I had convinced myself that, if I failed, it would be the end of my life — a "failure" being memory lapses.

I had set up the concert as a lecture-recital, and because of my deficiency in English I was allowed to read from my notes, which helped me cope with my anxieties.

My performance lasted no longer than sixty minutes, yet how many years of intense study and practice were necessary to accomplish this undertaking! Consequently it led up to the venture of communicating to the audience what the composers had expressed in musical terms and hopefully to let the beauty of the music transport them to emotional heights. You may object, Alicia, that every concert has this goal; but numerous factors can lead to success or disaster. Imagine your memory plays a trick on you, you lose your place in the music, or you get stuck and have to start the piece all over again. Or a string in the harpsichord breaks with a clang and you either play without that particular note and become a laughing stock or you try to put a new string into the harpsichord and the bored audience goes home.

So, wary of all those possibilities I entered the stage, acknowledged the polite applause with a bow and sat down at the harpsichord.

To introduce the sound of its plucked strings I played the hauntingly beautiful Tombeau by Louis Couperin. A tombeau is a lament, commemorating the death of a famous person — in this case Couperin's teacher, Chambonnieres. Right from the first arpeggiated chord on, the sound went through my hands right into my heart, which in turn made my fingers express the grief. When I finished the short Tombeau the moment of silence before the applause revealed to me that the audience was moved. I had them on my side now.

Scarlatti's Sonata in A-major was the next piece. It's pretty like most sonatas by Scarlatti, but this one requires crossed hands, your left hand jumps from its left side over your right hand many times. The audience perceives this as acrobatic and thinks the player is a keyboard athlete. A stormy applause is guaranteed. And I got it.

The next piece was long: J.S.Bach's great Italian Concerto, played also on the harpsichord. Its first and last movements are pretty rambunctious and, because of their obvious technical challenge, admired by the listener. If I, in contrast to the wild race, succeeded with expressing the grievance of the slow middle movement then the audience would applaud wildly. They did that night, and I knew I had done a good job with the Italian Concerto.

Then I read my notes on the difference between harpsichord and clavichord and asked the audience to hold their breath while I played a Fantasy by C.P.E. Bach, old Bach's second son, on the clavichord. That tiny, whispering predecessor of the piano made the audience strain to listen to the delicate sound.

For comparison I played the same piece on the modern Steinway grand piano, where it sounded ten times as loud and the piano sound itself was familiar to the modern audience. The applause was modest; I interpreted this as the listeners' indecisiveness about the two instruments. Or was it the style of the piece that was neither classical nor romantic?

I stayed at the Steinway for my last piece, Beethoven's Sonata in F-sharp major, opus 78. Knowing that it was Beethoven's favorite sonata I fantasized that he himself stood before me — not as the genius he was but as a suffering human. I imagined that his soul was soothed by listening to the beauty of this sonata, and so I tried to transfer this admiration to the audience. The stormy applause confirmed that I had succeeded.

Since I had no memory lapses, I knew I had won the battle and "my life was saved." My degree 'Master of Arts in Music' was secured, and now I knew what that really meant to me: I could hope to find a full-time job at a university. That was my goal and "my life."

I wish you'd been at my concert!

Cariños, Eva

My revels were brutally interrupted by Manfred's complaint about pain in his abdomen. Knowing that he mentioned an indisposition only when it was unbearable, I was thoroughly shocked.

Manfred's Diary. Los Angeles, April 27, 1972

During my annual physical my doctor discovered a painful spot when he pressed on my abdomen. He was suspicious and ordered X-rays. When those showed a shady area on the colon he sent me to a surgeon, Dr. Gordon in Hollywood, who suggested immediate surgery.

I wasn't very concerned about the suspected tumor because I'd had that little pain for the last ten years and therefore thought it couldn't be cancerous, but Dr.Gordon said only surgery would tell about the nature of the tumor. Finally, I yielded. But I told him I needed three days to get my work in order.

I had to make important decisions regarding my cover work,

and then another big problem came up: I was informed that one of the agents had to be present during my surgery to observe if, under the anesthetic, I told any secrets about our work. That was standard procedure, they told me. In a few cases a patient under anesthesia had mentioned secret code words and if that happened to me our project could be jeopardized.

The problem for me was I had to ask Dr. Gordon to allow an observer to be present from the moment they injected the anesthetic into me until I was fully awake again. Needless to say, I was not allowed to mention that a secret Customer was behind this demand. But how could I justify such a thing?

Harry, one of the agents at our Global Marine office and a doctor of geology, was a great guy with a tremendous sense of humor. I talked to him about my problem. While looking at his intelligent face with its many laugh-wrinkles, an idea came to mind. I asked him if he was ready to act as my personal priest, my confessor and giver-of-the-last-rites if I died under the knife. After all, religion was respected in this country, and a pious patient would probably not be prevented from exercising his religious fervor. Harry's laugh-wrinkles deepened and he agreed to play this role.

So I told Dr. Gordon about my desire to have my priest around. He wasn't too enthusiastic about the idea but gave in, saying, after all, this was his private hospital and he could allow or disallow whatever he wished.

In the early morning of my surgery nurses walked in and out of my room until I saw Harry, clad in a long, black habit and a white priestly collar, stride into my room with dignity. "Do you wish to confess, my son?" he asked with a deep voice.

To hide my laughter I made up a coughing spell, while the nurses discreetly disappeared. Harry sat down on my bed, lowering his ear to my mouth. "You son of a gun, you drove away all the pretty nurses," I whispered in his ear.

He stared at me and said under his breath, "You'd better behave, or I'll cast a curse on you." He got up from my bed and went to open the door for the waiting nurses.

They put me on a gurney and rolled me down the hall. Harry followed us into the surgery room. Dr. Gordon shot an anesthetic into my arm, and before darkness enveloped me I saw the priest at my side.

When I opened my eyes, I looked into the priestly eyes again, wondering why they wouldn't perform the surgery on me.

"It's over," the priest said.

I recognized Harry. I was lying in my bed and had neither recollection of the operation nor pain.

"You behaved well," Harry said and winked. "I've seen your inner self and can certify that you're clean. Now I'm no longer needed." My guard left.

A nurse entered to ask me how I was feeling. Only now I realized that I had a bandage around my belly. Dr. Gordon followed, checking on his patient. The surgery, he said, had been a partial colectomy, and the tumor he had taken out of my colon was sent to the lab. I stayed in the hospital until Dr. Gordon told me that the tumor was benign. Thank God in heaven!

Manfred's hospitalization happened at a time when West Los Angeles College called me to substitute for an ailing music instructor. So I drove back and forth between college, hospital and Pepperdine University, which had built its first buildings in Malibu. I went to see Manfred at least twice a day, always tense from worry and teaching.

Manfred's Diary. Los Angeles, March 15, 1973

The cover strategies ranged from minute details to wide-open events like the launching of the HUGHES GLOMAR EXPLORER in Pennsylvania, which had been camouflaged as a family event. Another way of disguise was the misleading destinations of The Customer's agents' meetings with Global Marine personnel. Whenever I was told to fly to Washington, Seattle, Denver, Houston or other cities I expected one of two outcomes: I would be told to leave the flight on its first leg, take a cab, stop at a restaurant, enter, but leave through the back door, be picked up by a car with tinted windows and driven to a small hotel with "safe" rooms where the meeting would be conducted. Or we, myself and some executives, would fly straight to a major city, be picked up by three cars and driven by different routes to a secure military camp forty-five minutes away or an equally safe government facility in the

Nevada Desert.

Invariably our names were changed. To prevent confusion between us we kept our first names, but the last names were always changed. Forever I was Manfred Krause on the documents. Since we called each other by first names I didn't mind the change; on the contrary, Krause was easier to pronounce than Krutein.

"Ermgord Crusteen," sounded from the loudspeaker at the high school graduation ceremony, as Irmie stepped forward to receive her diploma.

"We should have changed our names when we became citizens," I whispered to Manfred. "Nobody can pronounce them."

I sighed. My youngest child, my baby, was fully fledged! Our house was getting emptier. Wernher was in New Mexico, filming with our neighbor-director. "Soon we'll be alone," I said to Manfred.

"Before you get the empty-nest syndrome let's go on vacation."

"Would they find manganese nodules without you?" I asked in mock-irony.

"We're far from sampling nodules yet. But everything is under control. So I can take off."

"Where would you like to go?" I asked.

"Your choice."

"Iceland!" I blurted out. "I've longed for it since childhood."

"I know. But I thought you would say Chile or Hawaii."

I contemplated it. "I've conquered my nostalgia for Chile and Hawaii. Now there's only my last and very old nostalgia — for Iceland."

Back at home, I pulled the atlas from the bookshelf. "Chile, Hawaii, Iceland and California have one thing in common, they are all volcanic." I thumbed through the pages until I found Iceland. "Recently Iceland had a volcano eruption. I wonder what the Westman Islands must look like now." I pointed to the islands south of Iceland. "The volcano erupted a few days ago and buried a whole town, and a brand-new island was born. It's not even on this map yet."

Manfred smiled. "Your wonderland."

"And it will be mine, when I touch it."

"Okay, let's go to Iceland. Do you know anybody over there?"

"Not yet. I know the population is Scandinavian and highly educated. They read a lot, and more books are published per capita in Iceland than in any other country."

"Amazing. Probably that's their entertainment during the winter, when it stays dark for months."

"Most of their wonderful books have been translated into German. The Edda. I read Jón Sveinsson's children's books as a child, and in later years the many excellent novelists, Gunnarsson, Kamban, Laxness. I really got to know the Icelandic people through their literature."

"Weren't they Danish at one time?"

"Until 1944. Now they're independent."

Next morning I called the Icelandic Consulate in Los Angeles, asking for the name and address of the largest Icelandic newspaper. *Morgunbladid*, they said. I wrote to the paper, asking to put an ad in:

"German-born American couple, an ocean mining engineer and a piano teacher, interested in Iceland and its people, want to travel to Iceland and are looking for people to talk to." Plus our name and address.

The long-awaited first letter came from the land of my dreams. Overjoyed, I sat down in my favorite chair and read:

> *Mrs. Eva Krutein, I just noticed your name in the most fascist newspaper in Iceland. You say you are interested in Iceland and Icelanders; if so, you should turn your interest to the interest of Icelanders and help us in fighting against the American imperialist occupation of Iceland. And that you can do best by not traveling to Iceland but instead helping the Attica-prisoners, the Soledad-brothers and other victims of U.S. imperialism with active protests. The Nazis murdered in concentration camps; the U.S. imperialists turn whole countries into*

concentration camps.

Birna, University of Iceland.

Devastated I collapsed in my chair, paralyzed by the hatred. The fall from joy by this slap in my face was too deep. Yearning for communication, I searched for someone. Wernher was home, so I went to his room.

He was lying on his bed, reading. Seeing my face, he cried out: "Mom, what's the matter?"

I stammered, "You know how much I was waiting for a letter from Iceland. This is the answer." I dragged myself to his bed and showed him the letter.

He read it, jumped up from his bed and said, "What an outrageous smear! Mom, do you want me to answer him?"

His sympathy and unexpected assistance helped me recover. "Birna is a woman's name. I don't know yet what the most effective way is to answer this hate letter. Let's sleep on it."

"Let me know tomorrow. I'd love to write to her."

As usual, Manfred was unavailable, for he had flown to Philadelphia, to Chester's Sun Shipyard, to caress his ocean mining ship. The next day I made two photocopies of the letter and gave one to Wernher.

"So you can let go of your rebellious steam and write to that Icelandic communist," I said.

I wrote to the *Morgunbladid* again, included a copy of the infamous letter and asked for a second chance to find a pen pal. This time I had more luck.

The new letter read:

Dear Mrs. Krutein,

My name is Assy. I am afraid I am too late to answer your ad. I am thirty years old. I am the manager and a waitress in a small cafeteria. My father's name was Nixon. He was an American soldier. I have never met him. Maybe I will find him through you. I have the same name as your president. That is probably a good omen. I hope to hear from you soon.

Sincerely, Assy Nixon.

Happy as a child at Christmas, I answered her immediately.

There was also good news from Geneva, Switzerland. In one of my letters to Anne Fenton I'd told her about the bad letter from Reykjavík. She answered by return.

> *Go see our friends Vilí and Lára in Reykjavík. (The Icelanders use only their first names, even in their phone books.) Vilí is an engineer, with whom Doug attended the university in Berlin.*

I carefully saved Vilí's and Lára's address. Everything seemed to be under control. Ronnie and Peter came back from Europe in time to stay with Irmie and Wernher for as long as we were in Iceland.

Iceland Interlude

For me the flight to Iceland was a pilgrimage to the saga-island at the edge of the Arctic and I felt its magnetic pull.

Flying over Greenland, I said with surprise, "Look at the land that's supposed to be green. It's white!"

"That's the eternal ice cover. It's a mile thick."

"Definitely a misnomer."

Flying over Iceland, I said with surprise, "Look at the land that's supposed to be icy. It's green!"

"Also a misnomer."

Nowhere in the world can one find a capital like Reykjavík. The buildings are white and all roofs have different colors, with red and green prevailing — possibly to make up for the gloominess of the night seasons, when the sun doesn't rise for months.

After landing at Reykjavík's airport, my eyes wandered over the overwhelmingly blond crowd awaiting visitors. We immediately recognized Assy, who stood out because of her dark hair and eyes. Her stature, though, resembled her peers: Tall and proudly erect. Unfortunately, her cool Scandinavian nature prohibited us from hugging and kissing her.

She led us out into the cold wind and to a 1970 Ford. "I'm borrowing my mother's car. I'm taking a vacation during your visit so I can drive you everywhere."

"How sweet of you, Assy," I responded gratefully.

She corrected my pronunciation of her name, "Assy rhymes with fussy."

With rain blocking our view we saw little of Reykjavík. "If you don't like the weather in Iceland, just wait five minutes," Assy said. Her words stopped the rain immediately, and we arrived at her snow-white apartment building dry, only the cold wind continued to blow.

In her small apartment she led us to her bedroom with a double bed. "You two are going to sleep in here. I'll sleep on the couch in the living room."

"Oh Assy, you are a wonderful person," I said.

The living room was decorated in European fashion: A huge bookcase, replicas of ancient masters on the walls and no kitsch or knick-knacks around.

Manfred took off his jacket. "It's warm in here." He looked at the heater under the window. "You must be paying a fortune for heating."

"Very little and only for the installation. The hot water in the radiators comes from the hot springs and is free for all of us."

Soon she asked us to sit down for dinner. She served an appetizer of caviar with mayonnaise and smoked lamb chops, basted with butter, and broiled ptarmigans for the entree—those birds with oversized beaks. They tasted good.

Vegetables and salads accompanied every dish. "Home-grown," Assy explained with pride in her voice. "In our greenhouses. We have many of them. All heated by thermal energy from the hot springs. We also grow flowers and bananas."

Manfred shook his head and smiled. "And all this with a free energy source."

For dessert we ate *skyr*, a delicious, sweet yogurt-like foamy dish, loaded with calories. I indulged in these delicacies with the silent promise to go on a diet when I got home. Manfred was blessed with a metabolism that processed any over-indulgence.

After two days we had adjusted to the new time and learned how Nordic people led their lives under the bright light of midnight. Although the sun crawled along just below the horizon, it was clear as day.

At about 10 p.m. Assy drove us out of the city into the green rolling hills, which were hissing and steaming from the hot-water pipes that harnessed Iceland's natural forces. A few miles east, a big geyser had attracted lots of tourists. Parents with little children had brought raw eggs along and cooked them in the boiling water.

Downtown Reykjavík sported a public swimming pool. The water from the hot springs steamed in the cold air, giving the impression the swimmers were being boiled. We joined them and, swimming, played hide-and-seek in the vapor.

At 1 a.m. we drove around the capital and saw people playing golf and laborers building roads and bridges. "We have to make use of the long days," Assy explained. "In the winter months there's hardly any light."

Passing by a bus stop at 2 a.m., we saw a mother waiting with two small children, flower bouquet in hand, perhaps about to visit a friend. No one looked tired. Neither were we, and it felt strange to go to bed at daylight.

After a few days Assy returned the car to her mother and went back to work, while we rented a car for a drive along Iceland's ragged coast. Long and calm blue fjords, shimmering in the eternal sun, made up for the bad condition of the roads.

"I don't understand why the Icelanders who are so clean and so modern don't fix their roads," I said.

Our car rumbled through dozens of miles of green, rolling hills with hundreds of thick-fleeced, black-headed sheep, running for their lives when our car approached.

On a lava field with fantastic dark-brown formations I asked Manfred to stop. "What's the matter?" he asked.

"You know I'm always enchanted by lava. Look at this." I left the car and walked over to a bizarre lava block.

"It looks like a space creature or a sculpture by Picasso," Manfred said.

Silently I touched the shiny, almost black structure with both hands, and thus it became mine. I knew Manfred understood my magic way of treasure hunting. While my accumulations required no space, their image remained within me forever: Chile's Andes, Hawaii's Diamond Head and now Iceland's many treasures.

On a meadow stood half a dozen Icelandic ponies, brown-skinned and blond-maned, grazing on the fresh grass. We stopped and got out. In amazement we stared at a display of animal affection we'd never seen: one of the ponies had put his head over a beloved one's neck and remained so — an embrace without arms, but with a tenderness unequaled in the animal kingdom.

"Have you ever seen anything like it?" I asked Manfred in an undertone, not wanting to disturb the touching scene.

The two ponies remained in their tender pose even as we went back to the car and drove away.

The road led to some farm houses. Before one a small truck was parked. Next to it stood a light-brown pony whose blond mane and long, white-blond tail wafted in the wind.

"Now look at that," I said.

Six white-blond small children, one after the other, climbed into the truck's empty bed and from up there jumped onto the little horse. The one who landed without falling from the pony's back got applause. "Yay!!"

"The pony has the patience of an angel," I said.

Suddenly a door opened and a tall, blond woman in dark, wide farm garb appeared. We stepped out of the car and wished her a good morning in English, which she returned. I had read that there was hardly a person in Iceland who hadn't learned Danish and English. She shooed the children from the truck.

I began to pet the little horse. It turned its head to see who I was and must have decided I was okay.

"I love your little horses," I said to the woman.

"They are good animals, intelligent and affectionate," she replied. "And they love children."

"What do you use them for?" Manfred asked.

"For nothing. Machines and trucks do better jobs."

I searched my brain to continue the conversation. "Do you use them for horseback riding?"

She nodded, petting the pony's neck. "Do you want to ride him?"

A jolt of surprise and joy raced through me. "Not ride him, because I don't know how, but I'd like to sit on him."

"Come on, I'll help you up," she encouraged, cupping her hands ready. She and Manfred helped me mount the pony, and I just felt happy to sit on this lovable creature.

Suddenly the pony bolted away as if catapulted. I was scared to death. *No saddle, no bridle, nothing to hold on to, nothing to stop it!* It ran and ran and I began to wonder why the little horse's gait was so smooth — I was almost floating. Now the pony approached the river and "flew" into it. *Will it swim in the icy water? Will my legs get in the river?* Before I could react the pony reached the other shore, climbed onto land, turned around, floated through the shallow river again, up the bank and toward Manfred and the farm woman and stopped. I was so stunned it took me a while to dismount to their outstretched arms.

"I thought you'd fall off any minute," Manfred said.

Still breathless, I said, "Me too. But the ride was smoother than I ever thought it could be on a horse."

"That's because of the *tölt*," the woman said. "Only Icelandic ponies have this fifth gait. Back left, front left, back right, front right."

"In rapid speed," Manfred said. "And it sounded like a constant four-beat staccato."

"No other horse in the world can do that." Her voice was full of pride.

I petted the little brown horse and ran my hand through its blond mane. And the animal became mine.

Anxious to see Iceland's natural resources, we flew north to Akúreyri, rented a car and drove to the idyllic Lake Myvatn with its extraordinary lava formations along its shore, dwarfed birch trees and an abundant bird-life.

At one point we left the car and began to walk inland on a smooth moss carpet. We passed by Iceland's famous natural and cheap power resources: Geysers spewing out huge white steam columns that reeked of sulphur.

"Listen to the two different sounds," I said. We listened intently: A high-pitched hissing and low-pitched thundering. And the ground trembled like a perpetual earthquake.

"Jules Verne labeled this place, 'the path to the Center of the Earth,'" I said. "And our astronauts trained here before going to the moon."

Manfred looked at the rock-strewn field and nodded. "That's what the moon pictures look like."

Back at Lake Myvatn we booked a bus tour to the volcano Askja in Iceland's uninhabited interior. Askja was said to be the most beautiful of Iceland's thirty active volcanoes. Specially equipped, our bus lurched over rock and lava, on a humped-up narrow track and sometimes even through shallow rivers — at a speed of three miles per hour in first gear up and down, up and down, right, left, right, left. To drive under such conditions would be prohibited anywhere else in the world.

After two hours of riding through rough lava we had made about six miles, when the driver stopped. "This is as close to Askja as I can get," he said in Icelandic and English. "You have to walk now. The caldera is a forty-five-minute walk from here. Do not fall into the sulphur lake. See you in three hours."

We followed the crowd, walking up the caldera over black ash from the volcano's last eruption in 1961, gray rain-heavy clouds above us. Despite the gloomy scenery I was excited and could hardly wait to get to the crater.

Arriving at the caldera rim we stood spellbound by the glistening glaciers in the distance. And here, at the 4,500-foot altitude, a large blue lake lay before us, its bed created by a tremendous eruption. Right next to us, two stories lower, a small crater called "Vití," meaning Hell, sank its steep walls into the turquoise waters of a sulphuric lake that lay about 600 feet lower than the large caldera lake. Steam rose from the surface into the 32 degree cold.

"Are you going to swim?" a bearded man with a rucksack on his back asked us. "The water is about 80 degrees."

First I thought it was a joke. But then I saw him and others half-climb, half-slide down the steep crater wall. Now I noticed people in the water. "Come on, let's go," I said to Manfred.

More sliding on the rubble than climbing, we reached the bank. We saw the Icelanders walk into the water in the nude. For Scandinavians this was normal. So with only a slight hesitation we became instant Scandinavians, stripped in the cold air and quickly walked into the warm lake.

The water, loaded with sulphur, felt silky like soap suds. It also smelled like its name — Hell.

The comfortable warmth and the people's laughter relaxed us

and made me feel in heaven. Some feet away from us a young couple, face-to-face, self-forgetting, rocked back and forth, rapture in their faces. Blessed be Iceland!

As we hiked back to the bus we were bombarded with hailstones the size of ping-pong balls. An icy wind lowered the temperature to 15 degrees. We rushed to the bus. Driving through the lava fields, we suddenly saw a huge lake before us.

The driver, in radio contact with his headquarters, announced, "A sudden melting of several glaciers has occurred. It was caused by a geothermal outbreak. All rivers are now fifty times wider than before. I'll try to cross them anyway."

He opened the door on his side to watch how high the flood would rise while he was driving. As the water entered the bus, we lifted our feet to avoid getting wet. Cool and skilled, the driver steered with his right hand, holding the door open with his left. Clinging to Manfred's arm, I couldn't take my eyes off the lake that hadn't been there a few hours before.

When the water level sank below the bus floor, the driver closed the door and continued "sailing" until we reached the other bank and civilization.

Still in the northern part of Iceland, we hired a small Cessna with a solemn pilot, to fly us to the small island of Grímsey up north to fulfill my dream of standing on the Arctic Circle.

My dream became true; we found a small plate, indicating the imaginary line, and I happily stood on the Arctic Circle, legs spread wide apart over it. While Manfred was adjusting his camera, arctic seagulls attacked me, disheveling my hair. Completely unaware, I was standing between their eggs, which I spotted only now on the wide-open breeding place.

After Manfred had shot the scenery, I brushed my hair, and we flew back to Akúreyri.

At midnight we stood on the bank of Akúreyri's long fjord, watching the clouds moving across the slopes. Sometimes they were like a gossamer film in which shadows flitted by, sometimes like cotton batting which completely enveloped us. With the sun crawling below the horizon, all of this cleared and we could see the peaks bathed in the low light of midnight. I was grateful beyond words.

On the flight back to Reykjavík I thanked Manfred for having come with me to my beloved Iceland and told him how much this meant to me. I asked him how much his thoughts were with his ocean-mining and semi-secret job. He looked out of the plane window and forgot to answer my question. Now I knew that his body was flying over the Atlantic, but his heart was in the Pacific ocean. I softly caressed his hand.

After resting at Assy's flat, I wondered what natural forces were waiting for us as we again hired a Cessna with a young, constantly whistling pilot, Sigurdur, to fly us to the devastated Westman Islands near Iceland's south coast.

I sat at his side as he, whistling opera arias and folksongs in turn, flew over the capital and its bright-red roofs. Suddenly the door on my side flew open. Terrified, I looked at Sigurdur. "The door opened!" I shouted over the motor's noise.

He interrupted his whistling. "Close it!" he shouted back, unmoved, and continued to whistle.

Although strapped in with the seat belt, I was horrified as I leaned over, halfway hanging out above Reykjavík, to grab the door handle and shut the door. My heart was pounding like mad.

Minutes later we landed on the black-ash runway of the Westman Islands' volcano. Having left the aircraft, I stood glued to the spot, spell-bound. Below us spread a landscape of black ash with ruins of houses burnt by the previous month's volcanic eruption.

Accompanied by Sigurdur's artistic whistling, we marched on the soft ash and approached the remainders of the former white residences.

Without being asked Sigurdur said, "The eruption destroyed the whole fishing town of 5,000 people within hours."

"How many were killed?" Manfred asked.

"None. They were evacuated by boats and airplanes."

Courageous Norsemen! "Did you have relatives here?" I asked.

"We are all more or less related," he answered, summing up

the Icelanders' general feeling of being one large family.

Walking through the ghost town was eerie. Most streets were filled with black cinder and therefore impassable. Several homes were burned out and many remained buried under lava and pumice forever.

"Can we walk up the ash mount?" I asked.

"Sure," Sigurdur replied. "I shall wait here."

As if entering hell we walked up the ash slope, under which more houses were buried. Suddenly clouds of sulphur vapors surrounded us from all sides.

"Oh God, how will we ever find our way back?" I asked Manfred.

"Just listen to Sigurdur's music," Manfred said.

Indeed, the sound of "*America, the Beautiful*" penetrated the sulphur cloud, directing us back.

He then led us to the only building that was not destroyed: The Lutheran Church at the edge of the town. Sigurdur opened the door for us and ushered us to the organ-loft. Miraculously, there was electricity, so I sat down, turned on the organ and played a Lutheran chorale. Sigurdur, who had interrupted his whistling, smiled and nodded. All Lutherans in the world, it seemed, sang the same hymns.

On our flight back Sigurdur kept whistling as before, but this time the door didn't open in flight.

Back in Reykjavík, we contacted Anne Fenton's friends Vilí and Lára, whom Anne had alerted of our arrival. They invited us to their home.

In pouring rain we drove to their Danish-style house — its walls white, roof red, and its windows wide. Vilí, a fifty-year-old herculean figure and full of pep, was the technical manager of an aluminum smelter. He dwarfed his pretty wife Lára, who by Icelandic standards was petite.

Their living room with Danish-modern furniture was dominated by large book cases on three walls, filled with hundreds of books. "'A man without a book is blind,' we say here in Iceland," Vilí said.

"You've even got a Nobel Prize Winner, Halldór Laxness,"

I said with admiration.

"We're very proud of him."

Lára served pancakes, generously covered with strawberry preserve and whipped cream, with vanilla ice cream on the side.

In the course of the evening I told them about Birna and her ugly letter to me.

"Birna? The leader of the young communists?" Lára asked. She thought for a moment. "There was a cartoon of her in one magazine." She got up and rummaged in a newspaper rack. "Here it is!" She showed me a cartoon of a long-haired, short-skirted young woman with the name tag "Birna," standing behind a lectern, preaching. Out of her mouth came the words "blah-blah-blah." We laughed and Vilí handed me the magazine. "Take it home as a souvenir. Iceland has a democracy and everybody can open his mouth and say and write nonsense like Birna. Just don't listen."

Manfred changed the subject. "Something strikes me as strange. Everything in Iceland is so clean and people so efficient, why then are the roads outside Reykjavík so bad?"

There was a second of hesitation before Vilí answered. "It's caused by our attitude against tourism. We are afraid foreigners might spoil our country as they've done everywhere else. By not developing the roads we hope to discourage them."

"Sorry, we're here anyway," I said. "But I love this country."

"Great," Vilí said without further elaboration, for Norsemen don't express emotions.

After we'd devoured the pancakes I helped Lára carry out the dishes. When we came back to the living room I heard Vilí say to Manfred, "Our bloodless conversion to Christianity happened around the year 1,000. The parliament then decided to legally adopt the new religion but left it up to the citizens to worship the old gods. When Lutheranism was established the gods shrank to ghosts. But in our minds they still remain very much alive."

"You folks have such a modern life style," I said. "But you still hang on to ghosts and such?"

Lára smiled. "There are even people on this island who want to revive the old pagan religion. A man named Sveinbjörn made himself a priest of the god Thór. He's a sheep farmer and a poet. With his followers he erected a throne-like altar for the god Thór, and that's where they worship in the old way."

I wondered how much I could bother our kind hosts with a request beyond their invitation. But my curiosity won. "Would it be possible to see Thór's altar?"

Vilí looked at his wrist watch. "Ten to midnight. I'll see if I can find out." He got up and walked over to the telephone. The rain had stopped, and in the twilight life obviously went on.

After four phone calls Vilí returned to the table. "Let's go."

Preparing for the ride to the god Thór, Vilí checked the gas tank and Lára packed midnight snacks — mainly dried, salted cod, whose strips one could see hanging from drying racks on many balconies.

In the low midnight light Vilí drove, while we were eating dried, salted cod strips. Rattling, the middle-aged Ford rumbled on the rough roads along the green-banked loops of shimmering fjords and then straight inland through lush, green meadows.

"What are the thousands of bulges in the lawn?" Manfred asked our friends.

"Chilblains," Lára answered. "Caused by frost."

Sheep were grazing peacefully on the grass until the car's approach made them run.

After the projected two hours of driving we finally spotted Sveinbjörn's farm in the distance. A young man with shoulder-long hair staggered toward us. Vilí stopped and talked to the obviously drunk man in Icelandic.

"We are right," Vilí confirmed. He drove directly to one of three white, low farm houses and parked. It was 2 o'clock in the morning. Brown ponies with long, stately blond tails and manes and black-white sheep dogs moved majestically around the courtyard, ignoring us.

We knocked at the door, heard a voice calling from inside and entered. In a small, poorly lit room sat three young men and an obvious center figure, who seemed to be the god Thór himself. Dignified, about sixty, his long, gray beard hanging over a crimson top with sewn-on, blue, nordic ornaments, he seemed to personify authority and wisdom.

The young men, looking very Germanic — tall, blond and blue-eyed — got up from their chairs, offered them to us and plopped on the floor. Vilí introduced us to Sveinbjörn and we sat down on the hard, wobbly chairs. The priest pointed to a vodka bottle, one of the young men got up, poured the contents in water glasses and served us. Thirsty from the salty cod, I gulped the stuff, before I realized it was pure alcohol. My throat burned.

Now the conversation was held in Icelandic. Once in a while Vilí translated for us, "He said lots of people come here to see Thór's statue or to hear Sveinbjörn's chanting."

My interest flared up. "Would you ask him if he could chant for us?"

The priest obviously understood my English, because he nodded, picked up a book, thumbed through it and stopped at a certain page. He took a deep breath before he began to chant in Icelandic. I listened intensely to the melody which used very short intervals. I took my notebook from my purse, quickly drew five lines and jotted down the notes. The shape of the melody resembled the Roman Catholic liturgy.

Our water glasses were never empty, the young man kept refilling them. I saw how Vilí made a gesture of car-steering to Lára, obviously meaning she should drive home and not drink now. A very wise thought.

When Sveinbjörn, who had not been drinking in our presence, got up and announced something, Vilí translated, "We shall walk to the Thór statue now."

Outside, the sun now was crawling below the horizon. It was 3 a.m. as we stumbled over the grassy chilblains. I tried to blame the little bulges for my staggers, but I knew they were caused by the vodka. The others had drunk much more than I, but apparently they were used to the strong stuff. The three young men were still with us, so Sveinbjörn had a flock of seven this morning.

Even from far away we could see the light-gray plaster statue, a bearded male sitting on a stony hill. Sveinbjörn placed himself before it, bowed and began chanting Icelandic words. As he turned to face us, I noticed the priest's great resemblance to the towering statue. The beards, the stern countenance and the majesty of both, god and priest, were awe-inspiring. Music began to ring out in my mind, Wagner's opera, "*Twilight of the Gods*." How often had I seen those gods on the stage — but now this was for real! Or did Sveinbjörn also just play a god, creating the statue in his own image?

Now Sveinbjörn produced a ram's horn and drank from it. He then preached a little in Icelandic, and in my mind I added Wagner's music to it.

The strange midnight service was over, and we stumbled back. In vain I tried to balance myself, yet someone's guiding hand slipped under my forearm, giving me support. For the first time in my life I was drunk. Blaming the old god for it, I would remember the scenario many times on the day which had been named after the god Thór — Thursday.

On Friday — named after Friya, the goddess of love — Assy took us to the airport. I had gained a good friend and was grateful for it. Now we were leaving Iceland, which I loved so dearly — how hard was it to say goodbye! Yet I knew I would return as soon as I could.

Ship Launching and Danzig Beckons

It was good I'd taken off during the summer, doing what I always wanted to do, because in the fall my teaching schedule reached breakneck proportions. I soon learned that money-tightening policies at colleges caused full-time positions to shrink and I had to be content with part-time assignments. I ended up teaching part-time at four different colleges, Pepperdine University included. Feeling like a morning paper's delivery boy whom no one ever sees, I rushed from one campus to the next, eating lunch and dinner while driving on the freeway.

This frenzied schedule was interrupted by an unusual event.

The Shipbuilding and Dry Dock Company in Chester, Pennsylvania, invited all of those working on the big ocean mining project and their families to the launching of the huge 51,000-ton ship that had been specially designed for Howard Hughes's ocean-mining enterprise.

I was setting the dinner table, when Manfred showed me the invitation to the "Launching and Family Day." I carried in the meatloaf, the green-salad bowl and potatoes, and sat down.

He didn't seem to be too impressed by the invitation. "I've attended dozens of ship launchings, and I've traveled so much on this business that I'd be happy to stay home and relax for a change."

I helped myself to the salad. "Not me! Do you realize how close Philadelphia is to New York? Let's fly to New York after the ship launching and see a performance at the Met!"

The prospect of seeing an opera at the Metropolitan Opera seemed to enliven Manfred. "That's not a bad idea. And we both deserve it. What's playing at the Met?"

"Der Rosenkavalier!"

Richard Strauss's opera alone was worth flying to the East Coast. So we flew to Philadelphia, rented a car and drove under a warm November sun to Chester's Sun Shipyard.

Even from afar we saw the black giant of a ship, about ten stories high, loom above the tall shipyard structures. The white letters HUGHES GLOMAR EXPLORER stood out from the black hull. Cranes, looking like steel giraffes, reached out to the readied hull. I smelled sea water and shipyard equipment. Our years of living in the middle of Manfred's shipyard in Germany came to mind, and I strained to hear the din of riveting and welding, but today was Sunday and no one was working. Instead I heard the noise of rejoicing children and chatting adults. The kids flew colorful balloons, and a band was playing, its music muffled in the open air.

The crowd, dwarfed by the dark ship's bow, was in a festive mood. Manfred seemed to know most of the important men around. "You've got to meet John Graham," Manfred said to me, approaching a man who visibly enjoyed each puff from his cigarette. We shook hands.

"John is the chief designer of that big ship," Manfred said, pointing to the Hughes Glomar Explorer.

"John also is a chain-smoker," Manfred said later when we were out of earshot. "I've never seen him without a cigarette in his mouth."

Soon a representative of Hughes Mining division climbed up on a platform and began his speech, praising the ocean mining effort and hopes for the future. Global Marine's chairman followed, saying more or less the same but adding, "Howard Hughes is always in seclusion. But who knows? Maybe he's watching us from around the corner." Laughter followed, for everyone knew about Hughes's self-imposed isolation.

At last, the wife of a Hughes Company executive ascended to the platform of honor, tried to throw a champagne bottle against the vessel, missed twice, then got help from a man who ran to her side and hurled the recalcitrant bottle with enough force that it splintered and the fizzing liquid gushed over the hull. Enthusiastic applause followed.

Now an elaborate lunch was ready for us in a large barracks, buffet style. When we sat down with our filled plates a couple, much younger than we, took a seat across from us. They introduced themselves as Bob and Halina Drake. Bob, athletic-looking, worked for the Hughes Company, and he and Manfred indulged themselves in a vivid conversation.

Halina, with her dark hair and eyes, was a real beauty. She spoke with an accent, and I asked her where she was born.

"In Warsaw, Poland," she said.

Immediately my interest woke up. "I'm from Gdansk, when it was still Danzig."

A spark appeared in her dark eyes. Of course, with my sparse information she must be able to imagine my past.

"Were you there during the war?" she asked.

"Yes. Now it's a heap of rubble," I said with bitterness.

She looked at me intensely. "No longer."

Confused, I asked, "What do you mean?"

"Our architects are rebuilding Gdansk in its old glory," she said, and in spite of the animated conversations around us I still could hear the pride in her voice. "Brick by brick, ornament by ornament. It looks exactly like before the war."

I sat thunderstruck. Was she, the former enemy, ridiculing me, or was she revealing an unheard-of miracle? Shutting off the noise around us, I stared at her beautiful face, clinging to her incredible words.

"I've seen your birthplace," she said. "Our people have achieved an architectural miracle. You should go see it."

The image of Danzig's destruction, which I had fixed as a final page of my war memories — pushing the experiences way down into my subconsciousness — now seemed to ruffle, shrink and vanish, leaving the final page empty. "Go there and see it." I kept hearing Halina's advice, which took on the sound of an overpowering force, a command of irresistible strength, drowning out the trivial plans of the present.

While the high-spirited company enjoyed themselves I heard someone say, "Look at the dark clouds moving in." Someone else said, "We'll be dry in the cars."

Halina and her husband said goodbye and left, not suspecting what a turmoil her information about Danzig's resurrection had left in me.

After the luncheon we ran through heavy rain to our rental car and Manfred began to drive toward Philadelphia's airport. The rain obscured the view, forcing him to slow down. A strong wind pushed the car every which way, and Manfred had to concentrate on making it through the foul weather.

I noticed the storm as if through a veil — soon we would escape it. Images of Danzig's glorious beauty and the horrible pictures of its near-total destruction were whirling around me like broken pieces in a kaleidoscope. Which images were true? Danzig intact or destroyed? Could I go home or must I remain in exile? New York? What did I expect to see there? The Met? Forget the Met! Forget New York!

Arriving late at the airport, Manfred said, "Go get tickets to New York. I'll return the car and meet up with you."

In the hall with the many airline counters I found American Airlines. No customers were around.

"May I help you?" the checker asked.

To my own surprise I heard myself say, "I want to fly to California immediately."

"How many people?"

"Two."

"The plane is leaving for Los Angeles in a minute." He picked up the phone to the pilot. "Hold it! Two more passengers are coming."

I handed our tickets over to the checker. Manfred came running up, dripping wet from the rain. "Manfred, do you want to fly to California now?"

Dripping with rain, he reacted in a flash. "Yes. Let's go home."

The clerk urged us, "Please hurry, we're holding the flight for you."

We hastened through the jetway into the plane, the flight attendant closed the door, and with us barely strapped in our seats, the jet started taxiing. Within a short time we were airborne and above the bad weather. A full moon gave the clouds a silvery appearance.

Were we going home? Home to Danzig? No, nothing had

changed there, the medieval towers and buildings of the Baltic Renaissance were destroyed — no, they were rebuilt, they were reachable, no longer a dream, they were home again, we were flying over to be home again…

I turned to Manfred to tell him, but he was already asleep. It was good this way. Maybe what I'd heard about Danzig was a dream. There was no way to go back in time. The past had to be expelled or suppressed, not allowed to interfere with the present.

Meanwhile, our jet sped through space and time, carrying us back to California.

In Concert

Life went on.

"I'm not a crook," President Nixon announced. It was spring of 1974. To our amazement we realized that the Watergate scandal was growing into unforeseen proportions and could topple the president.

I went outside to get some fresh air and watch the surf.

In the front yard of the house on the corner stood our Italian-looking neighbor, screen-writer and good friend Guerdon Trueblood. Curious what he'd have to say about Nixon, I greeted him. "Out for fresh air too?"

"Once in a while you just have to get out of your cage," he grumbled.

He's in a bad mood today, I thought, and turning toward the ocean, gave up on asking him about Nixon.

"Hey! Eva!" he called. I turned back to him. "I have a job for you. I need music for my new movie. I want you to write it for me."

"Sorry, I'm not a composer."

"Don't tell me you can't do it," he said with rage.

"Guerdon, I'm a music teacher, not a composer!"

His face was red with anger. "You're chicken! You're just chicken!"

"Goodbye," I said, turned and walked away. Although we usually accepted his frequent outbursts with equanimity, this time he had gotten me angry. He said I was chicken! I, a chicken? Too bad I couldn't show him my value as a composer, but I could show myself that I was not a chicken! My long-avoided quest for performing at the Public Library welled up with such force that I turned and walked downtown to the Library and asked for the head librarian. The gray-haired, dignified lady appeared at the checkout counter.

After introducing myself I asked, "Would you be interested in letting my group give a concert here at the library?"

A friendly smile appeared on her face. "I'd be happy to have you here. What kind of a group is it and what kind of music do you play?"

In an instant I planned my group. "We play Baroque music. A singer, a flutist and myself, a harpsichordist."

She seemed very interested and told me to let her know whenever I had a definite date in mind. I thanked her and left.

Terrified by my own assertiveness, I suddenly was doubtful. Had I done the right thing? I felt I'd shown — Trueblood or myself — that I was able to produce music, if not in composition at least in performance, but my confidence had sustained a loss. I'd had the nerve to ask for a concert date without even having a group! I bit my lip and commanded myself: Call some active music friends and create a group. Rehearse and perform. I thumbed through the Union members' list, called a singer and a flutist and received not only positive responses but found out how desperate they were to perform.

Queen-like, super-blond, mezzo-soprano, Kay Duke, and charming black flutist, Tony Brazier, agreed to get together at my home. I called the group "The Palisades Renaissance Ensemble," and we rehearsed every week. I also added my best harpsichord student from Pepperdine, Jackie Hart, so we could play Couperin's beautiful *Musette de Taverni* on two harpsichords.

Four months later the four of us played at the library before a full house with standing room only. Toni Brazier, looking exotic in his tuxedo, opened with a flute sonata by Blaver, and I accompanied him on the harpsichord. Kay Duke, in a tight silk dress showing off her good figure, sang Elizabethan songs by Dowland, and Handel arias with harpsichord accompaniment. Jackie and I played *Musette de Taverni* on our two harpsichords. Everything went well, and our joy of playing resounded in the hearts of the audience; they responded with enthusiasm.

Guerdon Trueblood, who unknowingly had been instrumental in giving life to this concert, wasn't there. Instead, program-chairs of various organizations approached us to book our group for concerts for their clubs.

One offer came from conductor Joel White to play with his Palisades Symphony Orchestra, "I suggest Bach's C-major double with you and Jackie Hart."

The concert for two harpsichords with orchestra — my dream for years! I felt a joyous wave flooding over me. Joel set the date on the spot, and Jackie and I discussed the rehearsals.

Another outgrowth of the library concert was the offer for our Palisades Renaissance Ensemble to play the first concert at the recently opened Paul Getty Museum in Malibu. The director invited me to come over and choose the best room for the concert. Walking with her through all the elegant rooms with the famous pictures by Raphael, Titian, Tintoretto and others, I decided on the Italian Renaissance Gallery, and the director immediately set the date for the concert. I felt like a queen.

Thanks for all this, Guerdon Trueblood! Your rage had been transformed into a lot of musical activity!

Manfred liked our concert so much that he came up with new ideas. "I'll build you a synthesizer," he said enthusiastically. "You can use it for your music appreciation classes."

He kept his promise, assembled it on weekends and in a short time put a small, one-oscillator synthesizer in my multi-purpose studio. "Now you can show how sound can be produced electronically."

Thoroughly excited, I began to learn how to use it.

Just a few days later I complained about the inefficiency of piano tuners who weren't up to my standards. "If the tones are even a tiny bit off pitch it hurts my ears," I explained.

"That's enough," Manfred said. "I'll learn to do it myself. Tell me where's the nearest college that teaches piano tuning."

"Manfred, I can't believe it. Do you have the time to do it?"

"Yes. There's a delay in our ocean mining project, and I don't have to travel at the moment. The Hughes Glomar Explorer had to be widened and now it can't go through the Panama Canal. She has to go around the tip of South America.

That takes a lot longer, and that gives me some free time. At last I have the time to do what I want." And so Manfred took an evening course in "Piano Tuning and Repairing" at nearby Santa Monica College where I was teaching.

"He's a Renaissance man," my harpsichord friend Susanne said. "Very knowledgeable in more than one field."

And he loved it! His musicality and his engineering background combined to form new skills which both of us could enjoy.

He also had fewer working hours at the office and was home more often. Now we did things together, laughed a lot and found enough opportunities to make love — in the backyard, under the pine trees in the San Gabriel Mountains, even on the San Andreas Fault, playing a trick on the earthquake demon. Manfred kept me on cloud nine and I hoped this would go on forever.

But nothing is permanent.

The Great Dismemberment

Manfred's Diary. Redwood City, May 9, 1974

Finally the day has come to travel to Redwood City to train for the recovery of the sunken submarine.

The HMB-1, the Hughes Mining Barge, whose launching I witnessed in San Diego in January 1972, had been towed to a facility in Redwood City, just south of San Francisco. In utmost secrecy the barge was being outfitted with a gigantic steel claw that would grab and lift the sunken submarine into the so-called Moon Pool, the belly of the rescue vessel Hughes Glomar Explorer.

I told you, Eve, I was flying to San Francisco where the testing of the nodule-collecting device would begin. This necessary lie was not too far from the truth, if one substituted "nodules" for "the sub."

Our group of twenty engineers left San Francisco Airport and drove to the facility in Redwood City. Even from far away we could see the huge, black-painted barge. It dwarfed all the nearby industrial structures. Passing through a tight security check, we were led to a large metal building next to HMB-1, where the secret training sessions for our future work on the Glomar Explorer would take place.

Access to the facility was heavily guarded to allow only briefed personnel into the fenced area. There was an A-crew, which consisted mainly of technicians who would lift the target and clean it. We engineers belonged to the B-crew, which would take apart the submarine and pack up the important parts for later analysis in government labs.

I looked up at the ten-story-high barge that stretched 350 feet from bow to stern. Its top was covered by a domed roof, whose several sections could be telescoped whenever a crane had to put parts in for the assemblage of the claw.

An agent led us into the barge, where the claw was in an advanced stage of construction. It was simply overwhelming to see this spider-like monster with its heavy steel legs moved by hydraulic force — a steel tarantula, loaded with the newest technology. Throughout its interior were sets of sensing devices, TV cameras and strobe lights, which would be used to observe how the claw was grabbing the submarine.

After that we were guided through digital-lock-controlled doors into the metal building where the training took place. With the help of experts in scientific and engineering fields The Customer had carefully prepared our training schedule. In a large classroom, complete with blackboard and chalk, we sat on chairs with folding desks.

Engineer John Hicks, in charge of the three-mile-long pipe, sat next to me. "Back to the classroom. Have you ever thought we'd go to school again at our age?"

"I'm ready for any surprise," I said.

One instructor whom we called Blackjack, because his hair, beard and outfit were black, told us what we would probably find in the Moon Pool of the Glomar Explorer. He drafted sketches of the submarine, its structure consisting of the cylindrical pressure hull and the outer hull. He showed us where fuel and diving tanks were located, where the conning tower, the nuclear missiles and torpedo tubes would be found. For me as a naval architect and former U-boat man the lecture was extremely interesting.

At one point Blackjack asked me, "Manfred, what can you add about German submarines? After WW II they'd become part of the Soviets' war booty. I understand the Russian designers copied them."

"You're right — the Soviets used the German type XXI submarine as a model for their postwar subs," I replied. "The Soviet G-class is one of them."

"You'll be a big help whenever we are inside it," Blackjack said.

Two hours later the "linguist" appeared, a short and stocky man with a heavy Russian accent. You talk about experts — The Customer got them. He gave us lessons in the Russian language.

"Above all," he said, "You have to learn the Cyrillic alphabet so you can recognize printed signs and warnings on parts of the submarine." He paused to let this sink in. "During the mission two or more linguists will be on board the Glomar

Explorer to translate on the spot. For instance, should you see the Russian words for danger, radioactive, secret or classified, you must call the linguist-on-duty and let him decide what the words mean."

All in all, we learned the Russian spelling of more than twenty words. Some of them — in phoneticized version:

Attention, watch out!	Vnimanie!
Caution	Ostorozhno!
Danger!	Opasno!
Nuclear materials	Yadernye materaly
Radioactive	Radioaktivno!
Radioactive hazard	Radiatsionnaya opasnost!
Secret, classified	Sekretny
Top secret	Sovershenno sekretno

At noon we left the fenced area to buy lunch from a vending truck. The afternoon was filled with a lecture on radioactivity, nuclear weapons, missiles and torpedoes. The instructor, Ralph Thorson, tall, slender and gray-haired, was a nuclear scientist with years of experience in radioactive material and decontamination procedures. He told us that the Soviet submarine would probably be radioactive. Although I had known this for years I now asked myself if I should go on this mission. I didn't want to be killed by radiation. But the lure of the unusual task before us swept away all my reservations.

"There are three different kinds," Ralph said. "Alpha, beta and gamma radiation. The latter is the most dangerous. But I assure you, before the sub is lifted into the Glomar Explorer it will be thoroughly investigated for the kind of radiation present. Should gamma radiation be found the sub will be immediately returned to the sea floor. Work on a wreck, infested with gamma radiation, will be out of the question. The probability of finding beta radiation is considered minimal. However, we assume we'll encounter alpha radiation. The best protection against that is a "space suit" which will cover you completely. There's sufficient experience with contaminated areas from nuclear accidents to show that they can be cleaned up without any danger to personnel."

I thought, since so many agents and nuclear experts are involved in the dissection of the submarine they will know how to protect themselves. And so I could trust their expertise and leave the rest up to fate.

The next day we entered a hall where a mock submarine was erected. We had to practice getting adequately dressed for protection against radiation. Over our own underwear we pulled on a set of thick and heavy long johns and a long-sleeved top. I struggled my way into a yellow suit with a reflective aluminum-type exterior, then into rubber galoshes, pulled on surgical gloves and over them ordinary work gloves. All parts were taped together to seal against air leaks. Lastly came a hard hat, an oxygen mask, complete with an oxygen pack on our back, and a hood with built-in earphones and a microphone. Once outfitted, we walked and moved as if we were working. I felt transported back to WW II in the German Navy when I was working under water as a diver, completely on my own, peeking through the small glass pane, which was opaque from the steam of my body, just as it was now.

Still muffled, we walked through a narrow passage to learn not to damage our "space suit" or to get caught by the oxygen pack on our back. Trying to hold my breath to minimize the fogging, I learned how to carry objects around without damaging my suit. My task was to photograph an E-motor at its location, tag a number on it and carry it to the registrar who would write down the number and a short description of the item. Then I had to pack it into two plastic bags and attach a duplicate of the tag on the outside of the bag so it could be shipped to laboratories for investigation.

At the same time Manfred came back from San Francisco, Nixon fell. "Good riddance!" Manfred said as we enjoyed one of our rare lunches together. Lately, they had become more and more scarce.

"I once read what Adlai Stevenson said about Nixon," Manfred said. "He was the kind of politician who would cut down a redwood tree and then mount the stump to make a speech for conservation."

"His speeches are over. Ford will be president now," I said and bit into my egg sandwich.

"Forget politics. How's the family? How's Lilo?"

"Lilo and family have moved to Cupertino, south of San Francisco. Jay got his Bachelor's and his first job at Sears & Roebuck in Cupertino. Imagine, Lilo has learned belly-dancing at a college and teaches it when the instructor can't make it."

"Our multi-talented daughter! She got it all from you," he said.

"No! I can't do very much besides music and writing."

He picked up another sandwich. "Don't belittle yourself. Where are you going to teach in the fall?"

"I haven't told you yet. Imagine, at UCLA Extension!"

"Wow! How did you get that job?"

"Four years ago I had lunch with Dr. Haas, the dean of the extension program. Since my subbing at West L.A. College is over, I called Haas, and he scheduled me to teach keyboard classes."

"Congrats!"

I felt bathed in luck.

Manfred's Diary. May 30, 1974

Today our office watched a movie: The true story of an unusual rendezvous. The famous barge HMB-1 — Hughes Mining Barge — had accomplished a great job again. It was a high class ocean encounter that occurred near a semi-deserted cove of Catalina Island.

The barge with its precious cargo, the steel claw, had been towed from Redwood City to Catalina Island, the playground for the venturesome people of southern California. Guards stood on the beach, ready to shoo away would-be observers, and divers swam around, looking for underwater spies. Both groups operated film cameras, so government officials and employees of Global Marine could watch the documentary.

Soon the giant Hughes Glomar Explorer from Long Beach arrived at the scene. Now was the time for the barge with its precious claw to begin the maneuver. It submerged. Then the huge Explorer with its sophisticated computers moved into precise position over the barge, hovering motionless in the water.

The secret undersea transfer began. The Explorer gradually filled its belly, the Moon Pool, with water. Then the Moon Pool gates opened by sliding along the entire underside of the ship.

At the same time the submerged barge telescoped its dome, exposing the claw. Two docking legs moved from the Explorer down toward the claw to pick it up, like chopsticks grabbing a shrimp on a plate, and pulled the claw up into the Moon Pool.

The Explorer closed its docking gates and sailed, the precious claw in its belly, home to Long Beach. The barge rose to the surface and was towed back to Redwood City.

Mission accomplished.

Manfred came home for lunch — worth noting on my calendar. We sat on the terrace, watched the leaves of the walnut tree float in the wind and ate sandwiches and fruits.

This luncheon turned out to be a prelude to Manfred's new assignment.

"I'm going to Hawaii again," he said.

I swallowed my last bite. "Again for months?"

"No. Just for three weeks."

No time for me to follow him, I couldn't leave my new assignments. I sighed and tried a smile. "Greetings to all my friends. Diamond Head, the rainbows, the flowers and my human friends."

"I'll blow them one big kiss," Manfred promised.

On my first evening alone the telephone rang, as I watched the news. It was Irmie, calling from San Diego, sobbing and stammering.

"Mom, I have to tell you something." Sobs. "Remember John?" The image of the nice young man rose in me. "We had an argument last night. I said I didn't want him around anymore. I went to bed. At five in the morning I got a phone call from the police. They found him collapsed on the street. They took him to the hospital." More sobs.

"Try to calm down, Irmie. Take your time."

"The policeman said John swallowed malathion to kill himself."

"Oh my God, Irmie!" How could he burden Irmie with guilt for having caused his attempted suicide!

"This morning I went to see him in the hospital," Irmie

continued. "He was awake but couldn't talk very much, because he burned his throat with the malathion. A psychiatrist came to see him too. He took me aside and explained that he'd asked John why he attempted suicide. John said, 'Nobody loves me.'" She cried again.

"Oh Irmie!" was all I managed to say. The burden of guilt might stay with her for a long time.

"You know, Mom, John was an orphan. As a child he was sent from one foster family to another."

"Poor John. How's he now?"

"Okay. He has to stay in the hospital for a few more days. I'll go see him everyday." Sobs. "Mom, it's all my fault!"

"No, Irmie, it's not your fault. You must not blame yourself. It's the fault of all the cold people in his childhood. Not yours!"

I hoped she would accept my assurance. As we kept talking she seemed to calm down.

"When you visit John again, give him my love. But remember, don't blame yourself!"

"I'll try. Thanks, Mom."

I hung up and sank into an armchair. *My gentle baby involved in a friend's suicide attempt! Of course, I don't mean she's a baby, but she is my youngest, well, my baby forever. Stop this nonsense!* I scolded myself. *She's a young woman whose boyfriend tried to make her miserable by a dramatic act of self-destruction. His likeable personality notwithstanding, it's he who has turned to violence to force her into loving him. His fault, not hers. I hope she's strong enough to cope with the situation. A good opportunity to grow, a psychologist would say.* Oh, where was Manfred when I needed him?

Manfred's Diary. September 7, 1974

At long last the day has come for me to fly to Hawaii to board the Hughes Glomar Explorer to dissect the submarine. About 170 men are involved in the "rescue" operation: the A-crew to lift the sub into the Hughes Glomar Explorer, and the B-crew to dissect it. I was part of the B-crew, but I wished I also belonged to the A-crew so I could experience every little bit of the procedure.

Before we flew to Hawaii we were brought up to date on the

situation by Blackjack, whom we all knew from the Redwood City training.

"The satellite-beam navigation system led the ship to the exact spot in the ocean above the submarine," he said. "The implosion and the tremendous water pressure have ripped the sub apart. During the lifting process a part of the sub slipped off the claw and fell back to the sea floor. However, the bow section has been lifted into the ship by the A-crew." He paused for a second. "During the operation Soviet trawlers were constantly around, observing and filming the A-crew's every movement."

While our chartered plane was flying us to Hawaii the Explorer was sailing to Lahaina, Maui, for the crew-exchange. I could hardly wait to be in the action.

We landed at Maui's airport, Kaluhui, and we were then bussed to Lahaina, where the Explorer had anchored a mile from shore. Hundreds of curious people stood on the quay, staring at the huge 'Howard Hughes ocean mining vessel,' which looked strange because of the tall, pyramid-like derrick and the two tower-like docking legs on each side, all three about twenty-five stories high. The unusual silhouette of the ship caused fascination but also anger. THE MAUI NEWS, which I read later, described us this way:

"...the tight-lipped crew with serious, non-expressive faces looked like a band of CIA agents headed for exile."

Did the Soviets still believe in our cover story? The ship had been in the North Pacific for its first "ocean mining test." Surely, the oceanographers in Moscow must know that only uneconomical manganese nodules could be found in that area. They must think, why does the ship sail to that location in the north for a mining test? Why don't they make their first test in shallower waters? Would they put two and two together — the loss of one of their submarines and the "test" at an obviously awkward location? I couldn't help worrying.

Meanwhile, motorboats moved us to the ship. The closer we came the more impressive the 618-foot Explorer became.

On deck we met the departing A-crew. They looked exhausted, and no wonder. The twelve-hour shifts every day took a heavy toll on them.

"Did you encounter dead bodies?" I asked one man.

"Yeah, about six of them."

"What do you mean, about six ?"

"They were in pieces. We put the parts together until we thought we could make out six bodies. We put them in bags and then in the freezer."

"Is the sub radiating?"

"Some alpha. Supposed to be safe."

He and the others were called to the motorboats, which took them to Lahaina, from where they would be flown in a charter plane to the mainland.

We received our sleeping assignments — twenty-five double bunks for fifty people in a big bunk room — and then entered the interior.

Impatient to finally see the Soviet sub, I walked through a steel door that led to a narrow catwalk at the fifty-foot level along the walls. From here I looked down at the rectangular 200-by-75-foot Moon Pool. And there it was: In that huge cavern lay a part of the retrieved Soviet sub. The gray lump was so crumpled that I wasn't sure it wasn't the residue of a crushed stock car. Tomorrow I'd enter the hellish cage.

Now I stared at the immobile monster and the some twenty vans around the walls. The huge claw with its steel arms, which had done the retrieving job, hung from the ceiling like a gigantic frozen crab. Mud and dirt covered the Moon Pool's entire floor. An almost unbearable stink of decomposing organic matter in the mud filled the air.

"I hope we don't have to haul that mud away," I said to John Hicks, who was staring down too.

"We'll suffocate before that," he replied.

"I need fresh air now," I said and went outside.

On deck, which was densely crowded with equipment, I took deep breaths. I looked at the tall derrick superstructure that had supported the 320 lift-pipe sections, the claw and part of the submarine, everything weighing several thousand tons. When the ship rolled, pitched and heaved in the swell this derrick would stand motionless. Besides that it could handle a 17,000-foot tapered string of gun-barrel steel pipe with the huge claw on it — a hell of a good job of engineering. The 36,000-ton Explorer in any case was the epitome of high marine technology. To everyone's regret John Graham, the ship's designer, had died of lung cancer two weeks ago without ever learning of his vessel's success.

From the slight vibrations I gathered that the ship was moving away from Maui. Soon the island would sink below the horizon. I turned around and saw a stranger walking in my direction. He wore a black beard, eye glasses and a name tag "Stan" on his jacket. "Hi, Manfred," he said.

I recognized him by his voice — it was Harry from my office, the agent who, disguised as a priest, had "guarded" me during my surgery. Only he'd been red-haired and without a beard then.

"What's with your masquerade?" I asked.

"Soviet satellites can read the headlines of a newspaper in your hands," he replied. "They shouldn't see me on board this ship." He touched his black beard. "This way I'm just another man." His laugh-wrinkles deepened as he smiled.

I would have loved to talk to him more, but the time for the planning meeting had come. I entered the ship and walked through one of the control rooms. Fascinated, I stopped for a minute, surveying the many computers and assorted screens lining the walls on all sides. Four agents manned the control consoles to send electronic commands, monitoring the activity of each piece of equipment. This ship was definitely the most sophisticated and innovative vessel ever built.

At the meeting a well-known face greeted us, Blackjack. He designated each of us for various jobs.

"Manfred, you have to inspect the sub and list all the components you can identify as those the Soviets copied from German submarines," he said. "Particularly study the welding seams and compare them with German welding techniques."

He again told us about the existing radiation we'd encounter in the Moon Pool and in the submarine, and reminded us how to keep safe.

"Now listen," he said. "At this point, if anyone of you decides not to take the risk of going down into the Moon Pool, which is alpha-radiating, we accept the decision and will think nothing about it."

We took a vote. "We're going," we all said.

We suited up in the heavy radiation outfits. Two layers of underwear, then the thin, almost paper-like radiation suit, regular clothes, heavy denims and steel-toed boots. We felt like astronauts as we were helped on with the surgical gloves and elastic rubber boots, everything taped airtight, then a helmet, a backpack and a white hood. They blew smoke over us to test for leaks and then declared us ready to perform our duties.

Down in the Moon Pool, on a small wooden staircase, we descended into the body of the sub. Clumsily sliding in the mud, I was excited to finally rummage through the Soviet submarine. Our suits filtered out most of the humming of the ventilators and other machines so that they seemed muffled to our ears.

I looked at the welding seams of the outer hull and found them much more uneven than the same work done by the Germans. The steel plates had already rusted to an ugly brownish color since the air had begun to oxidize them after six years in an oxygen-poor environment at 16,500 feet of water. The insides had collapsed like an accordion into the fore part of the hull. Bunks where the men had slept were now about one and a half feet long.

Before I removed any part for later inspection, I photographed it to show its location in the submarine. I cleaned mud from it, attached tags with numbers and brief descriptions, put it in a plastic bag, closed the bag tightly and put it in a second bag. Again sliding in the mud, I carried the part to the registration table, where it was recorded and packed in drums for later crating.

For hours I was busy preparing materials from the sub until we finally were called to come upstairs and to undress. Tapes and helmet off, we threw the radiation suits into a big drum. Scientists tested us with Geiger counters for traces of radiation on our bodies and sent us to the shower room. Fortunately, I was free of any radiation traces. Unfortunately two of our men had to scrub themselves until they were declared to be "clean."

Our shifts in the Moon Pool stretched over long hours and we were exhausted from the cumbersome work in the suits. We looked forward to strong coffee and a good meal. Reading the menu in the mess, I thought we were on a cruise ship with huge food selections.

"Do we really need that much food?" I asked John Hicks.

"Well, we have to work twelve hours every day, including the weekends," he replied.

After the twelve working hours we went to our bunks and slept like rocks.

Next day back to work in the Moon Pool again, I watched a bulldozer next to the submarine shovel sand and mud into steel drums. These would then be lifted and thrown overboard. Ironically there were small manganese nodules in the dirt; but they were of no use to us, being of poor economic value and in addition radioactive. So they were tossed overboard.

I helped Blackjack decide which sections of the pressure hull the welders should cut out for later analysis in metallurgical labs, in order to learn about the quality of steel the Soviets used in more than 400 submarines built since WW II. The remaining steel pieces were dumped overboard to make room in the Moon Pool.

In the sub, we found the bunks covered with only a very thin layer of horse hair, and no signs of a canteen to buy candies or chocolate bars.

New items were discovered — food cans. Some contained potatoes in excellent condition after lying in the nearly freezing water for six years. Potatoes, potatoes and more potatoes; once in a while red beets, cucumbers, tomatoes and rice. Meat was found only in the form of pig's feet with fat and bones, or pork bellies with fat and skin. Quite a repetitive menu for a three-month-long mission far away from home.

For entertainment they had movies of the Bolshoi Ballet, one sci-fi with the action in very slow motion and a faster one of a soccer game. Audio tapes, with patriotic speeches urging them to make their best effort for Rodina, Mother Russia, on the cruise along the enemy's coast, were probably the source of the young sailors' energy and enthusiasm. The superior value of the communist philosophy over the "already collapsing decadent capitalistic concept of the Western World" would convince the submariners that their sacrifice was not in vain and should be accepted day after day of their patrol.

Surprise: Instead of the expected pictures of Lenin or Stalin we discovered girly pictures and nudies — proof that the crew members were human. Otherwise life on a Soviet submarine must have been very monotonous and stressful without any comfortable environment or sufficient space for enduring a three-month-long patrol; surely they felt like the German U-boat personnel during WW II, locked up in a tight underwater fighting machine for a long time.

I recalled that the Soviet Navy was lacking any tradition or successes for their naval forces in the 20th century. Neither in the Pacific nor in the Atlantic had they had any victories in WW II. The only reported success came from two submarines in the Baltic Sea, where they sank three refugee ships and drowned 20,000 women and children in the icy sea water. One submarine commander was decorated for it, the other reprimanded for heavy drinking.

"Manfred," Blackjack's voice over the intercom pulled me from my pondering. "We need you in the chemistry van."

Carefully I slid over to the van with the document-recording system. A flood of books and papers had been discovered, single sheets, notebooks, instruction manuals and reference books. A whole library had been discovered in the submarine and carried into the chemistry van.

Now I stood, in the uncomfortable radiation suit, before the van's large wash basin, bathing the sticking sheets in a special liquid, adding more and more liquid to allow penetration between the different pages. With ultra-sound motion added, the pages separated and could easily be turned. A camera was installed above the sink, focused on the text of the page I shot by pressing a foot pedal. As soon as the page was recorded, I picked it up with a pincer and put it in a numbered and coded bag.

One of the items was a booklet with handwriting. I picked up the telephone and called Eugene, the linguist-on-call, to come in and determine the nature of the booklet.

Eugene glanced over the pages. "Hey!" he called out. "A sailor describes in detail the activities of an earlier mission, ending with this patrol. That's a real treasure! Be extra careful with these pages, Manfred."

So, I turned the pages with special care, shooting and recording them. Suddenly the ink was barely decipherable. The sailor must have changed his pen. I called the recording expert, who added a different liquid and turned the ultraviolet light on. Immediately the text became legible. My work began to be automatic, step by step, page by page, one journal after the other, recording, listing and packing them.

One book was big and heavy, like a reference or instruction book. I read the Russian words for nuclear and torpedo. I called in Eugene again.

"Manfred!" he shouted. "You've hit the jackpot! A book

about torpedoes! We need every page of it."

Apparently the book told how to handle a torpedo when away from port. Eugene called Blackjack in, and, as I heard through mikes and receivers, both were delirious with joy. I understood the importance of this treasure; it provided our Navy with knowledge about Soviet torpedo functions and the impact a nuclear torpedo would have on an aircraft carrier when shot from a long distance. The journal was considered so important a helicopter appeared to take the precious book to a plane that whisked it off to Washington.

One day when no ships were visible nearby or on the horizon and the Soviet satellite had passed the area, the six or so "assembled" Russian sailors were buried with proper respects. Their remains were taken out of the freezer, each plastic bag draped with a Soviet flag and put in a steel box. Before being video-taped the bizarre ceremony was rehearsed several times, accompanied by the taped Soviet anthem. The tune, new to me, was very pleasant. Only when the performance was declared to be perfect was it videotaped, complete with sound. Then a crane hooked onto the metal box, lifted it up, swung it over the side and then lowered it into the ocean. It sank to the sea floor where the bodies would never be disturbed again.

After fourteen days the Moon Pool was almost empty. Workers were busy washing and scrubbing its deck clean of all mud and radioactive debris, pumping it overboard. The air was constantly sucked through special filters to prevent any contaminated air from leaving the ship when in port. The Explorer could now sail back to Lahaina and look her best. She left us there and continued to her home port in Long Beach, while we flew back to Los Angeles.

After three weeks on "his" ship Manfred came home and promised he'd stay in town for a while. Thank God! I sighed. We could do things together again.

The mailman arrived, and Manfred brought in the letters.

"What's in the big envelope?" I asked. I opened it. "It's from Golly." My parents' former sales manager in Danzig and my dear friend, who now lived in East Berlin, was sending me sheet music of songs from East Germany. I took it to the piano and began to play one song after the other. They were all new to me. Also the last one, the Russian anthem. I'd hardly begun to play it, when Manfred whistled along. I turned around. "How do you know the Russian anthem?"

He kept reading a letter. "Oh, I must have heard it once," he said nonchalantly.

I knew about his great musical memory, which surpassed mine. "It's new to me," I said. "But it's a pleasant tune."

"Yup," he said.

The Great Revelation

Today, the second day of the new year, 1975, I received another letter from my Danzig friend, Golly.

> *The Poles have rebuilt Danzig! Almost all the historical buildings and whatever else was destroyed are reconstructed. Pictures are in newspapers and magazines. The Polish architects are doing it brick by brick, and it all looks like it was before. Go there and see it!*

With a jolt, Halina came to mind, the Polish woman at the Pennsylvania shipyard's luncheon and her tale about Danzig's resurrection. In her letter Golly used the same words Halina had spoken, "Go there and see it." This was the second call back to Danzig — no matter its new name Gdansk. My hometown was calling! I felt unrestricted desire wash over me. *How much longer shall I stay away? I've been away for thirty years, isn't it time to go back? What will Manfred say? Will he understand my nostalgia?*

We were remodeling the house, and he was busy, supervising his two assistants. I went to look for him to tell him, to get some support, hoping for his usual optimism. He was in the living room, trying to rip off a wooden wall paneling.

"I want to put an electrical outlet in here," he said. "You came just in time. Pull on this end. I'll pull on the other."

With all our might we ripped off the panel — and stared with horror at dozens of panicked termites. They all disappeared into the ground, leaving an intricate, almost artistic pattern of roads carved in the wall, the dust softly sailing down behind the insects.

"Dammit!" Manfred shouted. "That's all we need. I've got to

call an exterminator."

The termite man came the next day and said these were rare ground termites and he could easily take care of them. He drilled forty-eight holes in the floor, sprayed poison in, plugged the holes and declared the area "clean."

When the exterminator had left and Manfred had put back the wood paneling he said, "Before the sun sets, let's go for a walk on the beach."

"Now? It's dinner time. I'm cooking your favorite dish: Spaghetti."

"Hold it. I want to tell you something no one else should hear."

Bursting with curiosity, I put off my desired trip to Danzig and followed him to the ocean. We took off our shoes, left them on the dry sand and walked where the cold waves came in, washing over our feet.

"I must tell you something before you read it in the newspaper," he began.

Wild assumptions flooded my head. A crime at his office? Another money-cut-off by the government?

"I haven't been mining the ocean for manganese nodules," he said. "I helped raise a sunken Russian submarine in secrecy."

I was shocked to my bones. Speechless, I followed his explanations, and many doubts and questions that I'd had over the years and ignored, now found an answer. The inconsistencies when he told the neighbor about the good weather in New York, while it had been raining there for days; or his whistling when I played the Russian anthem — all this was now explained.

"After all these years of secrecy how would this come out now?" I asked.

"During a burglary of the Howard Hughes offices a note to Hughes disappeared, which mentioned the plan to raise the sub. Journalists dug for more info on the deal. Meanwhile, the government pleaded with the newspapers not to run the story in the paper. It now looks as if that begging won't help and the story will be in the news."

A blood-red sun hung low above the rolling hills. The waves were getting stronger and already reached my calves; sometimes they were louder than Manfred's voice. I thought high-tide was approaching and, like the spy story, would soon flood over us.

"I'm sorry that I had to lie to you all the time, but we all stated in writing that we wouldn't talk to anyone about it."

"I understand that," I said, although I was unable to grasp the meaning of the whole affair. "Now what?"

"We have to wait. But don't talk to anybody about it while it's basically still a secret. It may not stay one for very long." He stopped, turned to me and took me in his arms. "Forgive me for hiding and lying, Little Bear."

I managed a smile. "No problem with that. But what will happen if it blows?"

"Life will go on."

The sun had disappeared behind the hills, leaving fiery cloud strips on the horizon. Immediately, the air cooled. We continued to stroll but soon had to get away from the rising tides. We rescued our shoes, left the beach and walked home through the canyon.

"I know it will take me a while to absorb your revelations," I said. "But I'm happy for you that you had this adventure."

Just four days later our neighbor Guerdon came over. Without saying a word he handed us the morning edition of *The Los Angeles Times,* opening it to the front page.

U.S. RECOVERS PART OF SOVIET SUBMARINE

"So, it wasn't ocean mining, huh?" Guerdon asked.

Alarmed but ready to cooperate, I shrugged and said, "Baloney."

Guerdon looked at Manfred, who said nothing and showed no feelings. He now stood before his friends and neighbors as a liar. Guerdon left with a grin.

Only later I read the whole article which described the adventure. "Is all this true, Manfred?" I asked in disbelief at the operation's enormity.

"Yes."

"A James Bond, a Jules Verne cloak-and-dagger thriller?"

"Absolutely. Only it was true."

Suddenly I saw Manfred in a new light. He, always so correct and dependable, had been a spy! For a moment the thought made me shudder, yet immediately I realized that he had been chosen to create a cover story around this spy project, to betray the Soviets, to be a principal figure in this all-important game — he was a star! My Manfred, my multi-talented husband had shown his versatility again. Erect, handsome and sun-tanned, he was my hero, my lover, my one-and-only, and I'd be grateful for him forever.

I had one big question. "How could all this happen without anybody's suspicion?"

"I'll show you." He got up and went outside to his car. When he came back he handed me a glossy, blue-covered notebook. "My diary. I wrote every little bit down for you for the time when the adventure would be over. It's over now. Read it. There are a hundred times more details than you'll ever read anywhere else."

Fascinated, I thumbed through the 80-plus hand-written pages, which contained the spy story in which my husband played a major role.

It was Saturday, there were no piano lessons, and reading Manfred's diary would be the treat of the day. I slid open the wide glass doors to the backyard, marveling at Manfred's work of the last weeks: the ready-made lawn, created within minutes by rolling out sod, thus outwitting nature; oleander shrubs, not in bloom yet, covering the garden walls; birds-of-paradise, rose bushes and several citrus trees promised an early blooming — a beautiful background for reading Manfred's diary. I took a blanket out, placed it under a shady spot, laid down flat on my stomach and began to read.

A spy story! Incredible years Manfred had experienced without letting me know even a tiny part of it. Stirred up, I felt many contradicting emotions fight in me: Excitement about his experience, resentment because of his silence and his hoodwinking me for years, pride in his star position in the spy game.

When the midday sun slowly heated me up I rose, looking for some shade. In vain I searched for an adequate shady spot, picked up the blanket and went into the house. The smell of paint and woodwork lingered from the restoration work. Sounds of sawing and hammering came from different directions.

Looking for Manfred, I found him in the studio-cum-bedroom, hanging up the new curtains. There was the star of the thriller I had been reading for the last hours! He must have noticed my entrance, because without looking up, he asked, "How's your reading coming along?"

"It's an incredible story. I almost finished it except for the last four pages. It got too warm outside."

He pointed to the chair near the baby grand. "Sit over there and keep reading."

"I prefer lying on my stomach as before." I laid down on the new thick, beige wall-to-wall carpet and finished the last pages. I looked up from the diary. "Wow!"

He tried out his latest work, opening and closing the curtains. "Any questions?"

"Lots!"

"Let's get out of here. The story may be out, but not the details. And I don't want any big-ears listening."

I got up from the carpet. "Where can we go?"

"How about that Self-Realization Park? It's nice and cool there. Let me give our handymen some new jobs."

A few minutes later we climbed into his Toyota, drove a mile west on Sunset Boulevard and parked before the Self-Realization Center.

Striding through the square wooden gate always gave me the feeling of entering a sanctuary. Hindus had created these peaceful surroundings, dedicating them to every human looking for beauty and tranquility. It presented the closest place to Buddhism possible. No wonder the Buddha, born into Hinduism, had had a solid foundation to develop his message of compassion and peace.

Today, as always, the Park was for all of us a place to relax and enjoy. The quiet lake was enhanced by two swans, which nobly glided over the water, carefully avoiding the netting of the water-lilies. A path looped around the lake, intersected by a white chapel in the form of a windmill and the Golden Lotus Archway. It ran along low slopes, trees and bushes, engulfing the walker in total nature — shade and half-light, bird-song and fragrance.

We were walking slowly on the path, a dome of a variety of trees above us. "We are the only humans here," I said. "How wonderful."

"That's what I wanted, nobody eavesdropping."

"Wouldn't you call this a 'safe house'? Or a 'safe lake'? It doesn't even have to be de-bugged."

"You are learning fast."

I placed myself before him, looking in his eyes. "How did you feel in this secrecy all those five years?"

Forced to stop and confess, he followed the swans with his eyes. After a while he answered, "I had the time of my life. It definitely was a masterpiece of espionage."

"It didn't bother you to be a spy?" I urged.

He took my arm and made me walk again. "I was never a spy. Not even hired by the government. The government had hired Global Marine, and Global Marine had hired me and all the other engineers. The job was the rescue of a sunken ship. That international relations were involved was the framework of the job."

"I see your point," I said, relieved. "What were the highlights of your job?"

"Undoubtedly the discovery of the Soviet sailor's notebook, when I worked on separating the sticking pages with chemicals and ultrasound and ultraviolet light, and it turned out to be a jackpot — an instruction book on how to use Russian torpedoes." He pondered for a moment. "Another highlight was the Soviet sailors' burial at sea with English and Russian ceremonies and the Russian anthem."

I grinned. "You whistled it while I played it."

He stopped abruptly, laughed and took me in his arms. "Of course! But I couldn't tell you where I'd heard it."

We kissed and then continued walking arm-in-arm.

"It was just a hell of an operation!" he said, the excitement vibrating in his voice.

"Were you ever scared doing whatever you were doing?"

"Yes," he answered in a low voice. He stopped for a

moment, looked around — as if checking for safety. "In Honolulu, during the camouflage drive with the underwater pictures of the sub, I was really scared. I thought I could be shot any moment." A rock lay in the middle of the path; he gave it a kick so it fell in the lake, creating concentric rings around the plunge and causing the swans to flee to the opposite side of the lake. Even the bird-song stopped.

"Also one time on the Glomar Explorer," Manfred continued, "when a Soviet trawler appeared and moved closer and closer to us, obviously photographing us with large telephoto lenses. We expected them to open fire. We were trained to surrender and let them take us prisoners. That idea was no fun." He sighed. "Then one day a Soviet helicopter flew so close to our ship that we feared it would land on our heliport. We quickly put several oil barrels on the platform to prevent the chopper from landing."

We had come half-way around the lake and passed through the Golden Lotus Archway. There was a bench, and we sat down. Bird-song picked up again.

"How many people were involved in the adventure? And how could you guys keep all this so secret?" I asked.

"About 4,000 people were involved. Spy organizations know how to keep things secret. Remember the man who attended my surgery, disguised as a priest? That's one of thousands of tricks."

"But the story did come out."

"Only slowly. *The Los Angeles Times* was printing the story. The government learned about it; a representative flew to L.A. and tried to persuade *The Times* not to run the story. So the paper buried it on page 18, which few people read. Then *The New York Times* and *The Washington Post* announced that they'd publish it. The representative ran from one place to the other, begging to keep the story away from the public. At the end, journalist Jack Anderson broadcast it, and that was the end of the secrecy."

I couldn't believe it. "The government asked for secrecy and the media didn't obey?"

"That's democracy at work."

"Hats off to democracy!" I was deeply impressed. "The

whole thing must have cost a fortune. Do you know how much the government spent for the project?"

"Some say 450 million dollars, others say 500 million."

The sun had dipped into the ocean. All colors lost their luminosity and a cool breeze wafted through the trees. We got up and circled the rest of the lake.

"Have the Soviets reacted?" I asked.

"Not yet. And I don't think they ever will. It's an embarrassment to them and the best thing for them is to keep their mouths shut. And we'll say the affair was a failure. Period."

"But what are the consequences for you and our future?"

"Well, my job is over. And so is Global Marine's. Since the ocean is my field, I'll discuss new ocean projects with the company like going into ocean energy, OTEC, Ocean Thermal Energy Conversion."

"My God, what is that?"

"Generating electrical energy through the temperature differences between the warm surface water in the tropics and the cool water several thousand feet below."

In frustration I put my hands on my forehead. "Who brewed up this idea? You?"

"Oh, no, it's a consequence of the rise of oil prices. That led to the search for alternative energy resources."

Dusk fell on our surroundings. I could hardly see the path and clutched Manfred's arm. "Ocean energy research — it sounds like you're going to do futuristic work. You are always doing fascinating things."

We left the pleasant sanctuary through the square wooden gate and climbed into the Toyota.

On the way home I asked, "Do you think the spy story will become a scandal?"

"It might."

So, this wasn't the end of it. Yet before the nation could ponder the importance of the secret enterprise, it had to come to terms with the end of a tragedy which we had thought would never cease.

Danzig-Gdansk and Home to America

"Saigon has fallen!" Manfred announced one morning as he returned from his jogging, bringing in *The Los Angeles Times*. "The war is over. The North Vietnamese have won. We've lost it."

"Hardly because of military incapacity," I said with bitterness. "It's because the nation demanded an end. Unfortunately, it took the government a long time to accept this demand."

"Democracy at work," Manfred said.

"A super-slow process."

Taking off shorts and T-shirt, Manfred walked into the shower and turned the water on.

While I prepared the coffee, my thoughts flew to the far-away battlefields. The death toll must be in the millions. And what was the result of this latest slaughter? Millions of human beings dead, infinite pain for the survivors and a destroyed country. The horrors of WW II flooded in, depressing me. I sighed. Nobody ever learned from history.

Manfred appeared from the bedroom fully dressed.

"How glad I am you came back from the U-boat patrols," I said. "After all, eighty percent were lost."

"Yup," he answered. "It's all a matter of luck. I wonder how our soldiers coming home from Vietnam will be received. They'll arrive intact or crippled, but I'm afraid they'll face a hostile welcome."

I sighed. "Poor guys." Seeing him grab his briefcase, I asked, "What about breakfast?"

"We have a breakfast meeting today. There'll be more than we can eat." He kissed me and left the house. Through the window I saw him climb into his Toyota and leave. *How good to have him, and to have him here and to live in this wonderful town and to have this nice house. I'm grateful for all this.*

When he returned in the evening, we sat down in the living room, and news report after news report followed in rapid succession. He sat on a chair and I on the piano bench.

"Guess what," he said. "Global Marine is moving to Irvine. That's near Newport Beach." I sat in shock. He said he'd buy a house in Irvine and work there. Irvine was a planned community and supposed to be nice. "I've got more news. I'm flying to Canada next week." I felt as meek as a lamb and held onto the piano for support. "The United Nations are holding a Geothermal Symposium in Montreal. I'll be back right after Memorial Day."

On Memorial Day I was home alone. Home in Pacific Palisades. *Home? Where is home? Here in the Palisades or in Danzig? I wish I had never heard about Danzig's rebuilding. Then it would have lived in my memory as a rubbish-heap, a symbol of impermanence. But now Danzig, or, with its new appearance as Gdansk, is beckoning. Yet don't I belong to California now? Danzig has once been home, so has Chile and Hawaii, but now it's California.*

Or is it? I walked through the house, sat down at my desk, automatically picked up the phone and called Berlin, East Germany.

"Hulloh," Golly's warm voice said.

"Eva calling from California."

"Oh, Eva! What a nice surprise! How are you?"

I'm confused and homesick, I was tempted to say. Instead, I said, "I'm okay. Thanks for your letter. You were in Danzig. Tell me more about it."

"It was great. I cried when I walked through the streets. Almost everything looks like in the old days. I'm going there again. Do you want to come along?"

Baffled, caught between desire and reason, I hesitated. Then I heard myself say, "Yes." And suddenly I knew why I had picked up the phone.

"Get your passport in order," Golly said. "Get a Polish visa and pick me up in Berlin. We'll drive in my Opel."

I heard all this, registered it, but it seemed unreal, and my emotions were pushed into the background. "I'll do that. Just tell me when you want to leave."

"August 2."

The date had magical power, suddenly making the trip real and definite; it opened the door to the banned emotions, and excitement and travel fever flooded over me. "I can hardly wait," I said at last.

"What a treat, we're going together!"

We discussed details of the trip and then I said, "See you in Berlin."

After I hung up, I felt I was in another world. Only now I realized how much I had suppressed my nostalgia for Danzig. As soon as I heard about the resurrection of Danzig's beauty my old desire had driven me to take steps to go see it. And now I had even committed myself to travel there in a few weeks.

I thought of Manfred and what he would say. Would he want to come along? Would he be afraid to let me travel to a communist country that had been at war with us?

As usual, Manfred came home in time for dinner. While he was washing his hands I put the meal on the table: tossed green salad from the backyard garden, Orange Roughy from the Indian Ocean, broccoli and mashed potatoes from Safeway — a luxury dinner, compared to what most people ate all over the world.

"How was your day?" Manfred asked as he sat down and filled his plate.

"I called Golly in Hamburg. She's going to Danzig in August. She asked me to come along."

He didn't look up in surprise, just kept eating. "Are you going?"

This is going too fast! My long-held-back jump to the past is treated too casually! "Guess what I decided."

Now he looked at me, smiled. "You said yes, right?"

I nodded. "In August."

He got another helping. "By then I'll be back from Kuwait."

I stopped eating. "What are you going to do in Kuwait?"

"Get an ocean mining job for Global Marine."

I couldn't help but laugh. "You unabashed nomad!"

"Don't we have an enviable life?"

"Absolutely," I said.

Manfred, who had made the trip to Kuwait together with his vice president, returned from that little monarchy without the ocean mining job but with lots of interesting pictures of Muslim women and children, sitting in their black, floor-long chadors at the hot beach and wading into the ocean fully dressed.

"It was a real culture shock to see women so degraded," Manfred said. "On the other hand, there's no flirting, and, I was told, no raping."

We were sitting at the dinner table across from each other. Still looking at Manfred's pictures I asked myself, *will I experience a culture shock in Gdansk?*

He must have had an inkling of my feelings, because he asked: "What do you expect from your trip to Danzig?"

Thoroughly confused by all those places, Kuwait, Danzig and last, but not least, Irvine, I said, "Finding my home." I knew that sounded vague and romantic, but that was exactly how I felt.

He gently put his hand on mine. "You must prepare yourself for a culture shock, Little Bear. I don't know how much the Poles have rebuilt of Old Town, and if your house is still there, and how you'll feel in a Polish environment." I sighed. "Then where are you going to stay? With Golly's relatives?" I nodded. He took his hand from mine. "I'd love to see the rebuilt city also, but I can't do it now. The company is moving to Irvine soon, and the employees are already buying property there."

"It should be no big deal to buy a house in Irvine and sell this one here," I said. "But to leave the Palisades isn't easy for me. I like it a lot. This is the nicest town we've ever lived in."

Manfred got up. "Irvine is supposed to be nice too. Do you want to see it before you go to Danzig?"

I shook my head. "I'll do that when I'm back." This time I wanted to move to a new area without any strings to the past.

August came. I flew to Europe and landed in Berlin.

And Golly was there, big, radiant and affectionate. We hugged long; we were Danzig for each other, part of each other's past, survivors of the inferno of WW II, and Golly even a survivor of the Holocaust.

She and her spindly, friendly husband, Gerd, also from Danzig, were now well-established owners of an upholstery factory in Berlin. Their cozy home was a piece of Danzig's past, the walls decorated with shiny sconces — those brackets for candles to mirror the light in the polished brass. Even Danzig's coat-of-arms hung there, the golden crown above the two white crosses, on a red background. Seeing the large, framed pictures of Danzig's medieval towers and churches I felt my desire to go home intensify.

Gerd and Golly insisted I sleep off my jet lag, and I reluctantly obeyed them.

A day later Golly drove us in her Opel to our homeland. For six hours we rode through dense pine forests — one part of it belonging to East Germany, the other now to Poland. The border between them was not more than a hut, a turnpike and an uninterested frontier guard.

However, the ride seemed endless. I'd flown halfway around the world in the past twelve hours, and now we were crawling the last 300 miles at fifty miles per hour, the old Opel's maximum speed. My impatience grew from minute to minute. *I want to be in Danzig!* I silently screamed to the trees.

And as dusk fell, there it was: From a slight elevation of the road we saw the well-known skyline of my beloved hometown as it had been during my childhood and early adulthood, as if no war or bombing had happened.

"Oh my God," I said. "Never in my life had I expected to see it again after its total destruction."

"The Polish architects really have done wonders."

We reached a suburb of Gdansk, now called Wrzeszcz. Golly turned into a tree-lined street and at last stopped in front of a visibly old, one-story row house. "This is where my relatives live." We stepped out.

I hesitated. *I don't want to be in this suburb, I want to walk through Danzig! Be it day or night!* But here we had to stay overnight. I was Golly's guest, and I had to follow her.

With overwhelming friendliness we were welcomed by her relatives and spent the evening with half a dozen Polish-speaking people, drinking *Danziger Goldwasser* in a blue cloud of cigarette smoke — and drinking. During the muggy night I slept on a bumpy sofa, warding off flies and killing mosquitos. I yearned for California's cool nights and screened windows.

In the morning Golly drove me to the Mottlau River right at the St. Mary's Gate and dropped me there. "To walk through the streets the first time you may want to be alone. I'll pick you up right here at four o'clock. Okay with you?" I nodded.

Spellbound, I stood before the ancient, vaulted Gate that in the Middle Ages was one of the nine guarded entrances to the medieval castle-town. Now I walked through it and stepped onto the quay, high above the Mottlau River.

Six hundred years ago Danzig was the mighty headquarters of the Hanseatic League, which promoted commerce and made its citizens rich. They in turn laid the foundation-stones to the glorious medieval buildings. Leaning over the bulwark, I looked down on the river, which thirty years ago had carried me, baby Lilo and two million other refugees from the Soviets to freedom. I felt that day's panic return. Exactly here I had left Danzig in January 1945, and only weeks later it was ninety-five percent destroyed by Soviet bombers. With effort I managed to curb the panic and turned around to face the unprecedented resurrection of the almost 1000-year-old city.

I passed through the Gate again and walked down cobblestoned St. Mary's Street. Only a few people were around — a woman, carrying a small milk can, an old man with a cane, and a young, uniformed mail carrier walking up and down the steps to the ornate Renaissance terraces in front of every house. Amazing, the Polish architects had even rebuilt the wrought-iron balustrades and the stone reliefs with biblical scenes, which we once had to draw for art class.

Unwillingly my memory filled the street with panicking refugees. Here I'd run for my life and the life of my child. As soon as I shooed away these images, pictures of rubble and ruins imposed themselves on me. *Stop it!* I yelled in my mind. The horror pictures disappeared.

I kept walking toward St. Mary's Cathedral. From the year 1343 it had taken 150 years to erect this church. I smiled in memory of an essay I had to write in school about the cathedral and its art treasures inside. Later I had the privilege of playing on its big organ with the five manuals. People were afraid the powerful thunder of the lower organ tones would cause the cathedral's walls to collapse, but it had only made the organist's chest vibrate, until the Russian bombs put an end to organ sound and edifice.

Seeing again the well-known towers and narrow, winding streets with their old gaslamps, I caressed them in my mind, and at the same time I felt I was embracing my past.

I arrived at St. Katherine's church, where I was christened and confirmed. At a side door I read with awe the year of St. Katherine's founding: 1185. All my life I had heard its carillon, every quarter of the hour, with a half-hour "concert" at noon sounding over a wide neighborhood. I felt the tears running down my cheeks, took out some tissues and blew my nose. *Just go ahead! You're only two blocks from your house!* Now I walked faster than before to reach it.

With a jolt I was pulled from my daydreaming by the absence of one block of rowhouses which should have contained my parents' home. It and some neighboring buildings had not been rebuilt, and a lawn with tulip beds and two benches was there instead. *Where's my house? What did you do with it? I'm coming home and there is no home!*

I felt terribly alone. The two benches were empty, and I shuffled to one, slumped on it and let the tears come. I cried as I had when I learned about Danzig's destruction and my parents' violent deaths. No one disturbed me here. Life around the lawn went on as if no hatred and violence had ever occurred in this place.

After a while I realized that the bench on which I was sitting was about the spot where Manfred's and my bedroom and Lilo's crib had been. Gone, gone forever. But no, I suddenly saw, only the matter had disappeared, but not life itself. Manfred and Lilo were very much alive in a sunny, bustling place called

California, and after this journey into the past I would return to them. We would laugh together, I would tell them about my trip and no one would care if my old house stood tall or was replaced by a lawn. I blew my nose one last time, got up from the bench and left this tomb and the ghosts of the past behind.

Flying over the Atlantic Ocean, I relived all the kaleidoscopic events of the last days. Hours ago I'd seen Europe and my past sink below the horizon. Now I was waiting for the rise of America and my future on the other side of the world.

In contrast to the time, fifteen years ago, when I reluctantly neared Amerika, the K expressing fear and resentment, I now approached the Land of the Free with anticipation and a feeling of home-coming — America!

For five hours we flew over the immense American continent until the airplane landed in Los Angeles.

And, like fifteen years ago, Manfred was at the airport, waiting for me with a bouquet of red roses, handsome, with a warm smile and loving as always. The sun had set, giving way to another of California's cool summer nights.

We climbed into his Toyota.

Fastening his seatbelt, he asked, "How was it in Gdansk?"

"It was a place to relive my past and also to leave it behind. I don't think I'll ever have the desire to go back."

"Not even to Danzig's 1000th birthday in 1997?"

I chuckled. "If we live that long." I sighed. "I'm so glad I'm back in this country. There's no place like America. And everything I need is here: you and the children and my music."

We were driving north on the crowded San Diego Freeway.

"Our children feel the same," Manfred said. "From time to time they thank me for having brought them to this country."

I grinned. "They can't thank *me* for it. I resisted Amerika as long as possible, I was the last one to adjust." After a while I added, "We're lucky they all married Americans and their children were born here."

Manfred exited the freeway and drove west on Sunset Boulevard.

I rejoiced, "Home to Pacific Palisades!"

"Not for very long," Manfred said. "Soon home will be Irvine."

"Moving for the eighth time in fifteen years," I said. "Have we become typical Americans, moving so much?" I was fighting down that old feeling of panic and resentment at again being uprooted.

But the roots come along, I assured myself, realizing that Danzig had never left me, even though I had tried so hard to leave her. And Chile, Hawaii — all of the places I had called "home" — I still possessed. *Finally I have become at home with myself,* I thought, *and home is within me, no matter where we live.*

I turned back to Manfred, the joy of being reunited flooding over me. "Do you think we're typical Americans by now?" I asked again.

He laughed. "I think we're real and loyal Americans. But we're not typical at all!"

EVA'S WAR: A TRUE STORY OF SURVIVAL

by Eva Krutein

ISBN: 0-938513-09-5 [Trade $17]
ISBN: 0-938513-08-7 [Paper $9]
260 pp.

This gripping story of flight, refugees, privation, defeat, moral quandaries, growth and finally healing is strangely moving and compelling. It becomes a powerful anti-war statement from a woman's perspective. One year is recounted, beginning in January, 1945. Danzig, a Free City between the Great Wars, was seized by Hitler in 1939, and threatened by Soviet troops as Eva flees with her daughter.

They say that history is written by the winners, yet this bit of history comes from that nation which lost the war. Now that that nation is recovered and reunited, this sort of remembering is all the more important. And Eva Krutein is no loser. She and her family now live in California, where she is an accomplished musician and writer.

"A marvelously moving and often humorous real-life story... sad revelations, painful memories, excruciating experiences are tempered by compassion, love and a powerful, contagious optimism. Music permeates this tale."

-- Alfred-Maurice de Zayas, JD, PhD,
Senior Legal Officer, The United Nations, Geneva, Switzerland

"Her novel-like presentation makes for exciting reading. The story of German refugees has not been well covered, so this should find a p2lace in academic and public libraries."

-- THE LIBRARY JOURNAL

"Eva's account is one of fervent desire for peace in a setting of chaos, deprivation and horror... Yet EVA'S WAR is not exclusively about grief and guilt. It is about forgiveness, trust, accomplishment and love of life."

-- Thora Guinn, ALBUQUERQUE PEACE CENTER NEWS

"A gripping, unforgettable family odyssey through the terror of war and its aftermath. Definitely a page-turner... A different view of both the victors and the vanquished. One woman's spellbinding adventure in keeping her family intact."

-- Douglas Muir, author of TIDES OF WAR

"An excellent, provocative and important book." --Laurel Speer

PARADISE FOUND, AND LOST
ODYSSEY IN CHILE

by Eva Krutein

ISBN: 0-938513-16-8 [Paper $11.00]
241 pp.

Sequel to EVA'S WAR, this book tells of the Krutein family's nine years in Chile, where they are warmed by the beauty of the land and the openness of the people. Eva is sensitive to social injustice and *machismo*, and senses the pending violence of revolution and counter-revolution.

As in EVA'S WAR, we see important world-events from a new perspective. These are real people, and the events described are not imaginary. The account mounts to its sharp climax -- the decision that the family must emigrate again.

"The family's personal events are intertwined with Chile's social and political history from 1950 to 1989. Krutein witnesses the suffering of children with no future and women under the thumb of machismo, which only fuels her commitment to fight such injustices."

-- PUBLISHERS WEEKLY

"The author's abundant love for people provides the source of her political understanding."

-- Cecilia Pollock
Citizens for Peace, Laguna Hills, CA

"A loving account of the two faces of Chile. A necessary reading, for those interested in social processes from the view of a 'foreigner,' who adopted the country as her own."

Juani Funez Gonzalez
School of Social Sciences
University of California, Irvine, CA

"This is a book in the great tradition of sensitive participant-observer foreigners, who by their perspective help reveal the essence of a culture."

-- Timothy F. Harding
Professor of Latin American History
California State University, Los Angeles
Coordinating Editor, LATIN AMERICAN PERSPECTIVES

HITLER'S LAST GASP:
THE MIRACLE WEAPON
Manfred Krutein
ISBN: 0-938513-19-2 [193 pp. $12]

As the end of World War II approached, many Germans believed rumors about a Miracle Weapon. This novel shows a dramatic encounter between an American OSS officer, a German U-Boat commander and a Nazi SS officer, who wants to become Hitler's successor. They fight for control of the weapon, directed at the U.S. East Coast. At the end the action is declared a national secret, with all documents sealed for fifty years.

"Manfred Krutein knows his U-Boats from first hand experience gained during war patrols in U-123 while serving in Admiral Dönitz' Atlantic Submarine Force. This background provides unique authenticity to the U-Boat setting Krutein has chosen for his gripping and all too plausible tale of Nazi terrorism and desperation at the close of World War II. Suspenseful and fast moving in the Clancy style, HITLER'S LAST GASP will hold his readers, be they sailors or landlubbers, to the last paragraph."

William L. Read, Vice-Admiral, U.S. Navy, Ret.

"This exciting book combines the thrill of the chase with an intimate view of Allied spy and intelligence operations which helped defeat Hitler. If you enjoyed RED OCTOBER, you will want to read this book."

Robert Mulcahy, Historian for Edward Air Force Base, California

"Manfred Krutein's time aboard German U-boats shows on every page of this vivid and exciting suspense novel, which roams from fjords of Norway to the North Atlantic to Cuba, Italy and Mexico, packed with action every step and mile of the way."

Theodore Taylor, Author of TO KILL THE LEOPARD and THE CAY

"A former ***Kriegsmarine*** *officer, Krutein writes a vivid page-turner, interweaving accurate historical fact with audacious fantasy."*

Henry Cord Meyer, Emeritus Professor of German History, U of Cal.

"A well-written saga of the last throw of Hitler's dice. Packed with human-interest stories, full of suspense, intrigue and tragedy!"

Wm. Harold Campbell, Commander, U.S. Coast Guard, Ret.

AMADOR PUBLISHERS
P. O. Box 12335
Albuquerque, NM 87195
Phone/FAX 505-877-4395
To Order: 800-730-4395
e-mail amador@dump.com
http://www.amadorbooks.com

ORDER BLANK

# of copies		price	
_____	AMERIKA? AMERICA!	@ 14.00	_________
_____	EVA'S WAR[paperback]	@ 9.00	_________
_____	EVA'S WAR[hardcover]	@ 17.00	_________
_____	PARADISE FOUND, & LOST	@ 11.00	_________
_____	HITLER'S LAST GASP	@ 12.00	_________
_____	THE TIME DANCER	@ 10.00	_________
_____	ANCESTRAL NOTES	@ 10.00	_________

postage & handling 2.00

Total _________

Send to: Name_________________________________

Address_________________________________

City, State, Zip_____________________________